Acquisition and Merger Negotiating Strategy

Acquisition and Merger Negotiating Strategy

Edited by

Mark Strage

Presidents Publishing House, Inc. • New York • 1971

Book designed by
GEORGE H. BUEHLER

Library of Congress Catalog No. 78-148496
ISBN 0-87856-005-x

Printed in the United States of America by Haddon Craftsmen

FIRST PRINTING

Contents

Preface xiii

1. BY WAY OF INTRODUCTION . . . 1
by Mark Strage

2. THE ART OF MAKING A SELLER HAPPY 7
by Nicholas M. Salgo, Chairman, Bangor Punta Corporation

"Let's assume you have every reason to go ahead with an acquisition. Before you do, there has to be a very serious amount of time spent on appraising the whole question from the other man's point of view."

3. THE POWER OF POSITIVE ORIENTATION 15
by Warren B. Hayes, Chairman of the Board, Fansteel, Inc.

"One of the first questions which must be answered is whether the prospective buyer's own decision-making mechanism is in fact positively oriented in respect to making acquisitions."

4. HOW TO SUCCEED WHERE OTHERS HAVE FAILED 31

by John K. Castle, Donaldson, Lufkin & Jenrette

"Rarely do we find a corporate president of a desirable company who does not receive at least one offer a month to buy his company, yet most of these companies are still independent."

5. THE MAKING OF A NEGOTIATOR 49

by Donald H. Putnam, President, Conrac Corporation

"The person who negotiates must be the man who knows the purpose best, the rationale, the position on the other side."

6. TACTICS: THE DISTINCTION BETWEEN A MERGER AND AN ACQUISITION 71

by Fred R. Sullivan, Chairman and Chief Executive Officer, Walter Kidde & Company, Inc.

"The man who is going to be involved in merger negotiation must begin by appreciating the non-existent difference between seemingly similar words such as merger and acquisition."

7. THE USE—AND MISUSE—OF FINANCIAL SPECIALISTS 89

by H. Corbin Day, Vice President, Corporate Finance Department, Goldman, Sachs & Co.

"In theory we like to think there is one right company for everybody to merger with. Participation of an investment banker adds to the probability that this right partner can be found."

8. HOW TO ESTABLISH A PRICE RANGE 105

by Harry W. Keidan, Lybrand, Ross Bros. & Montgomery

"Determining price is a relatively simple exercise in decision-making, requiring the same procedure which would be applied to any prospective capital investment."

9. CONTINGENCY PAYOUTS: A POWERFUL TOOL IN ACQUISITION 125

by Thomas A. Steele, III and W. Robert Reum, Executive Assistants, City Investing Company

"On balance, the contingency payout method enables acquisitions to be consummated that otherwise might have fallen through."

10. THE EFFECTIVE USE OF TIMING IN ACQUISITIONS 147
by Stephen F. Snyder, Vice President, Corporate Development, The Greyhound Corporation

"The reason a seller will seriously consider the sale of his company is because he feels it will be worth less to him in the future."

11. EFFECTIVE HANDLING OF RISK IN ACQUISITIONS 167
by E.P. Fillion, Jr., Executive Vice President, W.T. Grimm & Company

"Probably the greatest difference between companies that make successful acquisitions and those that are still trying is the seemingly trite recognition that business is still a risk."

12. A MARKETING APPROACH TO ACQUISITIONS 179
by Thomas C. O'Connell, President, Northstar Industries, Inc.

"Values vary among people and there are many important factors of which only one is money. In many cases, it is not the key concern."

13. CREATING A FAVORABLE CLIMATE FOR NEGOTIATION 191
by Marshall Butler, President, Alloys Unlimited

"It takes something more than a perfect match-up of numbers to achieve a successful merger, and provide the basis for fruitful collaboration."

14. HOW TO MAKE THE "IMPOSSIBLE" MERGER 205
by John S. R. Shad, Executive Vice President, E.F. Hutton and Company

"It is one of the axioms of acquisition wisdom that buyers should avoid making dilutionary transactions. Yet in three out of five cases studied, this is exactly what happens."

15. INTELLIGENT USE OF LAWYERS IN ACQUISITIONS 235
by Warren G. Haskin, Partner, Bell, Boyd, Lloyd, Haddad, and Burns

"Used properly, there are a number of things a lawyer can do to expedite negotiations, and quite possibly to make their result more favorable."

16. INTELLIGENT USE OF ACCOUNTANTS IN ACQUISITIONS 251
by Warren G. Wintrub, Partner, Lybrand, Ross Bros. and Montgomery

"Very often, the problem is not to come up with the right answers, but to ask the right questions."

17. THE ANATOMY OF A SUCCESSFUL CLOSING 263
by Charles A. Scharf, Partner, Ide & Haigney

"A merger agreement informally begins to take shape as soon as the parties hold their first meeting, and continues to evolve as an integral part of the negotiating process."

18. AN ANALYTICAL APPROACH TO MERGER NEGOTIATIONS 281
by Gary E. MacDougal, Chairman and Chief Executive Officer, Clayton Mark & Company, and Fred V. Malek, Special Assistant to President Richard M. Nixon

"It is necessary, in an acquisition work, to develop an analytical approach which can be understood and communicated effectively."

19. **DISCLOSURE: A COMMON-SENSE APPROACH** 305
by Crosby M. Kelly, President, Crosby M. Kelly Associates, Ltd.

"The intent behind the law was not in the negative sense of disclosure, but in the positive context of dissemination of information."

20. **DISCLOSURE: A POSITIVE APPROACH** 317
by John P. Kehoe, President, Shareholder Perspectives, Inc.

"Through proper, consistent communication, there is opportunity to help shape the attitudes that lead to investment decision."

Index 335

Preface

Most of the material in this book, revised and updated, was originally presented at a series of informal two-day discussion and workshop sessions sponsored by Corporate Seminars, Inc., during the past two years.

Corporate Seminars, Inc., is a management education and information gathering organization which for the past five years has served the executive community by providing opportunities for corporate policy makers and outside specialists to exchange their expert knowledge of vital problems in modern business practice.

The sessions in question were held in New York and Chicago, and brought together unusually qualified groups of professional experts in the field of acquisition and merger—corporate chief executives and staff officers, investment bankers, legal, accounting and financial relations specialists.

Most of them came with predominant experience as buyers rather than sellers, for the simple statistical reason that a man usually sells a company only once. However, their observations have equal pertinence to both parties in negotiations. In fact, as will be explained in detail, a potential seller can profit substantially by placing himself, for purposes of establishing strategy, in the seat of the buyer.

I wish to thank the editors of the HARVARD BUSINESS REVIEW for permission to reprint *Master plan for merger negotiations* by Gary E. MacDougal and Fred V. Malek, and *Contingent payouts cut acquisition risks* by Robert Reum and Thomas A. Steele III, which originally appeared in the January-February 1970 and March-April 1970 issues of that magazine; and also thank Robert E. Jones, executive editor of Presidents Publishing House, Inc., who with gentle firmness guided this book to completion.

New York
March 1971

Mark Strage

Acquisition and Merger Negotiating Strategy

1

BY WAY OF INTRODUCTION...

by Mark Strage

In providing the introduction to a complicated subject, perhaps the most useful service an editor can perform for the reader is to isolate one workable generalization.

The subject of this book is complicated indeed. Acquisitions and mergers are among the most powerful instruments of business policy ever devised. Used well, they can telescope time and vault distance, multiply physical resources and permit the spectacular leverage of human energy.

Understandably, they are likely to engage the full interplay of points of view, business philosophy and value systems of both participants. For one of them at least, the negotiating process will lead to the single most important decision of his professional career.

Because they do involve human elements, no two acquisitions are alike; there is no such thing as one right way to proceed. If there were, books such as this one would be unnecessary; a simple set of forms would do.

The twenty-one authors in this book are all skilled, experienced specialists. Together, they have been personally involved in perhaps one thousand successful acquisitions, representing tens of billions of dollars worth of enterprise. From everything they have to say, and much that they have simply assumed and left unsaid, one main generalization can be drawn.

Stated simply, it is that the essence of successful economic activity is satisfaction on both sides. For an acquisition to succeed, both the buyer and the seller must be better off after the transaction than before.

This appears to be so simple as to be virtually self-evident, a business corollary to the golden rule. Yet some negotiations succeed while others, the far greater majority, fail. Somebody—many people—must be doing something wrong.

In scope, this book will attempt to focus on the generalization and follow it through the entire negotiating process, from beginning to end. The end, of course, comes with public announcement of the completed transaction. The beginning starts some time *before* the prospective buyer even begins to approach his first prospective seller.

Strategy by definition involves the deployment of known and available resources to achieve predetermined goals. So our discussion begins with the identification and disposition of these resources.

"Probably the most crucial part of doing acquisition work must be done, and done well, before you ever start talking to anyone," one of our authors points out. Specifically, he adds, "Anyone who is to get involved in the acquisition process must first address himself to the question of whether the decision-making mechanism of his own company is in fact positively oriented with respect to making acquisitions."

Next, we see what can be learned from other people's mistakes. "Rarely do we find," says one author, "a corporate president of a desirable company who does not receive at least one offer a month to buy his company." Yet, he notes, most of these companies are still independent. And he suggests one very cogent reason why this may be so.

Having done the necessary homework and prepared a basic strategy, the next logical question is: who should set it into motion? Since the human element is so important in carrying on negotiations, three chapters are devoted to aspects of what makes a good negotiator, what he should do—and avoid doing. There is also consideration of the advantages and possible disadvantages of using third parties. A highly knowledgeable and experienced investment banker explains in some detail what is actually meant by the phrase, celebrated in "tombstone" ads, "So-and-So assisted in the transaction."

Then we come—as all negotiations inevitably do—to the delicate subject of price. How do you bring it up? How do you handle it? Who should broach it first?

Actually, if the problem is approached correctly, it need never come up in this possibly embarrassing form. One chapter demonstrates, with examples, how price determination can be handled as a perfectly straightforward and simple exercise in executive decision-making. Another chapter describes, again in detail and with specific examples, various techniques of price determination to meet specific needs of both sellers and buyers.

Since we are now within the core of the negotiating process, and alternative possibilities are numerous and potentially confusing, the next three chapters provide opportunities to stop, step back, and review the situation from three different and often-overlooked points of view. In turn, we consider the strategic implications of timing, of risk-taking, and of value. At each step of the way, we weigh alternatives against the basic principle: that a successful deal benefits both sides. Our purpose is *not* to see how we can gain an advantage but how, through innovative consideration of existing factors, mutual advantage can be achieved.

So far we have been talking in general about *buying* companies, and the resources and skills needed to achieve this goal. There are also skills involved in *selling* companies. In fact, our next chapter suggests that, in the current marketplace, sellers may be doing better as a group than buyers. The author discusses the results of a private survey of 65 recent important mergers, and suggests specific tactics that should be considered by both successful sellers and successful buyers.

There is a technical side to all acquisitions. However firm the understanding between principals, the arrangements must still be put clearly on paper. This is a job for specialists, including accountants and lawyers. In the next two chapters, two specialists—one an accountant, the other a lawyer—have their say. Their subject: how can they be of maximum use to you in helping to achieve your goal. You may not wholly agree with what they have to say, but it is well worth the time to listen to them.

One of the crucial stages of the negotiating process is the closing, and we have therefore devoted one chapter to this subject alone. Closing is crucial because it is, in its own way, the "moment of truth"—the point at which misunderstandings or breakdowns in communication suddenly emerge, usually with disastrous results. The purpose of the chapter, written by an expert in corporate law, is to show how these misunderstandings can be avoided.

Now, having taken up each of the separate parts of our strategic review, we put them all together into a unified plan. It is not intended to be a master key to *all* successful mergers, because we know that no such thing exists. Rather, it is a guide and check-list that should, if properly used, make *any* mergers easier to achieve.

And finally, having brought the deal home, all that remains is to tell the world about it. The final two chapters take up the subject of disclosure. There are certain rules—unfortunately not all of them fully explicit—about disclosure requirements, and the first chapter tackles the problem head-on, and proposes a commonsense approach. But disclosure can be an opportunity as well as an obligation, and the last chapter suggests ways in which a company can use financial communication as an effective tool in its long-term relations with the investment community.

Empathy—the imaginative projection of one's own consciousness into another being—is the soundest platform from which to launch any program of acquisitions. The author, a leading exponent of growth through acquisition and merger, has been the chief architect of his own company's corporate development.

2

THE ART OF MAKING A SELLER HAPPY

by Nicholas M. Salgo,
Chairman, Bangor Punta Corporation

There is a natural tendency, in approaching any kind of negotiation, to bring oneself "up" psychologically and mentally. The nearest analogy that comes to mind is of an athlete who has been in training preparing finally to compete, or of a performer about to step out in front of an audience.

The tendency is natural, I believe, because there is an inevitable sense of competition in any negotiating situation —your brains and skill against those of the other fellow; the desirability of taking the offensive and controlling events.

In dealing with acquisitions, I think it is the better part of wisdom first to recognize this tendency, and second to hold it in check.

Let us assume that you are at the critical point in an acquisition situation. You have gathered all the necessary information and, from your point of view, the proposition is desirable.

In my opinion, there should be no proposal made until you have arrived at as clear an idea as is possible of the seller's desires, scope and expectations.

After you have brought yourself "up" psychologically, you should devote a serious amount of time and thinking to appraise the whole question from the other man's point of view.

GAUGING A SELLER'S INTENTIONS

You should, for instance, determine whether he is really ready to sell, or merely entertaining a semi-serious notion. It is difficult to answer such a question on the basis of words alone. You must try to understand the other man's situation —not just listen to him, but to understand. If he is in his late fifties, and there is no obvious line of succession, he may indeed want to wind things up and move to Florida. Usually, however, it is not so clear-cut as this, and before you can start using your skills as a negotiator, you must use your skills at understanding human behavior and motivation.

In most cases, the man himself will give you all the necessary hints and indications, if you are alert. The exceptions are people who are either unusually unscrupulous or unusually shrewd, and these *will* be the exceptions rather than the rule. In the vast majority of cases, your success will depend on your ability to evaluate and empathize.

I have been thinking until now of privately-owned or family-held companies, since they make up such a large share of potential sellers. But even in dealing with a publicly-held company, the premise is valid. Here, you must get an accurate reading of the thinking of one or a few key men—the board chairman, the chief executive officer, a principal shareholder.

If anything, it is even more important to get a clear reading in this instance, because the likelihood of continued relations with the selling management is greater, and an evaluation of how those relations may develop is often important in assessing the desirability of the entire deal. It is easy to imagine conditions under which you may decide you absolutely want to retain a key manager. There are also, unfortunately, circumstances where your hope will be that he leaves as fast as possible. In either case, it is better all around if these circumstances are recognized and dealt with very early in the process.

TAILORING A PROPOSAL TO FIT THE SELLER

Once you have determined that you truly mean to understand the other fellow's position, the knowledge that you gain will help you in shaping the outline of your strategy. It will help you put together a more attractive offer, but it will also tend to dictate how you handle the negotiating process itself.

I recall an acquisition which we made some time ago in the boat business. The gentleman with whom we were dealing is still with us, but now as the chairman of a group. He was one of the finest human beings I'd ever met, and one of the plainest in his personal tastes. In the course of our discussions, I invited him to dinner and he accepted. After some hesitation, I took him to Nedick's.

He felt comfortable there; he ordered coffee and a sandwich, and we continued our discussion. He was and is an extremely frugal person, though no less excellent a businessman. To this day, I have the strong feeling that if I had taken him to one of the kinds of restaurants usually chosen to discuss major deals, he would have been scared off.

There was also the case of a man and his family in New York. After some digging into the situation, we found that this man was not really prepared to sell out. He had not the faintest desire. He had been told that it would be good for him.

He had been told how much he should ask for the company—a nice round figure, but with absolutely no relation to his company or its value. It was just a nice round figure: 750 thousand dollars after taxes. But when we really got to it, we found out that this was the sort of man who, regardless of his net worth, gets up at the same 6:00 in the morning, puts on the same work clothes, and works the same whole day.

He would do it even if they would take him off the payroll—just as long as they let him do it, because he doesn't know how to live otherwise. To take a man like that and give him a million dollars cash for his business would be actually doing him a disservice. You would make out of him, in a few weeks, the most unhappy person on earth.

So, instead of trying to buy him out, we made an offer which hinged on his remaining with the company. This not only gave him something to do, but it was absolute psychological knowledge and assurance that for the next five years he had to work to earn his money.

The next day after the closing was just another working day, with perhaps a little more motivation because even though it was no longer his own earnings alone that were on the line, there was the matter of pride.

This case was relatively simple, because it involved only one man. When the decision to sell is going to be made by a group, the matter is inevitably more difficult. Not only are you dealing with genuinely different desires and systems of values, but there is the likelihood that the interplay of factions will generate friction. People are likely to say and do things more for the effect they will have on other interested parties than on the deal itself.

I know of many negotiations that were carried on under these conditions. One in particular sticks in my mind. We were dealing with a group of three partners, but were conducting our discussions through one of them, who acted as spokesman. The talk dragged on for six months. There seemed to be something wrong with everything we offered, and we did our level best to be creative and accomodating.

Finally, as a last resort, we made contact individually with each of the three partners, and reviewed with each one all of the offers that had been made.

In quick order, we discovered that there was something in each of the offers that pleased one of the partners, but left the other two dissatisfied.

So we made what in effect were three separate offers. One of the partners accepted common stock for his share, another took a mixture of common and preferred at a fixed redemption rate, the third took only preferred stock.

Now, everybody was happy. It happened that the three men were entirely different in personality and outlook. One was essentially conservative—he wanted to know exactly what he would get, right to the penny, and when it would be paid to him. Another was more concerned about maximum achievement for maximum dollar. He was much more of the promoter-activist, and indeed had successfully played that role in the management of the company. The third one was much happier straddling the middle of the road. It was a position he had become accustomed to in his dealings with his two partners. In considering our many offers, each had weighed the terms on his own scales, and found them less than satisfactory. Finally, it was when we were able to put ourselves in the position of all three sellers, that we succeeded in closing the deal.

LOOKING BEYOND THE CLOSING

This was perhaps a complicated way of doing business, but it did carry with it the advantage of allowing us to become closely acquainted with the company involved, not only its balance sheet, products and markets, but with the people who were really its heart.

This knowledge in the strategy of negotiations can represent an enormous dividend. It can grant you insight into what you can expect from these people in the future, because if you understand what they want and why, you automatically get the benefit of being able to predict how they will function as a human part of your future organization, and you can also judge then whether you want them in this future organization.

In many negotiating situations, the test of whether empathy has been achieved between buyer and seller comes up very quickly and over a specific issue: price.

It is not appropriate here to discuss price strategy—several chapters are devoted to the subject elsewhere in this book

—but discussing an over-all approach to the question of price is relevant.

First of all, in many instances, the object on which you are planning a valuation is the result of most of a man's life-work. If the value to you is much less than what you know—or should know—the value is *in his own mind*, then don't even bring up a specific figure. You will only alienate or offend him.

Try rather to find out what he has on his mind—whether he actually is interested in the money as a quantity or money for himself or his family, or whether it is a way of achieving an aim and merely a numerical expression of that aim. Perhaps ways can be found to achieve this otherwise.

If you can see that you are going to be very far apart, I think you are doing yourself a disservice by even entering serious negotiations. If I were in such a situation I would point out very plainly why we are miles apart, and I would close the discussions in a most friendly manner, saying that if and when I can see that you are worth more to me, I will come back. If you can see that your own aims change, you come back.

Don't tell him that he is way out of line; because, first of all, he will never believe you. He realizes that you have adverse interests: you want to get it for the least amount. You just have to explain to him that although you believe there is tremendous value in putting the two together, and that you can see tremendous additional values created, still, adding all this up, you are not there. Let him then think it over, whether he is realistic or has exaggerated or not. But, in my opinion, you should not start telling him that his company is worth just exactly half of what he is asking for it.

Should you find that you are in the same ball park—which is to say that you can negotiate without risking or hurting the ego of the person with whom you would have to work and live, because I assume that in most cases you would want the people who run the business to continue—should you be in this position, by all means start to negotiate. But if your judgement or instinct tell you that the gap is still too wide, then leave matters alone. I do not believe that much is accomplished with a formal, written proposal, either. It certainly does nothing to narrow the gulf or encourage closer mutual understanding.

What *will* tend to narrow it, and most certainly *will* encourage the kind of understanding that makes for good acquisitions and good long-term relations, is the applied exercise of empathy.

The ultimate price has to be one which is good both ways. The correct deal is one where both parties sit down to sign a paper with pleasure, and a sense of constructive accomplishment.

To want to make acquisitions, and to be ready to make acquisitions, are two entirely different things. Failure to make this distinction has probably caused more negotiations to fall through than any other single factor. The author was principally responsible for leading his own company to more than a dozen technically-related acquisitions.

3

THE POWER OF POSITIVE ORIENTATION

by Warren B. Hayes,
Chairman of the Board, Fansteel, Inc.

Somewhere in the files of practically every company active in acquisition work there sits a document which, whatever its actual title, functions as a master check-list.

Typically, it will contain financial criteria, operational guidelines, legal *caveats.* Depending on its thoroughness, it may even include such details as executive perquisites, and what is to be done about hunting lodges carried on the books of the acquired company.

These lists are enormously useful and I have no quarrel with them, not even with the details. Anyone with even limited experience in acquisitions quickly learns that it is the details *not* covered before the final signing which end up causing the most trouble afterwards.

My criticism of check-lists is that too many of them fail to include one certain question—in fact *the* question which should be at the very head of the list. Stated simply, it is this: "Do we have a decision-making mechanism which is positively oriented toward making acquisitions?"

This is not the same as asking "Do we want to buy companies?" The difference lies in the phrase "positively oriented," and the purpose of this chapter is to investigate that difference and explore some of its implications.

THE OBJECTIVE OF BUYING

It may well happen, for instance, that a company's decision-makers—in this context the term could include a formal committee, a small *ad hoc* group, or even a single person—are really interested in acquisitions as an end in itself, rather than as one of several possible means to an end. I have in mind the example of one specific company which had a history of spectacular technical growth. As often happens, its growth rate began in time to moderate. Both its technology and marketing capability approached maturity, but it nonetheless remained an attractive and successful company.

Some time just after the growth curve began to flatten, control of the company passed into the hands of new management which was more financially than technologically oriented. The new management—in this case it happened to be an individual—had originally been attracted to the company because of its growth rate, and could see no reason why it should be allowed to slow down. He proceeded to steer the company into a series of acquisitions.

They were "good" acquisitions in terms of the balance sheet, but made very little operational sense. Gradually, the company began slipping in the estimation of the investment public. People simply couldn't understand—and the new management couldn't convincingly explain—what the company was trying to achieve. As a result, earnings continued to rise while the multiple dropped. This "successful" acquisition program did not solve problems, it created new and thorny ones.

THE EVALUATION OF RISK

Positive orientation requires the willingness to make a commitment. Even the stodgiest company likes to think of itself as "acquisition-minded"—it just isn't modern to be anything else. Yet when the chips are called for, something happens. Often, it is a simple case of cold feet.

It is easier and more comfortable for a decision-maker who, after years of service, has risen to a position of great responsibility, to vote "no." He risks little that way. The loss to his company may never be accurately assessed; even if it is, no criticism can be levelled directly at him. Fear may come from another quarter: the possible dilution of control through the introduction, by way of acquisition, of new managers, or directors. Here again, a negative vote may be justified on objective grounds. The decision-maker may quite sincerely believe that he is acting prudently and in the best interests of his company. No one—not even his psychiatrist—will know for sure.

My point is not to quarrel with motivations—the subject is complex enough without *that*—but only to suggest that it is extremely difficult to press decision-makers into making acquisitions if they themselves are not committed to the concept.

All of the positive acquisition programs which I am personally acquainted with involve decision-makers who believe that acquisition can be a viable and constructive business technique, who are willing to take the risks associated with acquisition, who understand the value of intangibles that are usually found in good acquisitions, who are ambitious for their company, who want to make their company grow, and who are, above all else, secure in their positions and are willing, because of their sense of security and confidence in themselves, to assume the risks that acquisition implies.

THE CHOICE OF TECHNIQUE

Having made the commitment, decision-makers must still determine how they are going to use various basic techniques. There is a choice: go out after acquisitions or wait for someone to bring them around for your appraisal. Neither approach is necessarily right or wrong—it depends on a number of factors. But one fact—in my experience, at least—is clear: if someone comes around and wants to sell you a company, you had better start with the premise that he knows why he wants to do it. He knows the situation a lot better than you do, and you are going to have to work hard just to catch up with him.

There is nothing sinister about this; it is just a fact of life.

Under the circumstances I have described, the seller is more likely to be "right" than the buyer. It therefore follows that, other things being equal, it is better to be an active buyer of companies on the basis of organized strategy and reasoning, than to assume the passive role of potential purchaser of companies which someone proposes selling to you.

All the acquisition work that I have been involved with has been based on some kind of a specific business strategy. That is, it was possible within the framework of an industry or a market or a technology, to identify what could be described as business opportunity, a sense of how the technology was going to evolve, a sense of the deficiencies of the industry structure as it existed, a sense of the opportunities that were going to unfold, and what their technical impact would be on the structure of the industry. From this would come a strategy.

THE DEVELOPMENT OF STRATEGY

In Fansteel, for instance, we found ourselves, more or less as a function of history, rather deeply involved in the aerospace business. Different aspects of it were potentially promising on the one hand and unattractive on the other. A number of years ago, we sat down and decided that we were irrevocably committed to the aerospace business by virtue of the materials in which we were involved, and that as long as this was going to be true we ought to try to optimize our tactical processes with respect to that industry. We concluded that what we really wanted to do was to get into the jet engine business.

This particular product area was attractive to us because it has a relatively long production life. Jet engine models have lifetimes of something on the order of ten years. In the space business in which we were heavily involved, if we ever made more than ten of anything we were lucky, and usually we became involved in very difficult and critical commitments with technical problems. By the time we achieved mastery of these problems the program was over, and we were starting from scratch on something else. Continuity was one of the major factors that attracted us to the jet engine.

Having made the decision, we acquired a producer of investment castings, because we knew that investment castings were part of jet engines. We worked in the field of powder metallurgy, which we considered to be promising. We found ourselves with an opportunity to acquire a vapor deposition company. This is a technique by which one can deposit metallic layers by growing metal out of vapor, a very interesting and very promising process. We went after one of the most important high temperature sheet metal fabricators in the country. Sheet metal fabrication doesn't sound like a very exotic kind of activity, until you consider the sort of metals that we were working with. We were making rocket nozzles out of columbium, doing extensive titanium fabrication, using super alloys. The particular company that we went after was the most competent operation of its kind in the country. We also acquired a division of duPont which had as its basis a materials technology—the only material that looked as if it would be serviceable between about 1700 F and 2100 F. Almost all the advancements in jet engine technology have to do with being able to operate at a higher temperature.

Some of these companies were already involved with the jet engine business but all were in technologies related to the jet engine market. Then, as the engine companies went into the new generation of engine designs, into the JT-9 which powers the Boeing 747, into the TF-39 which powers the C-5, and the commercial versions of it which power the DC-10, we were in an excellent position to respond to the need of this market.

Our strategy was to get deeply involved with the new technologies, to go after and establish a relationship with the principal producers of jet engines, to work our way in because we were able to do jobs that nobody else could do as a function of our technical competence. I think we've got a foothold in what ought to become one of the most important businesses of Fansteel over the years ahead. This is a direct product of strategy. In almost every acquisition we made, we specifically pursued a company. We knew what we wanted, the capability we wanted, we identified it, we went after it. We knew, for instance, we wanted a vapor deposition capability. There was a rather small laboratory in California that was reputed to have the best capability in the United States. We went after them. And we did the same thing in almost every case.

I believe very strongly in business strategy, and I believe very strongly in relating acquisitions to strategy. I believe that it makes a lot more sense to identify companies that fit within the structure of the strategy and pursue them, rather than be in the receiving line hoping that somebody will bring an attractive acquisition along. I do not think I can make a more important comment about the whole process of acquisition than that.

PERSPECTIVE ON RISK-TAKING

Even in the context of a reasoned strategy, there are several risks in analyzing potential acquisitions. One of them —a basic one—hinges on whether there is, within the buyer, a capacity for capable judgment with respect to the acquisition to be made. It is very possible, especially when dealing with companies engaged in dynamic technology, to run into two kinds of problems. One is that you may find yourself deciding on the basis of historical evidence—especially on the typical kind of information that is easily available—that you have a very attractive operation on your hands, only to discover that you have bought a company with a technology that is absolutely going to die in the next three years. If you do not have the capacity to penetrate the unfolding technology in the market which the company serves, you certainly can get into a bundle of trouble by buying something that is going to go downhill.

The other kind of risk is on the opposite end of the scale. You can get involved with a new technology that is demonstrable on a laboratory basis and is sincerely represented by the developer as being on the threshold of sweeping the industry and revolutionizing the market. This can seem very, very attractive and you can become committed and discover that it is absolutely not true. If you have sufficient insight into the problem, you are going to be able to identify this, but if it is, relatively speaking, a new and different sort of field and you are not expert in it, you face difficulty with respect to your capacity for judgment.

In my own experience, the most important area of technical evolution in electronics in the last two or three years has been the development of circuit technology, and in particular the impact of integrated circuits, thin film and thick film circuitry. When I came to Fansteel I had a feeling that we could profitably expand in the direction of electronics by way of acquisition. I was somewhat overwhelmed at that particular time, however, by uncertainty as to what the pattern of circuitry was really going to be over a four or five year period, and passed by an acquisition or two which I thought might be undermined by the impact of integrated circuits. One of the companies that I passed by almost went into bankruptcy because of the competitive impact of transistor circuitry on computers. Thereupon I became very much impressed with the importance, in an acquisition situation in which technology was dynamic, and where there was a significant possibility that the unfolding technology could undermine the logic of the acquisition, of the need to assure that the buyer does indeed possess capacity for judgment.

If such capacity does not exist, or is questionable, it is necessary when one makes acquisitions to put some analysts to work on the problem. Ideally, the buyer should try to find some bright people who have technical knowledge, who have analytical orientations and who are very good at exploring the facts with respect to the market. One caution: the analyst's whole orientation predisposes him toward making the acquisition. His job is to make acquisitions; it is not to turn them down.

In this context, I can recall one company which we looked at. Everything was right about it, the technology was right; we knew it was moving into a dynamic market. The company had had a history of sales and earnings growth followed by a year of trouble, but the president of the company, who was interested in selling it to our analyst, very conveniently, logically and efficiently rationalized the inadequate performance and very carefully presented a program for the succeeding year which made it perfectly clear that this company was going to bounce back and do very well. In the course of time the report came to me, and as I read and thought about it for a while, I came to the conclusion that at the given time the company wasn't going to do this. We decided not to go ahead, and as things turned out the company did just as badly the next year as it had done the year before. This was just a marvelous illustration of a perfectly sincere, dedicated analyst who was influenced to try to construct a believable case because he wanted it to be believable.

Another kind of a risk arises in dealing with internal company experts—and I would say that the technical breed is particularly guilty of this. Through loyalty and *esprit de corps,* they can easily become convinced that nobody can do things as well as "we" can, and anything that anybody else does on the outside is "dumb" and not going to go anywhere, and we can do it better than they can do it, and they're lacking in capability, and so forth. One of the worst mistakes I have made in the last five years happened when I looked at an operation that was in the casting business. I was reasonably new to casting technology, and I had a very bright technical young man who was working on a new casting technique and it was suggested that it might be useful to bring him in to take a look at the potential acquisition, which I did.

I have never heard anything put down as hard as this technical man put that casting operation down! In retrospect, I never should have listened to him, because we turned the deal down, and the company did nothing but make money and grow and do all the other things you would expect it to do. The fault, of course, was mine.

THE ELEMENT OF PERSONAL CONTACT

However useful experts are, there is still almost no substitute for direct contact between the decision-makers in the acquisition situation. Acquisition is not a remote project. If you are, let us say, significantly responsible for the acquisition decision, and ultimately for the acquisition negotiations, you cannot send a group of people out and tell them to analyze the acquisition situation and come back and decide whether or not it makes sense based on what they tell you. You can do a lot of spadework in terms of generating information and data, but in my experience there is practically no substitute for direct contact. There are also other reasons for direct contact, but I have found that you yourself must go see, look and feel and sense and talk with companies in order to make really good acquisition decisions. All the analysts notwithstanding, there is no substitute for direct contact.

I had an experience last year in which we did indeed go through the process of analyzing the situation and found that it all sounded good on paper. The price was too high, however, and my position, in a remote relationship to the situation, was that I just did not believe in the acquisition based on the kind of price that was being recited to me.

By accident, I happened to be in the vicinity of the company in question, and took a day off to visit it and become involved with it at first hand. The first thing that impressed me was that nobody in the world understood what the real asset value of the company was, that all of the people that had looked at it had missed the most important point of all, and that this had never come through. The crucial point had to do with the changing nature of the market the company was serving, and it became uniquely and perfectly clear in the course of a three-hour tour that this company would have a position that practically could not be attacked in terms of the market it was serving, and that therefore its business was bound to go up, and the profits were bound to go up with it. After the tour my reaction was "Buy it! Fast!" And that is what we did, and it turned out to be one of our best acquisitions. This again, I think, illustrates one of the benefits of direct contact. If you are going to be involved in making an acquisition decision, you should get involved in a direct way in order to have a basis for exercising judgment.

Now, if you have reached the point where you are convinced that a company fits your strategy and you really want to go, the next question is: what must happen in order to make that company want to go with you? I believe that the initial responsibility of a company that wants to make an acquisition is to secure a commitment from the prospective seller. All the orientation, all the energy, strength and determination in the initial phases of the relationship has only one real purpose, and that is to make the seller want to sell his company to *you.* Practically everything that goes on, as far as I am concerned, should be directed to switch the pressures around so that the other man wants to be bought more than I want to buy.

MAKING A SELLER WANT TO SELL

There are a lot of things that can relate to technique in this kind of a process, but the process itself is very simple. I want to go talk to the man about his business, and sit down with him and take the tour. I have mentioned that I think the tour relates in part to the decision-making process, but in this instance its importance lies in the effect of listening to the man talk about his business, in trying to understand what is going on and trying to identify the problems and the opportunities. Even as you are collecting information, you are demonstrating that you are that man's type of man, your company is that company's type of company, and if you can accomplish this, you have gone a long way toward making negotiations feasible.

I have often considered and have gone back over the history of the things that worked and the things that didn't work, and I think there is a good possibility that a deal is often made in the first three hours of association. By the time you are ready to get involved in negotiation, the chemistry is there, the mutual attraction and compatibility is established, and from that point on it is largely a mechanical matter. Very rarely, if that chemistry is strong, if that attraction is strong, is it impossible to work out acceptable financial terms. But I think almost never, if that chemistry is *not* there, will it be possible to come to a rational agreement.

There is ample time to take up the subject of price; there is ample time to take up the issues of organizational relationship. What *cannot* be done later is to get in and understand the business, and make its owner feel comfortable with respect to where he is going to live. I am sure that anyone who has given any thought at all to acquisition understands that a manager or owner who has put in years and years of work creating a company is very emotionally involved in what is going to happen to it as a follow-on of sale, and that this issue is as important as the financial arrangements. The objective is to empathize with that man's emotions, to put yourself in his place.

I had a recent experience in this regard with a company which had decided originally to go public. After they concluded a number of activities with respect to public sale, the president and principal owner decided that he did not really want the emotional burden of living with shareholders, and therefore it would be much better for him to be in another corporation. He decided to invite a list of bidders, which is always a very attractive situation if you are on the bid-receiving side, and can trade off one company against the others. Fortunately for us, he invited us first and we spent lots of time touring and then we spent lots of time, hours and hours, describing the Fansteel strategy and what we were trying to do, our philosophy of materials technology and how to build a growing business on it. By the time we were through we had never talked about price at all; we had talked a little bit about organizational relationships and operational matters.

The seller went on to the next bidder, who took a quick orientation tour and made a tentative offer to the company —probably within two or three hours of conversation. When the chips were finally down, that offer was several million dollars higher than the offer that we successfully made to the company. I might add that it took about six months of fighting before we finally got the deal settled, but in the final analysis we had convinced that man that Fansteel was the right company for him to join, and he may have passed up a significant short-term gain because he was drawn to Fansteel as the right home for his company.

As part of risk assessment, it is absolutely essential to understand why the owner wants to sell. He is going to have a lot of reasons for selling, but what I have found is that in almost no case will the owner tell *you* the reason for his selling; in some cases he may not even know what the reasons are. I can generalize to the extent that nearly all owners want to sell because they are frightened of something. They are afraid of technical obsolescence; they are afraid of losing the asset value they have created.

One of the first acquisitions I made had been considering going public. An underwriter was suggesting a multiple of 18 times earnings on public underwriting. It was an electronics company, which was fashionable back in the late 50's. We bought it for 10 times or 12 times their profit. The thing that the underwriter missed was that he was proposing to sell out a minority shareholder, and part of the condition of the underwriting was that the principals would continue to hold their own stock, because obviously nobody wanted to buy a company unless the principals were committed, and the demonstration of the confidence to the potential buying public was the fact that they would retain stock in the company. But on the other hand, these people had come to a point where they wanted to nail down something that would have real cash value. By giving them the opportunity to make a tax free-exchange of their stock where they could see it had real cash value in the sense that they could, if they wanted, go out and sell it, we were able to close at a much lower multiple than they might have expected by going public and ending up with paper which they couldn't conveniently sell.

The key to this whole negotiation came at the point when I realized that this was a significant factor in their emotions, and for the first time I realized I wasn't going to be beaten out by an 18 times multiple, but could make a reasonable supportable transaction.

The key here, as it so often is, lay in understanding the real dynamics of the situation, and then relating those dynamics to the buyer's own positive orientation—his true willingness on the decision-making level to make the necessary commitment.

Most companies that you are likely to approach as potential acquisitions have already turned down a number of prospective buyers. The author suggests that something can be learned from these failures, and proposes a generalized theory to account for them.

4

HOW TO SUCCEED WHERE OTHERS HAVE FAILED

by John K. Castle,
Donaldson, Lufkin & Jenrette

The subject of this chapter is: How does one go about structuring an acquisition package which is attractive to both the buyer and the seller? In other words, how are considerations of strategy actually implemented and put into action?

We have collected all available published material on the company we want to acquire. We have also done a certain amount of independent investigation. We have talked to people who have worked with the company or who have been closely associated with it. We know the predilections of the company's president and of the other key managers.

With this mass of information, we are at the stage where we can mold a package which, hopefully, will persuade the prospective seller that he should join forces with us.

THREE PACKAGES

Before doing this, however, I suggest we stop a moment and consider the fact that the corporate president of a desirable company who does not frequently receive offers to sell his company is rare indeed. This probably includes the man you are going to try to buy. The very fact that he is still independent indicates that historically he has always said "no" to prospective purchasers. The fact that he has said no, I believe, frequently has little to do with the actual value of the offer. It has a lot to do with the manner in which the offer was packaged.

My contention is that—in the eyes of the prospective seller at least—an offer consists of three distinct packages, and that his decision to sell or not to sell is based on an evaluation of all three of them. For purposes of discussion, let us call them the financial package, the business synergy package and the sellers' management package.

THE FINANCIAL PACKAGE

The financial package is the one which the public usually thinks about first, the one which eventually appears in the financial press. It advises shareholders that they will receive some security package such as one half a share of common stock and two-tenths of a share of convertible preferred stock, with perhaps some 7% notes and warrants attached.

In evaluating the importance of the financial package, I think it useful to remember that, in most instances, stockholders are not the principal determinants when it comes to deciding to sell a company. I do not mean that their interests are not important—indeed, paramount. But in the normal course of events, they are consulted after a preliminary agreement has been reached and most proposals are rejected before the stockholders are ever consulted. Given the nature of most public corporations, it is very infrequent that shareholders will reject a merger program suggested and recommended by management.

Therefore, while it is the financial package that received publicity in the press, it is in my judgment *not* the most important consideration in negotiating an acquisition.

THE BUSINESS SYNERGY PACKAGE

The second package, the business synergy package—it may be a written or an oral presentation—is the one in which you outline the various strengths and weaknesses of the two companies and try to demonstrate to the seller that union with you will result in a much stronger company—one which will generate more rapid growth and provide the seller's stockholders with a more exciting long-term investment.

THE SELLER'S MANAGEMENT PACKAGE

The third package, the seller's management package, is a presentation which goes beyond just salary and management contract to describe working environment and personal growth opportunities for management. All these are important factors in making it attractive for corporate executives to make the decision to sell their company.

Let's consider in more detail why I think the synergy and management packages are more important than the financial one.

If you have negotiated with a company and sold them only on a financial package, you will usually find that suddenly there appears somebody else who is more than willing to meet the price you offer.

PUTTING ALL THREE TOGETHER

A recent illustration of such a situation is a transaction in which I was involved, with a company whose common stock was trading at about $50 a share. We negotiated a transaction with a larger party who agreed to pay $75 a share and we signed a letter of agreement in principle. Within two business days of the announcement of the $75 offer, we had one counter offer for $100 a share and another offer for a package of $10 above our $75, or $85 a share.

The merger was ultimately successfully concluded at $75 a share—our original offer.

The moral is this: If we had simply negotiated a financial package, many other parties waiting in the wings would have been able to top our financial package. But it was the nonfinancial items—the business synergy and management seller's package that were so important in assuring that the deal was consummated by the buyer my firm represented.

Another of the critical reasons why I think the non-financial packages are so important is that today most substantial companies are regularly receiving offers to sell their firms. Usually these offers come from business brokers, investment bankers, or the president of the suitor company calling the president of the prospective ally. These initial offers are almost always cast in financial terms.

In some instances, the discussion is simply: "Your stock is $40. We will give you $60. Let us work out a package."

It is interesting that most of these prospective sellers are still independent. Their managements have been refusing all suitors.

This, I think, supports my judgment that the factors which usually make a seller are the non-financial, intangible ones. The management of the potential seller must be presented with a package stressing exciting opportunities for growth, opportunities for introduction and movement into new markets or new activities. The management must see something beyond a simple $75, $85 or even $100 a share. These are the keys necessary to make management want to sell—and it is the management of the company that sells it, not the stockholders.

An important aspect of the non-financial package is that it can enable a buyer to save money by persuading the management of the value of intangibles. For instance, if you can convince a company to sell for $75 instead of $85 per share, that is effectively 18% fewer shares, 18% fewer dollars. That helps you as a buyer to minimize your share dilution.

A POSITIVE APPROACH TO SYNERGY

Let's now discuss the business synergy package in greater depth. In most merger negotiations, the business synergy package is presented in a rather neutral manner. Frequently the discussion runs: "Here is Company X and here is Company Y. Let us compare the strengths and weaknesses of Company X and Company Y and, based on those comparisions, see what the strengths are for the combined company."

In my judgment, a more positive way to present the business synergy package is to discuss the buyer and seller, focusing on the seller in terms of what the transaction will mean to the seller; how the seller is going to be able to grow more rapidly, penetrate new markets, or participate in new activities because of its association with the buyer.

It seems to me that it is usually easier to communicate with corporate presidents in these business terms rather than in technical financial terms. Most corporate presidents are operating men. They usually have little expert understanding of the concepts involved in a financial package. They don't know the finer points of convertible preferred, debt with warrants, or of any other financial package. For them, the financial package is often the wall paper decoration of the modern corporate society.

In contrast, corporate presidents do understand marketing, product development, expanding sales distribution, cost reduction programs, new plants and so on. These are usually very tangible programs to corporate presidents. As a result, they tend to create excitement, and it is that excitement that may persuade them to sell to your operation.

The business benefits from mergers described in business synergy packages can go from the very obvious to the esoteric. An obvious example of synergy which I am familiar with involved two companies which had complimentary lines in the automobile "after-market" parts business. By combining the two companies it was possible to unify the sales forces of both firms, thereby gaining the greater leverage and penetration from the joint company's distribution system.

In other cases, more esoteric benefits are obtained in a business system. In fact, many acquisitions are so esoteric that one hears questions such as "Why did they merge? It doesn't make sense!" Usually, though, with a few exceptions, I think that if you dig deeply into a transaction you will find that it did make some substantial business sense.

One highly sophisticated advantage that a conglomerate offers to a seller is to be the conglomerate's core company within a product or market sector. This type of merger gives the benefit of forming a base for exploiting a new business for the conglomerate.

The business benefit to the seller may be that the conglomerate has a higher multiple than the seller and to the extent that the management of that core company wants to expand rapidly through the utilization of acquisitions, the core company management is going to have a high price-earning ratio paper to help it build its complex.

A conglomerate may therefore be able to offer an opportunity to a seller to acquire other companies which he could not buy with his own securities.

An additional benefit of a smaller company joining with a conglomerate is that the seller can greatly reduce his risk exposure. The smaller company can take on projects and activities which it would not have been able to take on otherwise, because if those activities are a failure, it does not mean a corporate catastrophe.

I think, too, one can frequently attract brighter and more dynamic people to work in a large corporate sphere. This is another characteristic that the conglomerate offers as a compelling argument to a hesitant seller.

For example, a small company may find it very hard to get very many people to relocate to its headquarters city if it happens to be a small town with limited attractions.

A larger company might be able to do it because they

would say to the person, "Look we have very special problems, very special needs, here, and if you will accept this assignment—of course, it is going to take three years or four years—there will be other opportunities in a nicer location, such as San Francisco or Seattle or somewhere else you'd rather go." This may seem like a small point, but it may loom large to the seller and that is what really counts.

There are many ways to present your business synergy package to a prospective seller. Sometimes, you have to resort simply to preparing a long letter and mailing it, although I think that usually means that you have lost your effort. In my judgment a verbal presentation in a face to face meeting is better.

After you have determined what you think the prospective benefits are, you must sit down with the seller and describe those merits in a discussion. By orally going through the business synergy package first, you are usually in a position to highlight the things that the seller seems to feel are most important. In other words, if his face glows when you describe a certain point, you can expand on that point, and if he frowns, you can ignore the item that he is not particularly pleased with, and you can build up a program that makes sense not only to you but also a business synergy package that makes a lot of sense to him. By doing that, you achieve a certain mutuality, some common interest, a basis for further discussions.

A POSITIVE APPROACH TO MANAGEMENT

The third package, the seller's management package, is frequently the most important of all when you actually sit down with the sellers. It is most important because it will be management that makes the decision to sell. This package is designed to affect that decision favorably.

You may be offering management face saving, or you may be giving it the benefits of joining in a merger for greater security and comfort. The actual content will depend on your evaluation of the situation. The important fact is that it be directed specifically to the seller as a human being, not just as a box on an organization chart.

Among some of the very important things that I think can be incorporated in a management package are, first of all, specific proposals related to management responsibility. Most corporate presidents don't want to sell because they feel they are going to be losing some of the responsibility, some of their personal opportunities to expand, and some of the prestige that they have enjoyed as the president of ABC Corporation, regardless of how small ABC Corporation may be, or how little known it may be anywhere except in Sioux Fall or North Platte.

In presenting a package which helps a management decide to sell, one of the opportunities is to demonstrate that they are going to have greater responsibility; that the package is structured in such a way that they will not only have greater responsibility, but greater responsibility in the areas in which they really want to participate.

In order to illustrate this, I would like to use the example of a buyer with \$200 million in sales. The buyer had two problems: One, that he wanted to merge with a company with \$50 million in sales; and two, that he had a management succession problem. As a result, the management of the \$200 million company went to the \$50 million company and said, "Not only do we like your product and think it is going to generate a lot of business for us, but we think we can give you management responsibility which goes far beyond what your management team is currently assuming."

The buyer easily excited the management of the selling company and induced them to accept the offer. The president of the selling company became president of the combined company, which was now a $250 million company, and thus gained for himself and his colleagues in the smaller corporation a more exciting management opportunity.

Let me cite a couple of other examples, not on such a grand scale as becoming president of a $250 million company. One was in the educational business, where a company had a sliver of the total educational market and the president felt rather competent in the marketing end of the business, but not nearly so competent in the manufacturing end of the business.

He was approached by a much larger corporation participating in the educational business. They said, "Look, we recognize that you don't really like the manufacturing end of this business, but that you have done a good job in the marketing end. So why don't we give you much more marketing responsibility, and we will help you out in the production and manufacturing problems?"

To this president, who had turned down dozens of prior offers, this was a very exciting opportunity. It meant gaining additional responsibility in an area which he felt was his forte. Of course he decided that this was a favorable merger.

Another example is the case of a man who had a small company, with about $5 million in annual sales. His company had developed a small capability in the graphic arts business, and he had used this capability rather extensively in advertising and other promotional types of products.

But he really felt that his capability went far beyond just that one isolated business. Someone finally figured that out and wanted to acquire the company.

The buyer went in with a proposal: "Look, we are in the packaging business. We are in the educational materials business. Both of them would be appropriate applications of your technology and manufacturing capabilities."

The prospective seller became intrigued at this possibility that he would be able to break out of his one current business, and move into other areas.

That kind of excitement eventually induced him to decide to sell his company. For the last thirty years, he had said "no" to all suitors.

Then, there are other kinds of people who want to reduce their workload. These gentlemen, at sixty or sixty-two years of age, may have decided that at the end of another three years they are probably going to want to retire. In anticipation of this, they may well consider selling their companies.

Currently in our firm, we are representing a firm very much like that. The president is sixty-one and he wants to pick his successor. He doesn't have a management team below him to provide that successor, so he is very interested in joining with a partner who will help him pick his successor, allowing him the next three or four years to reduce his commitment to the business activity.

Another example of a management wanting to reduce its responsibility is a Midwest firm whose corporate chairman (even though he is considerably under sixty-five) recently made a decision to reduce his workload and move into political and social activities. Here, once again, buyers were able to persuade him to sell his company.

UNDERSTANDING THE SELLER

There are many reasons why people sell, and if you can find the key reasons for any specific company, you can go far toward closing the deal.

For example, I know a particular company whose management had a major face-saving problem. The company's chief executive officer had told a lot of people at the New York Society of Security Analysts that his earnings were going to be excellent and his growth was going to be up for the next year. But as his fiscal year progressed, it became clear that he was not going to be able to achieve those financial goals. Rather than go back to the New York Society or call in the analysts or prepare a press release saying that his earnings were going to fall far below what he had expected, he decided to sell out and bury his company's results, thereby maintaining public appearances.

In this particular situation the gentleman was successful in selling his company. And all parties, including the purchaser, were aware of the fact that he had the reduced earnings and that things were not going so favorably, but he managed to keep his pride and his position in the community.

I would guess the pride element is extremely important today, when companies are so often being attacked by outsiders who take over corporations. As an element of pride, company managements may decide to join with buyers with the expectation that they will be able to help design their own destiny by doing so.

The last aspect of the management's package is the remuneration and security of the management team. Here, you have to decide just exactly what you are willing to give.

In most instances, titles are cheap but the board positions are not. Management contracts give a good indication of what you can settle for with the seller-management in the event a parting becomes necessary.

All these elements are important in designing your seller's management package—coming up with an interesting salary, interesting stock options or whatever other compensation your firm may have. You will probably also have to make a decision about whether you are going to give board positions to the company that you are trying to acquire.

All those things combined together—the responsibility, face saving, and remuneration package—usually are very important, I think, to effecting a successful merger. Without them, a company usually is unavailable.

DESIGNING THE FINANCIAL PACKAGE

Now, having examined the second and third packages, let us go back to the the first—the financial one. By stressing the others, I did not intend to slight this one. Financial terms are part of the basic vocabulary of negotiation.

The financial package will probably include these elements:

———the absolute price you are going to offer;
———the nature of dividends, if any (many corporate managements have very strong feelings about their dividend policy);
———the consideration of whether the transaction is going to be taxable or tax-free;
———the changes in liquidity which may be caused by the merger;
———the extent and nature of downside protection offered by the buyer to the seller;

The absolute price level has, of course, been determined as part of the over-all decision to seek the acquisition.

On the question of dividends, I think the general rule ought to be that stockholders continue to receive what they have in the past. From your corporate intelligence, you may find out that the management is not really interested in the dividend, or that the shareholders are not basically attracted by the dividend. You might, if it is advisable, be then able to eliminate the dividend or reduce it. But that is not normally a reasonable assumption as, for historic reasons, dividends carry tremendous significance in the business world. You can give a company the equivalent of ten years of dividends in increased stock prices, and it still does not serve as an alternative.

In order to achieve the level of dividends that is equivalent to the package the seller shareholders are currently receiving, the best alternatives probably are: 1) your own common stock, if its yield is high enough, 2) straight preferred, or 3) a convertible preferred.

A third aspect of the package is whether it is going to be a tax-free transaction or not. That can be rather important, not only to the seller, but to your company as well, because you must meet most of the criteria for a tax-free transaction in order to get pooling of interest accounting treatment. If you have a purchase accounting treatment, you may have to write off "good will," which makes the transaction financially less attractive to you. So it may be important to construct a tax-free deal, even if it is not of concern to the selling party. (Since this article was prepared, there have been substantial proposed changes in pooling of interest accounting. The result of these could have major impact on this analysis.)

The principal ingredients for constructing a tax-free transaction are voting securities. This usually limits you to preferred, convertible preferred or common. There is also a possibility of doing a Statutory Type A merger under which you can do a transaction partly on a non-taxable basis and partly on a taxable basis. I know instances where it has been done, but it is not common practice.

An important element in the financial package may be the fact that a buyer achieves greater liquidity for the seller. Of course, that is easily done if a buyer has listed securities. But a seller may, particularly if he has large stockholders, insist on piggy-back rights for registration or insist on registration very soon after completion of the merger, giving him an opportunity to gain liquidity and diversification in his portfolio.

The downside protection of a package, which again may or may not be very important to the seller, can be very easily achieved if a buyer uses something like convertible preferred, because with its dividend level this kind of security does not decline nearly as rapidly as common stock, particularly a common stock without much of a dividend.

In recent years, many special kinds of deals and guarantees have been made, particularly when people are buying private corporations and wish to provide downside protection. In these arrangements, the buyer agrees to add an additional payment in the form of stock in the event that the buyer's common stock declines or fails to perform well.

It may be relevant to refer to two financial packages in which I participated as examples of how financial packages can be constructed.

One of these was an extremely simple transaction, the other quite complex. In the simple case, the seller was a company that had about $50 million in sales, and was a tremendously profitable firm, earning about $7 million after taxes.

The seller's management decided that a fair price was 17 times earnings; the management also felt that it was important to maintain their $2 a share dividend level.

The other criteria they required were: listed securities, greater liquidity for their shareholders, and a certain amount of downside protection.

The acquiring company in this particular situation had a multiple of about 35 times earnings, no dividends—stock dividends, but no cash dividends—and it was listed.

Because of the buyer's own high multiple, he could easily pay the 17 times earnings. But there were two key problems: The seller's management wanted more downside protection and a $2 cash dividend. The solution was relatively easy: convertible preferred. A convertible preferred with a $2 dividend met the requirements of the seller shareholders and afforded them some downside protection. By making this preferred convertible into approximately $78 worth of buyer common stock, we had a package worth 17 times earnings. This dividend was subsequently quite important in supporting the value which the seller shareholders received when the buyer's company stock fell. So the sellers got what they wanted in this particular transaction.

Another somewhat more complex transaction illustrates the craftsmanship that makes an attractive financial arrangement for both parties. In this case, I can use names and I refer to the Squibb-Beech-Nut merger. The Beech-Nut Life Saver Company was a very attractive property, a company with a strong consumer franchise and a variety of product areas in the United States. It seemed to make a great deal of business sense to join with E. R. Squibb & Sons, since Squibb was a fully-owned subsidiary of Olin Mathieson Chemical Company, with no outstanding public common stock.

There were extensive negotiations between Beech-Nut and Olin Mathieson about the possibility of joining Beech-Nut with Olin Mathieson and the fact that this would make so much sense with the Squibb subsidiary.

The problem was financial. It was a difficult transaction because Olin Mathieson was selling at 11 times earnings and Beech-Nut was selling at 18 times earnings. And the Beech-Nut people wanted a price somewhat higher than the market.

It is nearly impossible, regardless of what kind of unusual paper you use, to take a company selling at 18 times earnings without dramatically reducing your own earnings per share.

In this particular case, we came up with an idea to get around the mechanical problem. The idea was that the Squibb Company would have a much higher multiple than either Olin Mathieson or Beech-Nut, and would be a more effective way to acquire Beech-Nut Life Saver.

That made a deal that was financially attractive to all parties because Squibb as the acquirer—if you are willing to look at it that way—was able to increase its earnings per share, whereas Olin Mathieson as a company would have had considerably diminished earnings per share in this transaction.

So there are deals that go from very simple ones, such as the first one, to the very complex ones, such as the Squibb-Beech-Nut. Sometimes the deals become financially impossible so that no way can be found to merge companies on terms favorable to both parties.

Or, more precisely, no way can be found to merge them by using only one third of the package.

Even if, for the moment, there is no agreement on financial terms, there are still the second and third packages—business synergy and the seller's management package.

Perhaps considerations arising from these packages may be applied to break the deadlock over financial terms.

My own feeling is that this is often the case. To make it stronger, I believe that many mergers fall through simply because little or no attention was paid to the other two packages. They include some of the most powerful arguments you have. It would be short-sighted indeed, in establishing strategy, to overlook them.

An experienced negotiator, the author examined the human aspects of the problem for clues to successful strategy. He notes, for instance, that "The fact that you are in a buying situation automatically gives you an aura of being a little bit worldly, a little bit sophisticated, a little bit of a city slicker."

5

THE MAKING OF A NEGOTIATOR

by Donald H. Putnam,
President, Conrac Corporation

I have a very strong suspicion that negotiating—successful negotiating—cannot really be taught as such. You can describe it and discuss it after the fact, but to talk about it in advance is something like trying to lecture on courtship—another very human endeavor.

It is like trying to teach selling. You can identify and teach all the points of good salesmanship, but it is very difficult to teach somebody how to sell. In fact, selling is a good analogy for merger negotiations because, in the last analysis, negotiation is no more nor less than a simultaneous exercise in sales by both parties.

UNDERSTANDING THE PROPOSITION

The single most important component of strategy must be a clear understanding of the proposition you are both considering. I do not now mean the financial details and the legal points; obviously you should be comfortable with those. I mean the more subtle dynamics within the situation which give it purpose.

You must, for instance, know the reason why you and the other party are talking in the first place, and trying to arrive at a common conclusion.

To be even more specific, you must know why he is selling—what is really motivating him to the point of sitting down with you to discuss selling the business that he controls.

Very often, the reason is not the one that you have been given, or may have inferred. This is not to say that you have been deliberately misled, but rather that this surface reason is usually only part of the story.

For instance, if there are operating problems in the business, usually they will have been carefully screened. If the seller has been moved by family circumstances, he may feel that these circumstances are too private to discuss with a relative stranger. Sometimes he himself may have personal motives that he would rather not discuss.

One thing is reasonably certain: if you expect to carry out a successful negotiation, you had better understand why he is really there—not only the surface reasons, but, if at all possible, those more subtle reasons.

WHY ARE YOU BUYING?

Next, and this may surprise you a bit, you had better know exactly why you are buying. You may be buying just because there is an opportunity to create an incremental gain in your profit-and-loss statement by the combination, but I think this is becoming less likely every day. New accounting rules are such that the incremental gain, or the one-shot advantage of making an acquisition, is rapidly disappearing.

Therefore, presumably you have some other substantial reason for feeling you should acquire this business. You must understand why you are buying, and why he is selling.

As you sit down to negotiate, you probably have some kind of operating rationale in mind. You may think there are sales advantages to you, or product advantages, or technological advantages. You probably see some reason why you and he can do better together than each can alone.

This you should have well developed, and you had better believe in it, because if it is not real, you probably will not be able to put your thinking across effectively.

The whole proposition—his standpoint and your standpoint—must have logic and purpose to you. Then, of course, you will be able to react instinctively to any position he may take.

WHY IS HE SELLING?

And finally, you will be well advised to go one step further and find out, in addition to why he is negotiating, what it is that motivates him. The motivations of a person are sometimes quite different from the objectives they are seeking.

These are frequently subordinate things, and alone they are not likely to make the deal. But they can kill it.

The seller usually seeks something in addition to the real objective of the negotiation; it may be personal position—position in his community as a matter of pride or prestige, or position in the resulting company.

He may have a special market enthusiasm. He may honestly want very much to go after a certain market that he cannot go after alone. Perhaps he has a desire to repeat his domestic success abroad, to show that he can do in international markets what he has done at home.

The path of motivation-seeking can become tricky, because sometimes in negotiations you will be dealing with more than one principal, who are all in agreement on the objectives, but may not be moved by the same personal motivations.

SELECTING THE NEGOTIATING TEAM

Understanding of the opposite party requires insight, and I think it helps dictate who should do the negotiating for the buyer. The negotiator's title is not important, he must be the man who knows the purpose best, the rationale, and the people on the other side.

Hopefully, he is the one who has developed the rationale, who has most clearly seen the advantages and the objectives of getting together. He can sell it well. He believes in it. If he is personally enthusiastic about it, he is unquestionably the right person to negotiate.

If he is weak on some of the details—technical, financial, historical—it really does not matter, because those can be taken care of by other people in the organization.

But it is supremely important that the person who negotiates for the buyer be the person who really understands and knows the proposition best.

If it is necessary to have other people in the negotiation to provide the support on technical or historical details, it is important that there be no uncertainty as to who in that room is speaking for the buyer.

Meetings of six and eight people on the side are not likely to be fruitful. If there have to be two or three people on the side, be sure it is clear who is the leader of the team.

Some people believe that the right man to do the negotiating is the man with the strongest leadership background. I cannot agree with that any more than I can agree that the man to negotiate must be the one with the best financial background. I think that it is the person who is most knowledgeable about the proposition. I also think this is one area —the choice of chief negotiator—where a third party is definitely not the right person.

Business brokers or go-betweens of various professions have a very useful role to fill but I do not think this role carries into the key negotiating sessions. For what it is worth, I have had unnecessarily unpleasant experiences along these lines. In one instance, we introduced a third party into the situation. The other side also introduced an outside party, so we had, in effect, two separate parties standing between the principals. It does not surprise me now that we got nowhere at all.

After wasting a few days on this, we pulled back and said, "It is either principal to principal, or no further discussions." That put the situation back on the track.

IDENTIFYING THE REAL SELLER

About who must speak for the seller, there can be no question. The person who controls the seller must do the talking.

Unfortunately, it is sometimes hard to reach this person because he is not always the man who is nominated to represent the seller.

It is not unusual, for instance, in a public or semi-public company to find a president who sincerely believes it is his responsibility as a chief executive to negotiate on behalf of the owners.

If he does not, in fact, have control of the situation, he is really not the right person. Obviously this presents an immediate diplomatic problem.

If you are dealing with a family-owned company, you may find one member of the family who sees himself as the leader of the clan, and he may well be just that—in everything except selling the family assets.

Sometimes, circumstances make it necessary for you to negotiate with one person, even though you know full well that there is more than one person in control of the situation. In that case, I urge you to repeat your presentation to as many control elements as you can find. It is a very risky thing to let the nominated control element carry your story secondhand to his own principals—not because he will deliberately mislead them, but because nobody can tell your story as well as you can yourself.

Sometimes it is difficult to identify the control. In one situation, we negotiated in a perfectly practical way with the trustees of a family trust who had full authority over the trust and full responsibility for the assets of the trust.

And yet, after the proposition was made, it turned out that it was the heirs of the trust who really controlled it.

This brought up an interesting legal point, because the heirs should not have had control, even as beneficiaries. But in this situation, legal niceties notwithstanding, the trustees were going to listen to the beneficiaries of the trust, and we found we were really talking to the wrong people. By following the right legal framework, we were ignoring the true control.

UNDERSTANDING THE SELLER

It may be useful to generalize a little about the seller. I will hazard the suggestion that he is usually misjudged by the buyer. This can be a fatal mistake.

In most operating companies of any size, including quite large ones that have not themselves been merger-oriented, you can assume that the seller is rather unsophisticated in the area of corporate finance and merger legalities.

But stop right here, because that is where the lack of sophistication ends.

This person knows his business better than he knows anything in the world. He certainly knows it better than you do.

Moreover, he has almost certainly been a success in his management of that business, and he knows it. Certainly, he has been successful enough to make the business attractive to you. And he knows that, too.

He is not a hayseed. He sees himself as astute in investment finance because he has a modest estate which he manages for himself and his family, and he feels he knows the investment world pretty well. He just does not happen to know that particular corner of it which has to do with mergers.

He is probably a fairly original and creative thinker, because he has been successful in managing his business. If he is the non-managing owner, he has been able to find someone else to build it on his behalf.

He is creative and original, and undoubtedly strong-willed.

He is probably a sophisticated man in every respect, except for mergers.

If you talk about his hobbies, you may find he flies his own airplane.

If you talk about travel, you will find he has done more of it than the average executive of a publicly-owned company.

His education has probably been very sound; if he is second-generation in a family business, it has been excellent, because he has probably been trained to take that business over.

His cultural interests are likely to be as wide as those of anyone he may be talking to about a merger.

As a matter of fact, he is probably very much like you in every way. He is to be respected for his success and his knowledge and experience.

The only thing he lacks is experience with mergers. As a result, he will be ill at ease because he is not used to being unknowing. He will feel as you probably do when you go to your daughter's school and sit down with her teacher and try to make small talk. You find you just don't have anything in common with a 22-year-old schoolteacher. That is the way he feels.

ESTABLISHING CONTACT

Obviously, it is up to you to try to eliminate that discomfort, and there are two ways to do it.

First, you must try to establish very careful contact on those interests you do share.

Second, and even more important, you must try to resist the human impulse to show that you know what he doesn't. By all means, play down the experience you have had and he has not.

I am not recommending that you act as if you were not informed; that would merely be insulting. If you insist on acting over-knowledgeable, you may derive a warm feeling of pride, but very likely you also will chill and frighten him, or at the least, make him feel he is up against a mysterious area which is dangerous to him personally. Also, you will accentuate your reputation as a city slicker. And you carry that reputation, deserved or not.

The fact that you are in a buying situation and representing a company that is to negotiate a merger automatically gives you an aura of being a little bit worldly, a little bit oversophisticated, a little bit of a city slicker.

For all the positive points I have made on behalf of potential sellers, I must add that they often come to the negotiation very badly prepared in two areas.

The first concerns the price or value of their business.

Oddly enough, even quite large companies seem to feel that it is entirely the province of the buying negotiator to put a value on the business.

This is nonsense. A seller must do enough research to form his own opinion. He must study similar companies, industry statistics, parallel sales of some of the companies he may know about. He must in fact do some of the same kind of research that the buyer has done, to determine what he thinks the value of his business really is.

He has access to the same resources the buyer does; he can get reports and industry statistics, he can spend the required hours in the library and with the calculating machine.

There is no reason why research cannot be done by both sides, and I think that any person giving thought to selling his business who has not bothered to devote the one or two days he needs to do this research is leaving himself vulnerable.

The second point is that sellers are often guilty of not having done their homework on how their company is going to be integrated into the buying company. Obviously, if the seller is the president of the company or is the principal owner and intends staying on, he will have a very natural desire to know how he fits into the company.

But even if this is not the case, the seller has good reason to question how his company is going to integrate into the buyer, because that can help tell him the unique value his business has for the buyer.

DETERMINING TRUE VALUE

In general, if you are attempting to sell a commodity and you feel that it has special value to one buyer, that is a valuable trading point. For instance, if you are selling a vacant lot, and you are talking to the man next door who happens to own a plant which needs parking space, it is quite different from dealing with someone who is just interested in your lot as an investment. This is simple common sense, yet many sellers overlook it.

The way to find the special value a business has for the buyer is to know what he is going to do with the business—what *his* rationale is.

When he talks about the values of your selling to him, what values do you see in his buying from you?

As a rule, I do not think sellers need to worry too much about architecture—about how the deal is actually put together, the tax and financial details, and the other technical things. Professionals are available who know these things better than any seller ever will, and they will ultimately pass judgment on the technical points. That is their function.

But I believe a seller must take responsibility for putting a value on his own business and he must know how his business is going to integrate into the buyer's.

Let us now assume that we have the best-qualified participants: on one side, the fellow who best knows why this is a sensible proposition for the buyer; on the other, a well-informed seller who is in control of the business being sold.

Most negotiations will not adhere to a formal agenda. In all likelihood, they will follow a plan which the buyer has in mind.

One of the first points in this plan will be to identify the biggest interest of the seller. It is usually price, but it may be something else. It may be to acquire capital support for certain ideas that the seller has, or perhaps to achieve liquidity of his investment. He may want to solve an estate problem that exists in his stockholders' group.

The buyer should try to identify this single area of major interest to the seller, and then make it almost his entire agenda.

The lesser details, important though they are to the deal, do not really make or break it.

That single area does.

It is almost impossible to arrange a balanced, attractive package that will sell itself. Assuming price is the first objective, there are still other factors such as liquidity or later income from the proposition or personal position, which must be considered.

But if the price discussion has not been satisfactory, no amount of advantage in the subordinate factors will make up for the gap in price discussion.

It is not possible to take a number of "pretty-good" arrangements and make them add up to a winning financial proposition. As a matter of fact, buyers who try too hard to bring the subordinate factors along may give away more than they need to.

An analogy for this can be made with the reasons why, according to researchers, people buy certain kinds of automobiles. They do not buy power and they do not buy accessories and they do not buy mechanical features. They buy style and personality.

If a man has convinced himself that he has a GTO personality, he will buy a GTO, given the opportunity to do so. And if he is convinced that he has a GTO personality, a dealer will have a difficult time selling him a Mercury. The fact that the Mercury has all kinds of gadgets makes no difference.

I can only guess that this is the way most selling works, but I *know* that this is the way merger negotiations work. If a man enters a merger negotiation seeking the maximum price on his business he can get, he will not be diverted from that purpose by any number of subsidiary attractions. A little more income, a little closer liquidity, prestige, tax advantages, will not make him waver from the primary goal he is after.

The part of the agenda that deals with this prime goal—whether it turns out to be price or something else—should be dealt with by the prime negotiator. Other details can be taken care of by staff people.

WRITTEN OR ORAL PROPOSALS?

The question almost always comes up: how early should we put things in writing? I never have been successful with a written proposal.

I do not really know why this should be so, because a written proposal is not hard to do very well. You can take your time and polish it, and structure it, and make a beautiful piece of prose. But for some reason, it does not seem to work —not in my experience.

Perhaps the reason is that in written form the proposal is not responsive enough, or that it slightly misses the mark, just enough to keep the dialogue from really beginning.

Or perhaps a written proposal may presume knowledge on the part of the reader which he does not have—a small technical point or a usage of a phrase he has not come up against before. If you are talking to your seller, you can immediately see this, but if you are writing to him, you may lose the thrust of your proposal.

For example, not long ago we negotiated quite seriously with a foreign company that would have been an ideal situation for some of the things we wanted to do in Europe. We held meetings in Rotterdam that seemed to develop clearly understood discussions of convertible debentures. These bonds were not as well understood there as they are here, but the gentlemen on the other side seemed to know what we were talking about. Because of the distance, we did in fact make a written proposal to them. It failed, and I have felt ever since that the reason it did not succeed is that the written proposal got us off on the wrong foot.

Their principals could not understand the debt quality of debentures, and did not understand the conversion premium. The whole thing had a negative feeling for them, and they did not really grasp it. By the time we attempted to recoup the situation and explain what these instruments were and how they can work to the advantages of the owner, the ball game had been lost.

Although I do not believe in written proposals—letters that say, "Here's our proposition. Will you accept, or make a counter-proposal?"—I do not suggest that you go entirely the other way and rely on purely verbal communications.

Usually, the situation is complicated enough so that *you* have trouble enough keeping it fully in mind and certainly a lot of the subject matter is going to be new to the listener.

He is going to need something more than his own memory, or the notes that he takes.

My own solution, not very popular with lawyers, is to use an informal outline. I sketch out the principal points for discussion, writing down the terms of the offer. It is a handwritten piece of paper and it covers the proposition we are making in a quite informal way. At the appropriate time, if the discussion has brought us to that point, I give a copy to the seller and use it as a talking paper.

It does not purport to be any kind of definitive offer or agreement; it is not signed or dated or anything else. It does have the value, however, of giving the other party, in your words, the proposition that you are making to him.

It is not a document; it is not a binding instrument on either side, of course; but at least you can feel when you have ended your discussion that this paper, or any changes you have made as you go through it, represents the substance of a reasonable understanding.

Obviously the final understanding, the final binding document, is drafted by the attorneys, not by the principals. But there can be no final agreement until there is agreement on the general substance.

HANDLING NEGATIVE FACTORS

Another point that comes up in every negotiation is: what about the negative factors? My view is that, however small they may seem, they should all be brought out.

For instance, if you are talking about an exchange of stock, it is very likely that the stock the seller receives will be restricted and that he will have to provide an investment letter that somewhat restricts his liquidity.

Or, if it's going to be a cash purchase, there may be a tax recapture on past depreciation.

By all means, bring out such negatives early in the negotiations. If you do not bring them out yourself in a forthright manner as small difficulties in your proposition, they will be brought back to you later as bargaining points by the seller.

Of one thing you may be certain: no such details, negative or positive, will be overlooked by the time the whole race is run, because between them the lawyers and accountants for both sides will eventually cover every possible aspect.

You are far better off in bargaining position to bring out such negative points at a time that suits you best, rather than have them brought up as a bargaining point by the seller.

TIMING THE NEGOTIATIONS

Do not start your final negotiations too fast. No matter how many days or weeks you sit, bear in mind that the man you are talking to is probably taking the one most important step of his entire business life.

It may have taken him thirty years of climbing through the organization to reach his position. Or perhaps he is the third generation of a family to control this particular business. Trying to bring a man to final negotiations too rapidly can turn off a negotiation before it starts.

I have talked to any number of selling people who have described their reaction to other companies that have attempted to pound out a purchase almost before they knew how to spell the company name. This is a most distasteful thing to a seller.

One final, fundamentally important point. When you get into the final negotiation stage, when you are about to make a deal, you must insist on access to all of the control elements of the company.

The person you are dealing with, for perfectly good reasons, may not have wanted you to talk too widely in his circle, to his directors or stockholders, until he himself can bring matters into shape.

If you are dealing with a company that has an inside board of directors, you could be in trouble, because while the president and owner may see the wisdom of a merger, it is very likely that career officers, who are serving as directors, will not see the benefits to them and are most likely to be negative as a first reaction.

If you can't reach them individually and attempt to tell your story individually, you almost know in advance that the board is going to vote against it.

If the owners are outsiders you have not met, you must insist on meeting all of them, to gauge their reaction to your proposal, and evaluate how successfully you have shaped the proposition to meet their interests.

Having said all of this, I must, in the final analysis, say I am still convinced that there cannot be any rules for the tactics of merger negotiation. Every situation has to be different. It requires great sensitivity to people, and a strong sense of purpose to be a successful negotiator.

By no coincidence whatever, these are also precisely the qualities required for success in any kind of enterprise.

Question: You stated that the man for the buyer who should do the negotiating is the man most knowledgeable about the situation.

What is the likely reaction, in your opinion, from the seller with respect to the man who is doing this, whether he be the president, director of the corporation or an outside investment banker?

Isn't there a sort of status effect?

Mr. Donald H. Putnam: Yes, I think there is a status effect. But I think what it really comes down to is this: the seller wants to feel that he is negotiating with the one person who controls the situation.

He might be momentarily flattered if he is negotiating with a senior title, but I think he will very quickly know that if he is negotiating with the person who controls on the other side, he is negotiating with the right person.

I would not run the risk of using a title to flatter the seller if that title did not happen to be on the best person to negotiate successfully.

Question: What is your opinion about having the seller establish his own selling price?

Mr. Putnam: Well, as I said, I feel that a seller who comes into a negotiation not knowing perfectly well what he thinks is the value of his business is just making himself hopelessly vulnerable. Who produces the price first depends on what side of the table I am sitting on.

I like to name my own price first. I have always been in a buyer's negotiation, and I always want to name my price before I hear the seller's price.

Question: Don't you feel, though, that you may be placing yourself at a disadvantage? That you might have offered more than he might have, or caused him to feel that your first go is merely an opener, and that he can raise his sights from whatever you establish?

Mr. Putnam: Yes, of course, that is a risk. But it cuts both ways.

If the other man speaks first, he may be shooting for the moon and he may start off at a level too far out of sight for you to work down from.

My feeling is if you do your homework right, you have a pretty good idea of what the value is. If the other fellow happens to think incorrectly that the value is a lot less, he is in for a pleasant surprise, but you cannot be hurt badly.

On the other hand, I think you have to control the negotiation yourself, and the price you name is the price to negotiate from.

Question: It has been my observation that frequently the chief executive officer or principal stockholder is not necessarily the most articulate or the best salesman, and you frequently have a better man down in the organization who may be the vice president or the owner, or somewhere down there who knows the deal just as well as you do, and can probably do a much better job of selling than the chief executive officer.

What is your feeling of who the choice should be?

Mr. Putnam: I did not mean to imply that I thought the chief executive officer or president should negotiate for the buyer. I meant to say that the person who understands the deal best should negotiate it, and it may well be a vice president or somebody else in the organization.

From the seller's standpoint it seems to me that there really can't be much discussion about who negotiates. It has to be the person who controls, and I think that a buyer who negotiates with someone else in the organization just as a negotiating exercise would be wasting his time.

If you are not negotiating with the seller who has control, you are not really negotiating.

Question: How can you realistically make an analysis of the proper price to offer without having full access to the company's records?

Mr. Putnam: Normally, before you get to the financial negotiation we have been discussing, you have pretty fair access to the records.

You may not have literal access to operating records, but you would normally have been given financial statements running back several years, and any supporting documents that you specifically ask for.

You may ask for order backlogs or you may ask for monthly new business, to see what the trend looks like.

Anyone negotiating seriously will provide basic financial data and answer specific questions even though he may not let you come in and examine all the records.

Question: Do you find that you often go through a series of negotiations with a privately held company only to educate them to the point where they go out and make a better deal than the one you gave them?

Mr. Putnam: I must give you two contradictory answers.

Yes, we often negotiate with privately held companies and don't bring about an acquisition. But I know of few cases in which we have sent them on to make a better deal.

Actually, I have been involved in a great many more negotiations than I have in actual mergers because the success ration in this business is not as high as we would all like it to be.

But in those unsuccessful negotiations, we have never lost the negotiation because we could not come to terms. We have lost the negotiation because the seller decided not to merge.

Of course, that is the hazard. If you are a reasonable and perceptive person, ready to pay value, you will purchase the company.

But very often the buyer comes to the table convinced that he is ready to negotiate, and at the last minute some factor makes him decide he is not. If someone else then makes the deal, it is not fair for the unsuccessful buyer to be resentful.

Question: A buyer will often ask certain personal questions and sometimes want to be very familiar with trade secrets, customers' activities, and so forth.

How far should one go in actually laying out this kind of information, and at what point during the negotiations are these things proper to be told, if told at all?

Mr. Putnam: Well, I don't think a seller should reveal anything that is not publicly available unless he is rather serious about negotiating a sale, or at least hearing an offer.

I think he is foolish to let information out until he is sitting down to listen to a proposition.

Once he has decided that, I think he ought to permit access to any financial information a buyer needs for the business.

If he holds anything back, he will not get a responsive offer.

I think there has to be a point where the seller decides, "I am serious about this."

Question: Do you feel that the seller need have any great fear of the potential buyer finding out about his business very deeply, starting negotiations, and using the information to his advantage, so to speak, by either competing with him or finding other companies in the industry and using the knowledge that he has gained?

Mr. Putnam: You are talking about the risk that the seller runs by letting proprietary information out.

I don't think this is too serious a risk. I am not dealing here with relatively small companies that may be talking merger, but I think if the buyer is a reasonably large firm or an established firm, he is really interested in that merger, and I don't think there is a great risk in your revealing proprietary information to him.

Question: Don't you think that there can often be a lot of time saved by the establishment of a price very, very early in negotiations, and then have this price deal subject to withdrawal by either party?

Mr. Putnam: Let me say that very likely you would have different answers from different people, and I am not going to pretend that my answer is conclusive. But I have strong feelings.

I say no, you can't save time this way. I feel that you have to develop the proposition. It has to feel right to both sides before you start talking price.

I personally feel that time cannot be saved by trying to establish a price, because I suppose my feeling goes back to this: there is no such thing as a tentative price in any merger.

Once a number is named, it is engraved in concrete. You might want to say that such and such a price would be the right one, presuming that the year comes out in such and such a way, or the current quarter is such and such, but there is no way of making even that tentative.

Question: In the strict sense, might the strategy for a merger negotiation and an acquisition negotiation be entirely different?

Mr. Putnam: No, they are really the same thing in the sense that we are using it.

We only are talking about one thing, and I suspect we are talking about acquisitions.

There are cases where mergers result. That is a legal technicality. That is what your lawyer decides.

I think in a semantic way we are simply talking about acquisitions. But you will notice that sellers in making announcements to employees or in discussion with associates will call it a merger, they will never say they are being acquired.

Question: What about a letter of intent, or a letter of understanding, a brief sketch that will fill in a period of time on a handshake or an agreement?

Mr. Putnam: That period will normally be at least two or three weeks. My own feeling is that such a document might be of value, but I have been assured by our counsel and our accountants that it has no value, because in order to be acceptable to the attorneys on both sides, it must in fact, be the definitive agreement.

In a lawyers' frame of reference there is no simple, sketchy document. There is an instrument or there is no instrument.

If it is an instrument, it had better receive the same care, research and polish that a definitive agreement receives.

I have come up against this from time to time when it seemed to me good to have an exchange of letters, and the lawyers involved found it a dangerous thing to play with.

Question: To what extent do you use your previous record in acquiring other companies to get new companies to join you?

Do you sometimes parade out the presidents of companies you acquired a while back and have them tell how happy they are?

Mr. Putnam: Yes, just as much as possible. It is the single most convincing thing you can do if you are dealing with people who are uneasy about becoming a part of a large company; to let them know how they will be treated.

We have several divisions managed by their former independent managers who are now very successful in our company and very flattering in their references to us as people to be purchased by. Believe me, we use that.

Walter Kidde & Company is one of the major firms that set the style for acquisition-oriented management strategy. The author, its chief executive officer, ranges over factors large and small that have played significant parts in determining the outcome of negotiations.

6

TACTICS: THE DISTINCTION BETWEEN A MERGER AND AN ACQUISITION

by Fred R. Sullivan, Chairman and Chief Executive Officer, Walter Kidde & Company

Based upon my experience, there is more than a little truth in the classic courtship analogy of mergers and acquisitions. Two parties are attracted to each other; they get together, both a little guarded at first; he tries to impress her that he's the smartest, most masculine and most courageous and courteous guy in the world, while she, of course, is trying to convince him that she's the most desirable woman that he'll ever know.

He's thinking about a possible acquisition and she's thinking in terms of a merger. Fortunately, that can't go on forever. They soon relax and a meaningful exchange begins. He discovers that her teeth aren't perfectly straight and she finds that he loves pro football. But nobody's perfect and if they learn that they're mutually compatible, they may decide to merge.

Of course, business merger negotiations are really a lot more complex than courtships. If the techniques of merger specialists were applied to the human relationship, our suitor would be calibrating exactly how far her teeth were out of line and calculating what it would cost to have them straightened.

But the man who's going to be involved in merger negotiations must not only learn a whole new vocabulary, he must also begin to appreciate the nonexisting differences between simple and seemingly similar words. Take the words merger and acquisition, for example. A company is never said to be acquired. It may be a merger, or better yet a joining of forces, or perhaps a blending of mutuality of interests.

Of course, that's hard to say with a straight face. But if you prefer sports phraseology, how about a melding of complementary entities into a new corporate team? And if you really want to confuse the issue, there's always an interplay of structural business components for the achievement of a combined enterprise whose concept is new in design.

Terms aside, merger discussions require a keen sensitivity which is basically a trait acquired through experience. To illustrate how important this sensitivity is, let me begin with step number one.

STARTING THE DIALOGUE

The first thing you have to decide is how to initiate talks with a company that has attracted your interest. My point of view throughout this discussion is generally going to be that of the acquiring company unless, as lawyers might say, it is specifically noted otherwise.

Your first awareness of the prospective merger partner can come in many ways. And here, again, we get back to our courtship analogy. Someone may introduce you, or it might be a sudden and casual discovery, or perhaps you've known each other for some time, but have never noticed a mutuality of interest.

If discussions are to proceed beyond the introductory stage, there must be significant ways in which a merger will be beneficial to both sides. It might be a good industrial fit, with the two already active in related fields. The merger might make financial sense, or market sense, but there must be some practical reason for both parties to proceed to more detailed discussion.

FINDING COMMON GROUND

Management sensitivity is called for in determining whether or not the apparent rationale is real. The merger possibility that appears very promising on the surface can look very unrewarding after a little bit of scrutiny. That scrutiny may involve a brief study of the company's entire industry, its competitive position, its reputation in the industry, the quality of its products or services, the kinds of customers it has, how long it has kept them and a whole host of other factors.

That scrutiny will also include an appraisal of whether or not the merger candidate can do for you what you think it can—whether the fit you think you see will actually materialize. Of course, you will also want to give their balance sheets a fairly good study.

After this homework is done, a decision must be made as to whether or not you wish to proceed with serious discussion. If you decide at this point not to go ahead, you will have saved a lot of wasted time and effort on the part of both companies.

Assuming, however, that after early scrutiny the merger still looks beneficial, it is now time to move to step two, which is the serious discussion.

ESTABLISHING A CLIMATE FOR NEGOTIATION

It will be critically important at this stage to develop a strong rapport with the top management people of your merger candidate. After all of the deal is completed, you'll want them to stay and run the business. In that case you're going to have to live with them for a long, long time. And when I say top management, I am talking about a fairly limited number of people. The more people involved, the greater the chance of information leaking out and this, naturally, can sour a potential deal very rapidly.

When a leak occurs, both sides can easily assume that the other was responsible for it, and a mutual distrust will begin to creep into the negotiations. In that case, it may be better to break off the talks, rather than continue when this crucial trust has been damaged.

Somewhere early in the serious discussion stage, after considerable give and take over what one can do for the other, the two managements may well decide that they do very much desire a merger. Now the real negotiating stage has been reached, and you get to the subject of price. This is where you get down to the real hard bargaining.

THE SUBJECT OF PRICE

Most merger candidates come into the discussion with a price in mind. They may be willing to accept anything within a certain range, or they may have a little flexibility, but unless they're simply shopping, and you had better be sensitive enough to discern that quickly, the management of the merger candidate will always know roughly what it wants.

Your price limit is pretty well fixed too. Your price earnings ratio often is a rule-of-thumb top limit, although there are a number of exceptions to that rule. Occasionally, you will find a very attractive merger prospect whose earnings are growing so rapidly that it will probably contribute materially to your earnings ratio in future years. Or, they might have certain technological expertise that will improve your present operation, or they may have unusually good potential.

For many reasons you cannot lock yourself into a hard and fast limit. If the candidate is a public company, currently selling at a ratio lower than yours, the price parameters are rather easily set. Let us assume that you are selling at twenty times earnings, and he is selling at ten. The final price is going to be somewhere between, and both of you know it.

Sometimes you will reach an impasse. You will have

come up to a price of fourteen times earnings, let us say, and they won't budge below sixteen because they are convinced that their future earnings are just too promising to permit a give-away at fourteen. One solution, of course, is the contingent pay-out.

We will tell him, "If you believe your future earnings will be so-and-so, and you can deliver in your belief, we will give you fourteen times now, and the remainder when you can show us that you're right." The contingent pay-out can be a wonderful concoction. It has saved a few excellent merger deals that otherwise would have fallen through, and if the acquired company delivers on its promises, everybody is made happy.

The timing of the discussion can sometimes have a bearing on the price negotiation. Perhaps the company being acquired is near the end of its fiscal period, and is projecting greater income next year. They may want to link the mutiple to next year's earnings. Perhaps your stock is currently selling at a lower multiple than usual; you may want to link the future pay-out to your future stock price. Often, at a time when your stock is selling below normal, this may be the only way an agreement can be made.

You or they may want to guard against price fluctuation between the time of the handshake and the time of the closing. It may then be desirable to make an agreement for an exchange of stock placing upper or lower limits on the value of your stock at the time of the closing.

For example, if your stock is selling for fifty, you may reach an agreement on a five million dollar settlement or a hundred thousand shares of your stock. Both parties may then agree that if the price of your stock at the time of closing is less than forty-five or more than fifty-five, the number of shares will be adjusted in accordance with a predetermined formula.

The central point in price negotiating is to maintain a posture of flexibility, and also creativity, in proposing terms that are both fair and feasible.

THE USE OF BARGAINING

Now, if you are in the game of mergers very actively, your most important possession is your reputation. You must be honest and worthy of trust first of all, but it's equally important to maintain a reputation as a hard but fair bargainer.

The management of merger candidates must, in fact, know that you are an astute negotiator. They will feel a lot more satisfied with the outcome if they can believe this, and they will also feel a lot more comfortable working with you in the future.

In one respect I dislike the word "sweethearting," which some people use. I dislike it to the extent that it implies a kind of sweet-talking of your candidate's management, a kind of razzle-dazzle. We prefer a straight businesslike approach to negotiations. It makes sense that if the candidate's management is good, the old soft-shoe routine is not going to impress them, and after all these are people you will want to work closely with after the merger is consummated.

This is not to say that there should not be some contact of a personal nature during the discussion. I think that aspect is very important. You will want to get to know them a little, as much as they will want to become familiar with you. If anyone on either side has some annoying idiosyncrasies, it is better to discover them early in the process.

Once the price has been decided upon, an agreement must be reached on the exact terms—exactly how the payment will be made. This can be the most complicated stage of the negotiation.

Management of the acquired company is naturally concerned with one thing—getting the best terms for its stockholders. The acquiring company has two problems, and they are of equal importance. It must protect itself and its equity and debt structure and its own stockholders, and it must be considerate of the interest of the candidate's shareholders as well. If any kind of stock swap is planned, they will become your shareholders, and as management you must be concerned with their needs.

SEEING SELLER'S PROBLEMS

Generally speaking, if the merger candidate is a privately held company, the terms of the deal are more flexible than if the company is publicly held. This is true because management is dealing in behalf of a limited number of owners who can be consulted on their wishes. For a publicly held company, the package must be tailored from the candidate's historical situation.

Kidde, for instance, has paid stock instead of cash dividends on its common over the past several years, and some of our acquired companies have had a history of cash dividends. In deciding on the package, we may assume that the stockholders of the merger candidate wish to continue receiving cash dividends in amounts roughly equal to what they are used to.

Where there have been no dividends, both parties might be satisfied with a straight swap of common and in another case we will probably have to design a package that includes both common and convertible preferred. Basically, you start with the preferred, awarding a sufficient amount to give the acquired company shareholders about the same cash dividend that they have been receiving, and the remainder of the price can then be filled out with common shares.

Of course, most merger deals aren't that simple. A lot of

things must be taken into consideration as the package is being constructed, not the least of which are the tax consequences of designing the deal in a particular way. After a handshake agreement has been reached, a more thorough scrutiny of the company's records is normally undertaken, and this is simply a protective mechanism.

I don't want to overstress this point because comprehensive analyses of balance sheets are certainly not all-important in evaluating the acquisition. In fact, quite the opposite is more often true. Just as some companies pay more attention to management techniques than management judgment, some pay more attention to acquisition techniques than judgment.

A FLEXIBLE APPROACH

In our company, we have no hard rules and no textbook approach for merger negotiations. Each of our merger candidates comes to us with different ideas, with different wishes and different hopes. All of them look to us to provide the impetus for accelerated growth through technological knowledge, or financial know-how, or marketing capability.

Some want to concentrate their efforts on running their business by turning time-consuming tasks like legal or financial work over to our corporate people, and some see more secure growth potential in our diversified operations than in their own single product or kind of business.

We recognize that our merger candidates are different, and we treat them in merger negotiations as special situations. There are no textbook formulas. As a general rule I don't personally get involved directly in all merger negotiations unless the company is a very large one. I do, however, keep constantly up to date on the progress of talks. Usually in the early stages of negotiations, the talks are turned over to divisional people who are closest to and most familiar with the business of the prospective merger candidate.

In this respect, our division managers are free to conduct merger programs of their own, and I can say that in the many divisions of our company, at least ninety percent of the merger ideas emanate from the fellows on the operational level. They know their own businesses much better than we do in corporate headquarters, and they know their needs. They know the people they are competing against, they know the people that have related lines, they know what's going on abroad and, generally speaking, they know a lot more about what should be done to help their business grow than we do at headquarters.

After the talks have gone beyond the exploratory stage, and our divisional managers have made their recommendations, negotiations do move to the corporate level. At that stage, our corporate specialists—legal and financial—become involved. The corporate staff includes no acquisition specialists as such, but because of the more than seventy acquisitions that we have made in the past five or six years, they are an exceptionally knowledgeable and capable group, able to move merger negotiations smoothly and quickly through the mass of detail work necessary.

MAINTAINING INTERNAL COMMUNICATION

Once we have reached the second stage of discussions at the corporate level, it is a foregone conclusion that we are quite interested in the prospective acquisition. We simply cannot afford to waste time and effort at this point on something which we are not fairly sure of.

Negotiations over price usually involve a senior management member of Kidde with the top management of the company being acquired. Whether members of the board of the acquired company become involved in negotiations depends entirely on the company that is being acquired. At

Kidde, our board rarely gets involved in negotiations; we have excellent rapport between our management group and our board, and both groups are well versed in our acquisition guidelines. In the seven years that we have been together, there has never been a failure to support management in approving a recommended merger.

All mergers, and especially those involving the issuance of a large percentage of shares of outstanding stock or requiring a new issue of stock, are subject to the approval of the board. Especially in the latter cases, we keep our directors as fully abreast of developments as possible, sometimes by calling special meetings, sometimes through informal meetings and through informal telephone briefings with those who are out of the New York area.

For some companies, especially the companies that are being acquired, it is imperative for the board to get involved. In fact, for the negotiations to proceed smoothly there must be some assurance that the board stands behind the management.

This will often mean that one or two directors should be involved in the direct merger negotiations and particularly in the final price settlement. Generally speaking, our negotiation philosophy is simply to adapt ourselves to the procedures that will best protect our interests and those of our prospective acquisitions, while making it as easy as possible for the selling company to get the kind of terms that will make its people satisfied and a working part of the new organization.

WHAT ARE YOU REALLY BUYING?

There is one point that I want to emphasize. In looking at the assets of a company, don't overlook the most important single asset of all. You'll never find it on the financial statements, but it will surely be reflected there. That, of course, is the management of the company.

The job of management is to employ all of the resources of the company, that is, the financial, the technical, the physical, the marketing or whatever, to bring the greatest return over a period of time, including short term. It is the responsibility of management to employ all company resources in the most productive and rational method possible under the circumstances that prevail.

The management should vary its course with economic and social changes which create new investment opportunities. This may be in the area in which the company is already operating or it may be in some other area, but I believe that it is incumbent on management to move these resources around to take advantage of existing growth and profit opportunity.

The most efficient and the most effective means of reaching the markets created by changes in the economic or social climate is through merger with companies that already have a stake in those markets, companies that have the know-how to keep pace with the growth of new and revitalized markets.

When we acquire a company whose markets are changing and expanding, both sides benefit. The acquired company gets the resources it needs for rapid growth, the acquiring company puts its resources to the most efficient use, and when two companies join together they can produce a total result in sales and profits greater than the sum of their separate outputs.

The companies benefit, the shareholders benefit, and the public benefits. The shareholder of thc acquiring company benefits in an increase of the earnings of his company, and ultimately and often immediately, there is a corresponding increase in the value of the common stock he holds because of the immediate or prospective earnings growth.

The shareholder of the acquired company also benefits. A good merger increases the value of his investment and gives him ownership in a broader-based company better protected from the risks that one-product-line companies are subject to: sudden technological obsolescence, a change in market structure, or the domination of a giant competitor.

The public benefits because mergers help bring newer and better products to the market faster. The demands of our increasingly affluent society require quick and massive response. In all this, the merger movement contributes to a stronger American economy.

In the narrow sense, mergers enable America to compete more effectively in world markets, and in the broad sense they enable free enterprise to compete more effectively against other economic systems.

Question: When you were first involved in building Kidde to a much more sizeable organization and a more diversified organization, there were only a handful of you. You mention the importance of quick response. How are you able to achieve this, now that you are such a large company?

Mr. Fred R. Sullivan: Actually, I think it is probably a lot easier to do it now with a bigger company. We do have a half dozen well trained fellows in the accounting and legal side, and we have very good fellows in the operating managements who bring these deals to us, and we have at least three or four fellows around the top of the company that are closers, and I'm always there. If anything looks that good and looks like it can be closed in a hurry, we can usually get to it.

We don't keep a running box score. We have never made any actual count of the number of acquisition possibilities that come in. In the last year or so we have hired a couple of young fellows to come along and train in this field. Our training policy is a very simple one. We give the man a telephone and a desk and tell him to go to work. They will say for the first few days, "Yes, but how do we start this?" Of course, there are a number of different ways that you can start it, and one of the ways is to let the world know about it. You let the world know about it by talking to commercial bankers, investment bankers and business brokers, and you even clip things out of the Wall Street Journal. There are all kinds of ways to start.

People know by now that we are a growing company and an acquisition-minded company, and there are a lot of things that come in every day. If we were to try to sort out all of this, I'm sure that only one out of ten of the possible things ever reach a stage where you'd have any serious negotiations. Maybe only one out of ten that get to that stage ever get to the handshake stage.

It seems pretty important to build a kind of selectivity and I wish I had a specific formula, but I think it's something you get at eventually, and that you develop in the light of your own company, of your own company's guidelines and your own company's philosophy and your own company's wishes for growth in the future.

Question: Who talks to potential candidates, divisional people or corporate specialists?

Mr. Sullivan: Well, it depends largely on the size. For example, we have a company called Sargent, which manufactures locks and architectural hardware.

We are very heavily engaged in the safety and security and protection fields. Sargent has been a fine growing company in this field, but there are certain parts of the architectural hardware line that they would like to be in. For us to sit in the home office and try to figure out how to do that would be a waste of time. We wouldn't know where to go. But the fellows at Sargent know very well what product lines they want. Recently Sargent brought us a company that is in a related line of architectural hardware, with sales of $5 or $6 million a year. Our division head talked to me on the phone, reporting that he had made his overtures to the management of the other company.

He determined in consultation with the president of that company what he thought could be arranged. Then he brought him in. We had lunch in New York one day, and we established what we thought was the right price range and then the division head went out and negotiated the final price.

The president of that company came in and met with our lawyers, and they drafted up a list of ten or fifteen points that a company should have. Now over a period of a couple of weeks we'll draw up a contract and the lawyers will be in almost daily contact on all of these provisions. There's a fair amount of boiler plate about a merger agreement, but there are also special provisions in every one of them.

Even though you pretty well know where you're going to end, sometimes the lawyer for the other side has to make certain requests and raise certain issues that take hours to debate. Sometimes, you tend to feel that the debating process is just for the benefit of the lawyers—to make sure that they've done their work properly. But you have to go through all of it.

After we get to the contract preparation state, we do make a serious analysis of the figures, and we make plant visitations and review our findings.

Question: Are the merger guidelines actually formalized in written memorandum or directive of some kind?

Mr. Sullivan: In our particular company they are not. I used to be on the board of a company which became part of the Reliance Electric Company. The name of it was Toledo Scale Company, a very fine company. One day as a director I was given a sheet of paper with the guidelines for the kind of merger that Toledo Scale would like to make. It is easy to sit down and write guidelines for the kind of company you want, but there are very, very few of those companies around. Typically, it must have fifteen percent of the market, it must have a good marketing organization, it must have good field service, it must have proper research and development. There aren't so many of those companies that are for sale.

Question: Do you have any minimal size limitations, and if so why?

Mr. Sullivan: No, not really. For instance, we're in the uniformed guard service business. Burns and Pinkerton are both bigger than we are, but we are looking for growth. In this particular case, if we're not very well covered in, let's say, Denver, and there's a little company that's doing a quarter of a million dollar business or a half a million dollars worth of business in Denver, it would be of interest to us.

We would certainly not be interested in anything that small, or even in the millions, if it took us into a new business or new industry—not even something that was a romantic thing for the 1970's or 80's. You get to a certain size, and you have certain resources and it does spread you out too thin if you get into too many small businesses.

Question: How much second guessing or conflict is there between division managements and the corporate managers on deals that one or the other initiates?

Mr. Sullivan: A fair amount. If part of what you have in mind is that one of your division operating people might say "Here's a good company, and you ought to have it, and it's worth $5 million," and you take a look at it and say, "It might be worth $5 million to you, but it seems to me that you're going to get into a lot of trouble by having to operate that company $5 million worth for the next five years," then I think you might have a lively debate, and sometimes the division people could be overruled.

But I don't think that we try to be arbitrary about the whole thing. Most of the fellows came into our picture through mergers, and they know pretty much what was paid at the time they joined us and what the parameters are, and they aren't likely to bring something to us unless they thought it had a chance of flying. As a matter of fact, I cannot remember a time that we went out to acquire a company over the head of a fellow who was going to have to operate it.

Question: Would you be willing to address yourself to the question of contingent payouts for a moment?

Mr. Sullivan: Well, contingent payouts are certainly difficult in large publicly held companies where there are thousands of stockholders. That's a whole special deal. There have been some that have been worked out on that basis, but they're pretty complicated. In small privately held companies where there are just a few shareholders, you can work those out quite often and we have a number of them.

I think that some of the problems have to do with who is responsible for the increased growth and health of the new enterprise, and it does mean that when you do have a contingency payout based upon the wonderful work that the new people are bringing, unless the people are people of good will, there are an awful lot of problems that can develop.

Question: What happened to the top managements in the seventy companies that your company acquired?

Mr. Sullivan: I don't know about all seventy of them. I'm not so sure that there were seventy presidents but they are, in the vast majority of those cases, still there. I think we have about fifty, or sixty, or even more presidents in our company.

Some of those presidents are presidents of very small operations. We've been at it now for more than seven years at Kidde, and I can say that certainly at least 75% of the presidents are still there. They may have moved to other jobs.

They've been promoted and they've been moved crosswise. In some cases, we've had to replace them. In one particular case we learned after about a year that the man didn't want to be president anymore, he wanted to go to Florida and spend his money. So we had to replace him.

That is a reason that you hear of a great deal. The management of a family company after working with it for a generation, or maybe two generations, sometimes just gets tired. It's a perfectly good business, but they're willing to put it into another business to get another stock, on the New York Stock Exchange. Eventually they'll sell our stock and get a diversified portfolio of stocks, and then they just go and live on the rewards that they've earned for working so hard.

A common sight on financial pages is the "tombstone" ad: "Company A has acquired Company B. So-and-so assisted in the transaction." The author, who has "assisted" in many transactions, describes in concrete terms the forms which this assistance may take, on behalf of buyer and seller both.

7

THE USE—AND MISUSE—OF FINANCIAL SPECIALISTS

by H. Corbin Day, Vice President,
Corporate Finance Department, Goldman, Sachs & Co.

Sooner or later, most companies that are involved in acquisition work—even larger companies that have internal staff specialists—ask themselves "Should we seek outside advice and counsel on this matter?" Many answer in the affirmative. To estimate just how many, it is only necessary to count the number of "tombstone" ads that appear in the financial press. "Tombstone" ads are those staid, discreet announcements that two companies have successfully completed merger negotiations. At the bottom is a modest line indicating that a particular investment banking firm had "assisted in the transaction."

Whether the transaction would have taken place with or without the assistance of financial advisors is a moot point. The purpose of this chapter is to describe what form this assistance can typically take.

WHAT DO INVESTMENT BANKERS DO?

As investment bankers, we can and do represent both sellers and buyers. I have chosen here to suppose that our role is to represent a prospective seller. This seems appropriate for two reasons: first, because the nature of our activities on the behalf of sellers should be understood by prospective buyers; and second, because our services for buyers are in many ways similar to those performed for seller companies.

Let us assume, therefore, that Company X comes to us for financial advice. Management and/or owners are not sure what future course the company should take, but feel the company is at a crossroads and must carefully analyze new directions.

Typically, X is a family-controlled company. In initial meetings with the principals we try generally to characterize the problems based on our experience in a large number of other transactions. This involves trying to understand what the real objectives of this company should be. These may not be the objectives that the management or the stockholders talk about. Our job is to identify what the realistic objectives ought to be by talking with the key people, the owners, and the management—bringing to bear our knowledge and experience in other transactions.

TO MERGE OR NOT TO MERGE?

Once we feel we understand the company's objectives, we have to analyze what we think is the right way to achieve them, both from a theoretical and practical point of view. A merger is not the only solution; objectives might be met by a public offering, private placement, joint venture or many other things. After preliminary evaluation, let us assume that we conclude a merger is the best alternative. What are some of the factors that usually lead to this? First, family control is expected to be less direct in the future due to the fact that there is no successor family management. It happens very often as sons and relatives pursue other professions. Second, stock has become widely held within a family with resultant wide divergence in investment criteria.

A good example of this was a company which had been very successful, had compiled a very good growth record, had public ownership, but still remained family controlled with about fifty percent of the stock in family hands. One man in the family was active in the company. He had, as I remember, three sisters, and they, in turn, each had two or three children. This man would not have been interested in selling his business except for the fact that he didn't want responsibility for the family's inheritance. He said "I can't hold this thing together and make the right business risk decisions that are necessary for future growth. There are too many people involved now."

Third, capital expansion may be necessary to move a business as fast as it should move. It is often too risky for a family to go into debt, or to build a new plant or capitalize on a development.

Fourth is estate tax problems. How do you pay inheritance taxes when the time comes?

Fifth is product diversification. I have saved it for last because it involves many things.

WHAT KIND OF MERGER?

I propose that there are many different types of mergers. I classify the first as a sell-out. This would be a combination where the seller tries to get the best price in cash or in stock, often with a big company, and is prepared to lose his identity in the vastly larger organization. Then there is the medium-sized merger in which you merge with a company that is going to be by far the dominant force in the merger, but is still small enough in size so that you will have some impact on the organization. Finally, there is the merger with a company two or three times the size of the seller. This I chacterize as really closer to going public than selling. There are many merger routes available, each with considerably different long-term implications.

Let us assume that the principals accept the decision that the best route for the company is to merge with a certain type of buyer. What does the investment banking firm do at this point?

WORKING TOGETHER

The first thing we do is to continue the discussions that we have had in the form of a detailed investigation of the business. We must understand what the strengths of that business are; we must know what the weaknesses are, we must build a rapport with the management because our role is never to try solely to take over the function of selling the business; it is to work jointly with the management, to be an expert sitting at its side so that when decisions must be made we can render advice as a professional who has been through similar decision-making processes many times before. The relationship is seldom successful if one or the other party tries to do everything. It must be a partnership.

Second, we usually prepare summary statements for a privately owned company, a brief brochure of the products, marketing, management, and other key points. We are careful to make sure that no confidential information is included in this brochure, which is always approved by the management of the company. I will later get into why we think that is very important.

ESTABLISHING PRICE

After we have a good understanding of the business we recommend to the owners what we believe is the appropriate asking price for the business. Price/earnings ratios are probably the most important single factor in our determination of price. An evaluation of similar publicly owned companies indicates what P/E's are generally prevailing in that industry. Once a base value is set, a premium is generally added which takes into consideration a higher value for control and many other factors which vary in each situation.

An important part of setting price is an accurate determination of the company's true earning power. Are salaries way out of line in this privately owned company compared to what they would be in a publicly owned company? How is depreciation and maintenance accounted for? Have capital expenditures been expensed? What other benefits may exist in a privately-owned company that will not continue under new ownership?

This homework must be done. Earnings must be reconstructed—not in a general fashion, but as specifically as possible. With the seller's help and with the accountant's help, we must put these things on paper, otherwise it is just talk.

We have said that P/E is the most important determinate of value. But, just as important is the bottom line number to which that P/E is applied.

There is a merger market today. There are so many potential buyers that a true market has developed. It is not, obviously, as structured as the New York Stock Exchange, but there is a market for companies today, and you can pretty closely define what fair values are. But to do so, it is necessary to have considered all relevant facts.

For instance, a company may have excess cash; how do you treat it? Is it fair to add it to the price after you have capitalized the earnings? I think you can. Do you get penalized for excess debt? I think the answer is yes, you do.

STRUCTURING THE TRANSACTION

Once a price is established, time must be spent analyzing the most appropriate way for this particular company to complete the transaction. Once again, homework. The seller may have particular qualities, or non-assignable licenses. What are the tax considerations involved for the controlling stockholders? Should only a tax-free transaction be pursued, or might a total cash transaction better meet objectives? An important part of our job is to analyze the stockholders' objective and recommend what we feel is best.

Very often a person will say on first meeting, "All I want is a tax-free deal, and I won't consider anything else." We just say, "Fine," and then perhaps the next time we meet suggest that we have done some homework and hope you have considered that if you take cash and pay the capital gains, this is what you should be able to earn after taxes, which compares with a significantly lower after-tax income from dividends in a tax-free transaction.

There are new types of securities appearing in mergers. We now have transactions in the form of debentures with warrants, or convertible debentures, and there are strong opinions of counsel that these can be treated as installment sales. As long as you don't sell the debentures, you don't pay a capital gains tax, so it is in effect tax-deferred.

What can something like a convertible debenture mean for the seller that we are looking at in this particular case? If it is appropriate for him, he can get more income because the buyer can probably put a higher coupon on the debenture because he is going to get the tax deduction, and he might even pay a higher price.

For a certain kind of seller—for instance, an elderly man who is going to have a large estate to pay—the transaction can be structured so that if he dies before the debentures are paid off, the effect will be the same as a tax-free stock deal because it is possible to get a deduction in your federal account on the part of your estate which is taxed as installment paper. In effect, a man in the 50 percent tax bracket that has installment sale notes in his estate will receive exactly the same thing as a common stock deal in terms of dollars paid out in income tax if he should die before converting or selling the debentures.

EVALUATING THE OFFER

If it is decided that a stock transaction is appropriate, care must be exercised. I think too many people fail to realize that this is probably the most important investment decision in their lives. When stock is received in a tax-free transaction the stockholder is frequently locked in. If I go out and buy a stock tomorrow in the market and two weeks later I don't like what I bought, I sell it and I take a loss or profit. When an owner takes stock in a tax-free transaction, there are restrictions. Generally at least 50-75 percent of the stock received must be held for two years. Many people don't take the time to look at a tax-free transaction from the investment viewpoint: "What is the long-term outlook for this stock? Is it the kind of stock I want to hold over a period of time?"

There is a classic example often cited: An owner of a privately-owned company had two offers, one for $36 million in stock, and one for $33 million in stock. He accepted the offer with the higher price, and that stock promptly went down from $65 to $15 over the next year and a half. The other stock tripled over the same period of time.

This means that an analysis must be done of the buying company. Research must be done; product areas analyzed; future forecasts made. Before leaving valuation, let me add that little tag-end: things left to the last can become very troublesome if you don't talk about them early. Depreciation recapture is a big factor today as is investment credit. Also, the appropriate way of handling real estate subsidiaries should be clearly spelled out.

Assume now that all the homework has been done, and assume also that the seller agrees with the price objective that we have mutually reached. (If his price ideas are substantially different from ours, we often will not proceed to work on the transaction: our investment is our time, and we don't get paid unless the transaction is completed.) Our role now shifts to identification of companies deemed to be appropriate buyers. Theoretically, there is only one right buyer for each company. How to find that company is a very difficult process.

As you look at what I term the business philosophy from

the seller's side, you must keep in mind the individual personalities involved. These are people who, in most cases, are going to have to work together toward the same ultimate business goals. Price is important, but in most cases—almost all cases—a buyer company is not going to be interested unless the management of the company acquired stays and will be there for some period of time. You have to look at people, at their philosophy of doing business, and make sure it is in juxtaposition to your own.

If you happen to be in a similar type of business, but the buyer's method of marketing is completely different from yours, or his method of advertising and promotion is completely different from yours, it is likely that the merger will not work out too well six months after the deal is closed. Degree of integration is important to the seller's future. Will the buyer leave you alone or fold you right in? What is the best way for your company to run?

There is the question of relative size of companies. A big company operates differently from a small company. A conglomerate will operate differently from a single-product company. Those are some of the considerations that go into this fairly detailed consideration of who we are going to talk to.

Up to this point, what we have tried to do, working with the management, is to say, "You have an objective. You want a certain kind of transaction. Let's do the homework so that we will be in a position to get the one right answer that meets most of the objectives that we want to obtain."

STARTING DISCUSSIONS

Now we are ready to go to the first candidate. We will probably suggest approaching as many as three candidates at one time. Our approach is to initially discuss the concept. If we sat down and spent so much time on why we are a good deal for a certain company, we will look foolish if there is no responsive chord. This first meeting with the prospective buyer, therefore, is usually attended only by the investment banker because we find a more frank discussion generally takes place.

If interest is exhibited, we give the facts. This is where the brochure is important. The brochure is used to put some pressure on the buyer to give us a fairly quick response. If we were to just go in and talk generalities, the prospective buyer may say, "I'm really interested. I would like to go visit the plant next week. I'll take Jack and Charlie and we'll spend two days down there." That is the last thing the seller wants. The purpose of the brochure is to make enough general information available to see if the buyer is truly interested or not interested, without upsetting the organization of the seller.

It is very important always to make the presentation to the top executive officer of the company. I think that he must be involved in all mergers regardless of size. It is better to deal with him right from the beginning than to bring him in later in the discussions. Most companies which run successful acquisition programs have the chief executive involved at an early time. That does not mean you will not work with other people in the company, but in the first instance you get the chief executive involved, if possible.

The reason why we feel it is appropriate for a sophisticated professional third party to make an approach is that it increases the likelihood of a meaningful response. People will more readily talk to an investment banker or some other intermediary because they recognize the professional role and respect our judgement. A candid response is less likely if management of the proposed seller is present.

At an early stage we establish price thinking. This does not mean an exact number, but an indication of what conclusions we have reached from our homework in terms of values.

There are, however, many considerations as important as price, and they will be taken up in due course. But, it is important at this stage to indicate ball park figures. This can be done in multiples or in dollars. If the buyer is thinking of something radically different, we don't want to waste time.

DETAILS ARE IMPORTANT

In negotiations we feel it is important not to avoid the small points once there is a strong degree of interest on both sides. Many deals fall apart and we know that more and more are falling apart because people don't look at the little details early.

This is not to say that you should let yourself get into lengthy arguments over fairly insignificant items. If you get into arguments make sure you're talking about fairly important points. Try to put a dollar value on each point that you're talking about. It's important to have homework done on depreciation and investment recapture structure and contingent liabilities that may exist in your company. Talk about them early, don't bring them up later, because people will tend to magnify them if unexpected.

It's important to understand the characteristics of the stock to be received. What are the registration rights? Is it all investment letter stock? If convertible, what are the antidilution and other provisions?

Most management desiring to effect a merger want to be reasonable. The middle man can play a very important role when you get down to the brass tacks. A deal is good if it's good for both parties. The professional intermediary can often be a sounding board to resolve points which otherwise could kill a deal. I would say that this is one of the most useful negotiating roles that the investment banker can try to play.

CREATING A COOPERATIVE CLIMATE

In concluding the transaction it is important to try to create the right atmosphere at the closing. Get the merger started off on the right foot. We have all seen, too many times, bitter arguments towards the end of negotiations that have left people in the wrong mood. I am not talking about the owners as much as the second-echelon management who have been drawn into negotiations. They may dislike the way certain things were done, or some of the surprises that came in the end, and I cannot stress enough the need to be politic in this very critical area. Business will have to go on after the merger is completed and it is people for the most part that make a business successful.

Try to make sure that by the time you get to the closing documents there are no more surprises, that all the homework is done. Make the closing a friendly affair, and get the merger off on the right foot.

In conclusion, I want to re-emphasize that the importance of handling people is the key ingredient to successful mergers. We like to say in our firm that if you have a merger that makes sense, and you have a management that want to do it, we're not good investment bankers if we can't figure out some way to make the numbers work out.

An investment banker, I think, also brings a viewpoint which is strictly financial. We never try to be business experts. We don't try to be consultants. We don't offer marketing services. We just look at numbers and sometimes in these discussions the outlook that some managements have for their business is quite different from the way we look at what those numbers say they are.

It is fine to have a good lawyer. There is nothing better in the world. But the president of the company or the other people involved in the discussions ought to know how important a point is when his lawyer is arguing for it on a break-the-deal basis. I know one big company whose lawyer is very powerful, has tremendous professional pride of authorship, and insists on the most restrictive warrants imaginable. The company has had an unsuccessful acquisition program.

Question: I'm a little confused about the role of the investment banker as an independent party, or as an intermediary. Actually, isn't he rather acting like an advocate for one party who's his client?

Mr. H. Corbin Day: Yes, sometimes it's difficult. The investment banker's role as the intermediary may conflict with his role as representing one party. This is a kind of hard thing to draw the line on and I didn't mean to make it sound confusing. Let me see if I can explain it.

We are respresenting one party, but we really are a specialist in one area. We're independent in a sense that we don't have a financial stake other than a fee as representing this company or that company. That differentiates us from owner or manager. There often comes a time in a negotiation when it is better to get the parties away from each other because they shouldn't talk directly. In that case you've got to be able to go to the other side and talk frankly with him about some of the problems.

Maybe we'll tell our client, the seller in this case, that we disagree with him on a certain point. We'll tell the buyer that we told the seller that we disagree on this point. Maybe there's another way we can get around it. In other words, there comes a time in negotiations where the buyer will look to us to help him solve some of the problems. It sounds like it might conflict with the role, but it really doesn't.

Question: Can I assume from your statements that you will not represent a client who wants an unreasonable deal?

Mr. Day: Yes, many times we've turned down prospects. If we come to the conclusion that a company is worth twelve million dollars and the owner says he wants twenty, it's not worth our time. We have that situation right now, it happened two weeks ago. We had one conclusion and the family in this case wanted a substantially higher price—double; we couldn't see it and refused the project.

Question: What has been your experience and batting average in contingency payouts?

Mr. Day: You mean are they successful or not successful? Let me say a couple of things and then I'll try to answer that. We basically are not proponents of contingency transactions and I'd say without going into a long talk that the two principal parties are starting off on the wrong foot if they have a contingency transaction.

Presumably the buyer has plans for growth, and wants to integrate the acquisition with other parts of his business. You've got a seller who doesn't want to do anything but make every dollar that he can out of that business for three years, or he's not going to get paid. There is a dichotomy of interests from the start and you can just see the personality problems which you could potentially create. When do you use a contingency transaction? I think it's most appropriately used when acquiring a new product. You'll know if that product is going to be successful based on sales. You don't even have to know what the profits are.

When Clairol merged into Bristol Myers a contingency was paid based on sales only. That was a three year contingency and was very successful. The Clairol management today runs Bristol Myers. There's one type of transaction.

A transaction I'm involved with now is a consulting business and the numbers are simple; no inventory, no machinery, no plants. It's strictly a people business. Management wants twenty-five times earnings for the business, but they can't get it. So, how do we break that gap? A contingency here does seem appropriate because of the necessity of locking people in.

Question: Putting yourself in the position of a representative of the seller, suppose you had been offered some common stock ratio of 25 or 35 times earnings. How do you price the value of that particular company?

Mr. Day: My answer to that is first to make a judgment of the stock. If it is overpriced, you have got to ask for a higher price and a higher number of shares. You have got to protect yourself from the downside risks.

If you make an investment decision that the stock should be selling at 20 times earnings, not 25 times earnings, you should ask for that stock at 20 times earnings. In other words, get more shares. Otherwise, you are locked in, and you are not going to be able to sell it. Why should you take any kind of alternative investment that you think is overpriced?

Question: Do you have a rule of thumb for price/earnings ratios for a company that is privately held? And does the size make any difference?

Mr. Day: No rules of thumb. They would vary anywhere from 12 times to 33 times in privately owned companies. I don't think there is much difference between public and private at all. The public market establishes prices at which stocks in a particular industry sell. The way we would price a seller company would be to compare it with publicly traded stocks in order to establish an estimate of where it might sell if publicly traded. To that price would be added an appropriate premium for selling all of the company.

Question: I would assume that investment banking firms, any one of them, would have strong points as well as weak ones. How does one select an investment banking firm?

Mr. Day: Go see four or five. Look for track records. If you are looking for a particular expertise don't go to a house, for example, that does not do any merger work.

Question: How do you charge?

Mr. Day: We charge in a merger only upon completed transactions. Generally speaking, this is always a negotiable fee in our firm because it depends upon what functions we perform in any given transaction.

There are five or six things that a banker can do, and if you only do two of them, you obviously charge less than if you do all five.

Question: When you represent a seller, do you talk to more than one buyer at a time?

Mr. Day: Yes. The practicalities of the situation have led us to do so. We did not used to, but we found ourselves getting in some situations where we were being held up for too long a period of time. So we have evolved a system where we like to talk initially to maybe three people at a time. And we tell each person that we are talking to two other companies. But in the same breath, we say that the first company that comes back to us with a bona fide interest to get into serious discussions we will give an exclusive. We will only talk with one company when negotiations become serious.

I think bidding situations are completely taboo, and you will lose your best prospects by getting into such a situation.

One of the most delicate subjects in any negotiation process is price. Who brings it up? How is it handled? By approaching the subject as a simple decision-making exercise, the author removes much of the mystique that has come to surround price determination, and outlines a rational, common-sense procedure.

8

HOW TO ESTABLISH A PRICE RANGE

by Harry W. Keidan,
Lybrand, Ross Bros. & Montgomery

Establishing the price range for bargaining is one of the less glamorous, though extremely important, areas of negotiating strategy. Although it may seem complicated, price determination actually fits directly into the pattern of the general decision-making process with which you are all well acquainted.

The effective decision maker approaches a situation with a clear understanding of his own position—his strengths, his weaknesses, and his objectives. He explores all the alternative courses of action and analyzes them carefully. He examines the costs and the benefits of each to him personally. He recognizes that emotional reactions may be hazardous if not tempered with clear-headed, rational judgment. Only after all these steps are taken is he in a position to make an effective decision—a decision in which the personal satisfaction potential is maximized and the risks of unsatisfied objectives are clearly understood.

Approaching the price determination process as simply another exercise in decision-making, this chapter will cover the following five areas:

1. The necessity for a clear preliminary formulation of objectives.
2. The need for a thorough analysis of the seller's earnings and cash flow.
3. The need to understand pricing concepts frequently used by parties to a negotiation—from price/earnings ratios to the all-important earnings-per-share effect on the buyer.
4. The necessity for the buyer to ascertain the intrinsic value of the seller and to view corporate valuation as an exercise in capital budgeting.
5. The importance of understanding the effects of alternative acquisition methods on the pricing determination.

FORMULATING OBJECTIVES

If the parties are to be successful negotiators, objectives and the relative degree of importance of each objective must be clearly defined. The carefully formulated goal will help narrow the merger search, and will enable your advisors to provide effective assistance in structuring the transaction.

Most important, however, goal formulation allows the buyer to determine the personal dollar value of his objectives. This helps the buyer determine how high a price he can offer, for he knows specifically what he wants and its dollar value.

There are many commonly mentioned buyer objectives:

1. An increase in earnings-per-share. Even if a price in excess of the intrinsic value of the seller must be paid, this might be irrelevant if earnings-per-share and, hopefully, the price of the buyer's stock increase. A seller/negotiator can often use this buyer objective to his own advantage to extract a price in excess of value. However, if the buyer is more concerned with objectives related to the intrinsic value of the seller, this negotiating strategy could prove fruitless for the seller. Of course, only buyers that are public or are planning to go public will be interested in book earnings. Others will be much more concerned with cash flow.
2. Acquisition of new personnel for management, sales, or research and development may be another buyer objective. The value of these assets to a buyer will be the total cost of recruiting, hiring, and training an equivalent group of people. Since the alternative cost is difficult to determine and trained personnel are in heavy demand, substantial prices are often paid.
3. Acquisition of additional plant capacity may be an-

other buyer objective. In this case, of course, the alternative costs of building a new facility will be relatively easy to estimate. Therefore, less room for price negotiation will be possible than when the buyer's objective is primarily the acquisition of human talent.

4. Additional buyer objectives might be the acquisition of a new market for present products, or new products; or, simply the investment of idle cash.

The seller's objectives will also be of great importance. They will affect the price that the seller will accept and, if known to the buyer, the price the buyer will offer. A listing of frequently mentioned seller objectives may include:

1. The desire to bail out of a business because the company is problem-ridden or has a questionable future. Here, of course, the seller might take a relatively low price and the buyer might be well-advised to avoid this sort of "bargain." The buyer/negotiator should hesitate and revaluate the seller when it appears that the seller will settle for too low a price.
2. At the other extreme is the seller who will sell out only if he is offered a price greatly in excess of his company's value. Here, negotiation can be difficult since the seller is not really interested in negotiating.
3. Acquisition of personnel or capital may be another seller objective. The seller does not really want to sell but the economic reality is unavoidable.
4. In addition, many sellers are for sale because the owner/managers wish to retire. This directly affects both the interest of the buyer and the price he will offer. Assets without management, as we all know, may be of limited value. However, the sel-

ler's principal asset may be its undeveloped real estate holdings and the buyer may not be at all interested in acquiring management.

In summary, the objectives of the parties can be of utmost importance in establishing the price range for bargaining. The objectives of the buyer affect the value he places on the seller, and the objectives of the seller affect the quantity and nature of consideration that he will accept for his business.

ANALYZING SELLER'S EARNINGS AND CASH FLOW

The review of objectives is the first step in the pricing decision-making process. The second step is an analysis of the seller's earnings and cash flow. Once the buyer has determined why he wants to acquire a given company, he should examine the seller's financial statements and see what he is really buying. How are the present earnings arrived at? Are they indicative of the future? What is the condition of the inventory, plant and equipment?

Typically, in pre-acquisition exploration we must rely on the seller's published financial statements. While this limits our research to a degree, these statements can be extremely revealing. Generally, when we look at financial statements we tend to examine a few areas such as sales, earnings, total assets, long term debt, and net worth. However, this type of review is totally inadequate for our purposes.

To begin with, we must read the accountant's opinion. Generally we find a clean and unqualified opinion, but we must look for the qualified or adverse opinion, or the disclaimer of opinion. If the opinion is qualified, we must examine the reasons for the qualification. These reasons may significantly affect our pricing decision and they should be thoroughly understood. We should also notice which financial statements are covered by the opinion.

The next step should be a careful reading of the footnotes to the financial statements. The footnotes often reveal many conditions which will directly affect the determination of the bargaining price range. For instance, a footnote may indicate that certain loan agreements place dividend payment restrictions on retained earnings. This, of course, may affect the buyer's plans and reduce the price that he will be willing to offer.

Another interesting piece of footnote information is the interest rate that the seller is paying on his long-term debt. If the interest rate is unusually high, it could reflect a low credit standing. However, this must be interpreted carefully in a period of tight money and generally high interest rates.

Also important when analyzing a seller's debt position and interest expense are the existing lease terms. What type of lease financing was used? Who was the lender? What percent of the original cost of the leased property is represented by the annual rental payments? And, are annual rental payments based in part on gross revenues?

Another significant area to watch for is the maximum equity dilution possible as a result of outstanding options, warrants, convertibles, and contingent payout possibilities. If the seller has a qualified option plan, are the exercise prices of outstanding options above or below the current market price? Although accounting principles now require a computation of "primary earnings-per-share" as well as "fully diluted earnings-per-share," historical data may have been prepared differently. How were earnings-per-share computed in the past?

Still another important area usually covered by footnotes is the presence of any contingent liabilities. This may be an important red flag. Not only may the bargaining price range be significantly affected, but the acquisition may be dropped if enough uncertainty exists.

Up to this point we have read the accountant's opinion and examined the footnotes. Now we should set up a comparative statements schedule for each available year's financial statements, look for variations from year-to-year, and try to explain them.

After the comparative statements schedules have been reviewed for the more obvious variations, a ratio analysis should be conducted by setting up ratios between various accounts for each year. These ratios can be very revealing in helping to determine the true level of earnings.

For example, ratios should be set up comparing each item of expense to annual sales. Particularly important are separate expense-to-sales ratios for maintenance, advertising, selling, and direct labor costs. If the ratio was reasonably constant for several years but declined in the current year, it could indicate that the seller has unreasonably reduced expenses such as advertising or maintenance to inflate the current year's earnings. The naive buyer might use the inflated reported earnings to reach an unreasonably high offering price under a price/earnings type of approach. However, earnings may well be lower in future years to make up for the passed-over maintenance or advertising.

Another significant relationship of particular importance to pricing determinations is the ratio of receivables to sales. If the ratio has increased sharply in the present year, it might indicate that the seller is now dealing with customers with lower credit ratings. The seller may be trying to boost the sales figure at any cost. Therefore, beware of sharp sales increases when coupled with a sharp rise in the ratio of receivables to sales.

Also of possible importance is the ratio of sales returns to sales. An increase in this ratio might result from poor craftsmanship or an inadequate customer service department. If the seller wants you to pay on the basis of his future projections, an increase in the sales returns to sales ratio may be a strong argument for a lower price offer.

Ratio analysis is helpful in raising issues, but the answers may not always be obvious. In price negotiations, however, ratios can be used effectively to confront the seller with questions and thereby shift the burden of persuasion onto the seller.

I will touch on one final area in the evaluation of financial statements. What accounting principles are used by the seller? And, what will be the effect on my earnings if the seller's reporting practices are changed to conform with the accounting principles that I employ?

For example, if we use straight-line depreciation and the seller uses accelerated depreciation, the seller's net earnings are probably lower than they would have been if we had made the accounting decisions. Policies of establishing useful lives will also directly affect net income through depreciation. In a period of rising prices, if the seller uses FIFO and a buyer uses LIFO for inventory valuation, the seller's earnings may be overstated.

As these examples indicate, we need to find out the seller's accounting practices so that we can evaluate his performance on an earnings basis consistent with our own. No technique, from price/earnings ratio analysis to discounted cash flow analysis, will produce valid results unless accounting practice comparability is first established.

HOW TO USE PRICING CONCEPTS

Now that we have examined the parties' objectives and scrutinized the seller's financial statements in detail, we are ready to work with commonly used pricing concepts to help determine the bargaining price range.

PRICE/EARNINGS RATIOS

Price/earnings ratios of businesses similar to the seller have a significant practical impact. Sellers tend to be unwilling to accept a price which represents a price/earnings ratio much below the market determined price/earnings ratio of comparable companies. If the seller manufactures mobile homes and publicly-traded mobile home firms are selling at multiples of 40 times earnings, an offer at 20 times earnings may well be futile. Here, however, we might be able to make use of our detailed financial analysis. If the seller is focusing on price/earnings ratios, we might be able to point out that earnings are really overstated as the result of certain business or accounting practices.

On the other hand, the seller's earnings may be understated, assuming that our business and accounting decisions were applied. In this situation, the seller's emphasis on price/earnings ratios may provide us with a bargain. The seller, too, can apply this approach to argue for higher prices.

The buyer's choice of negotiating arguments to support his pricing decisions should reflect his appraisal of the seller's financial and negotiating sophistication. Price/earnings ratios represent conclusions based on many facts and assumptions. If the earnings used are inaccurate from the buyer's point of view, or if comparable publicly traded companies are not truly comparable, the price/earnings ratio pricing conclusion may be distorted. However, if we have already analyzed the seller in detail, this risk will be minimized. If the seller wants to talk price/earnings ratio language, the buyer can also use this language to argue his pricing decision.

MARKET PRICE

If the seller is a publicly-traded company, it will be very difficult to make the acquisition without offering a premium over the stock market price. The market price may or may not reflect the seller's basic value, but as a practical matter the market price will significantly affect the seller's self-evaluation.

Exceptions, however, do occur. Storer Broadcasting Co., holder of approximately eighty percent of the common shares of Northeast Airlines, agreed to transfer its Northeast holdings to Northwest Airlines for a value of around seven dollars per share. At the same time, common shares of Northeast were being traded publicly at around fourteen dollars per share. Needless to say, many shareholders of Northeast were disappointed. All this really points out, however, is that the stock market public is not always as rational an appraiser of basic value as a sophisticated corporate acquirer. In this case neither party was confused by the price of Northeast shares on the public market.

The Northeast Airlines case drives home an important lesson. Except when stock market prices are beset by runaway inflation, a company's intrinsic value may be a much more realistic determinant of market value for corporate acquisition purposes than the stock market's appraisal. If a spread exists between the seller's intrinsic value, as determined by the buyer, and a higher stock-market-determined price, the spread represents a buyer's downside risk, and he should think twice before paying the stock market price.

BOOK VALUE

Book and liquidation values are additional concepts sometimes used in price range determinations. The book value of underlying net assets generally has little relationship to the economic value or potential value of a company's earning power. However, if we adjust the seller's book value to reflect replacement value or liquidation value, the result may be more helpful in bargaining price determinations.

If we are trying to determine an appropriate price for a personal service organization, neither the book nor the replacement values of the tangible and intangible assets recorded on the balance sheet will be of much importance. The true value of a personal service organization is the replacement cost of its human assets.

At the other extreme is the real estate or investment company. The bulk of the assets may be in the form of undeveloped real estate or marketable securities. Liquidation value is a realistic measure of value and should significantly control the buyer's offering price.

Although this concept seems simple enough, investors will often improperly evaluate real estate companies. Instead of looking at the fair market value of the company's net worth, they may well look at the earnings-per-share. However, earnings-per-share should be relatively irrelevant to a purchaser of stock in a real estate company, except for the continuing possibility that other purchasers will also look at the earnings-per-share.

SETTING A MAXIMUM PRICE

Price/earnings ratios, market prices, book values, and liquidation values may be significant and certainly must be considered since the seller may raise any one or all of these issues. However, the buyer also has certain practical internal considerations which will directly affect the maximum price he will offer.

First, and probably foremost, for a buyer whose shares are

publicly traded or who is contemplating a public offering, the effect on the buyer's earnings-per-share will be critical. Frequently, the maximum price that a buyer will pay is a price which will not result in the dilution of his earnings-per-share.

Since company performance is usually evaluated on the basis of earnings-per-share, this indicator is of prime importance. However, some buyers may accept short-run dilution if future earnings growth appears certain and substantial.

The buyer's costs of alternative means of fulfilling his objectives will also be a practical limitation on the maximum price that he can offer. The after-tax costs of internal expansion, plus the lost earnings during the development period, plus a risk of accomplishment factor, may all affect the maximum price determination. In addition, the cost of alternative corporate acquisitions may be critical if a particular seller does not have a unique value to the buyer.

VALUATION AS A MANAGEMENT BUDGETING PROBLEM

Essentially, corporate valuation is a straight capital budgeting problem for the buyer. And, since we are considering real economic value, the focus should be on cash flow and not on book earnings. The basic question should be whether the prospective acquisition will produce a favorable return on the investment.

The ultimate measure of profit or value is the rate of return which will be realized on an investment over its productive life. Phrasing it another way, the resulting cash flow —which represents the recovery of investment and the receipt of income produced by a particular investment—must provide an adequate return on the investment.

This is the only meaningful measure of profitability, because cash, or its equivalent, is the only ultimate form of economic realization. A business may show a large book income, and yet not produce a satisfactory economic return, if no cash is realized from the operations or from the disposition value which may exist upon termination.

For example, a company may be for sale at a relatively low price/earnings ratio, but if all funds to be generated in the foreseeable future must be used in retiring debt, the company's cash flow value to a buyer is questionable. The discounted value of income to be received ten or fifteen years into the future, after debt retirement, is minimal.

The buyer's stockholders should be able to expect that the allocation of the corporation's funds for all investment undertakings will result, in the aggregate, in an overall return significantly in excess of the prevailing cost of capital rates. Most companies maintain capital budgeting procedures which require that an approximate standard return be realized on major investments.

Acquisition investments should be required to meet these same minimum capital budgeting standards. Buyers should always remember that unless the expected return on a prospective acquisition is at least commensurate with the strategic earnings goals of his own company, the acquisition may not be wise.

In determining the cash flow component of the rate of return calculation, one should take account of the diminished value of money received in the future—i.e., one should discount future cash flows to their present value. This process of discounting is a technique used to find the value today, or the "present value," of money to be received in the future. The discount factor depends on the opportunity cost of capital expressed as an interest rate and a time period. The result is an amount which, if invested today at the given interest rate would, together with the compounded interest, equal the non-discounted cash value after the given period of time.

In the merger and acquisition area we can use this discounted cash flow theory to value a seller. The underlying concept is that the realistic valuation of any investment in income-producing property is directly related to the amount and timing of the future cash flow to be derived from that property. Cash rather than book income is used because only cash can be used for reinvestment and profit distributions.

An example of a shortened form of discounted cash flow analysis is included at the end of this chapter. In this analysis, the present value of the annual cash flow for the estimated productive life of the present assets is added to the present value of the net residual assets at the end of the same period.

This valuation procedure will give the seller a price floor for negotiations. The buyer can use the same technique to determine a maximum bargaining price. For this purpose, the seller's earnings projections should be used instead of the assumption of a level annual cash flow.

In either case, given a series of assumptions, we are talking real value terms. Therefore, the negotiator who understands discounted cash flow analyses is in an effective price bargaining position.

USING ALTERNATIVE ACQUISITION METHODS

Up to this point discussion has centered on how the bargaining price range should be affected by the parties' objectives, the buyer's financial statement analysis of the seller, the commonly used pricing concepts, and the discounted cash flow valuation analysis. Now we will briefly discuss the impact of alternative acquisition methods on the pricing decision.

Contingent pay-outs (see Chapter 9) are a common method of acquisition which may enable the buyer to offer a higher price than he otherwise could. The total price paid might vary with the future earnings of the seller or the future price level of the buyer's stock.

In addition, if the buyer uses his own stock with an inflated market value as the purchasing medium, he can offer what appears to be a much higher price than he could with cash. If the buyer manages a good stock financing, it more than compensates for the supposedly high price paid for the seller. The buyer's stock may move up higher as a result of the acquisition, thereby enabling higher prices to be offered to future acquisition candidates.

In another form of acquisition transaction, the buyer can purchase the seller's current assets for cash, and lease the fixed assets. The total of the cash paid and the present value of the long-term lease may be $10 million, but the seller may actually be receiving much more. The seller is able to defer any capital gain as well as any recapture of depreciation or investment credit. In addition, he might be able to borrow against the lease as collateral.

On the other side of the transaction, the buyer has deferred a portion of his cash obligation over the term of the long-term lease. Therefore, even though the seller was worth only $9 million, the net result of the transaction may be that the seller receives $12 million in total benefits. The method of acquisition has enabled the buyer to offer the seller a benefit package that exceeds both the buyer's dollar cost and his own present cash resources.

Sometimes a buyer sees a great future in a seller who is presently generating losses. The buyer wants to make the acquisition but does not want to reduce his own current earnings. The seller believes in his own future but needs capital. One way to solve the problem is for the buyer to loan funds to the seller corporation and take back a purchase option from the seller's shareholders. Another method might be for the buyer to receive a stock purchase option and, in turn, provide the seller with management and loan negotiating assistance. Using these acquisition methods, the buyer again might be able to offer a purchase price far in excess of the value of a present cash offer.

The purchase price may also be affected by the decision to use debt or equity as the exchange medium. Interest payments, not dividends, are usually deductible for tax purposes. However, the use of debt could eliminate the possibility of a tax-free reorganization or a pooling of interests for accounting purposes.

CONCLUSION

We have seen that many factors may affect the determination of a bargaining price range. First, the parties' objectives are controlling determinants. Second, the analysis of the seller's earnings and cash flow is critical. Third, commonly-used pricing techniques must be understood in order to appreciate both their usefulness and their limitations. Fourth, the intrinsic value of the seller may help determine the price and define the downside risk potential. And fifth, the selection of an acquisition method may also significantly influence price determinations.

The price determination process, however, is really not as complicated as it may appear. It is simply an interesting exercise in the familiar process of decision-making. If the buyer clarifies his objectives, gathers all of the facts, and compares the alternatives accurately, the proper decision will usually become quite obvious.

XYZ COMPANY ESTIMATED VALUATION BASED on DISCOUNTED CASH FLOW — 1970

Net income, for 1968			$ 10,000
Add:			
Depreciation and depletion		$ 6,000	
Interest expense		2,000	
Research and Development		2,000	10,000
			$ 20,000
Less, Interest on temporary cash investments			500
"Adjusted cash flow"			$ 19,500
Present value of adjusted cash flow discounted at 10% per annum for 13 years			
Factor 7.103			$139,000
Less, Long-term debt			38,000
			$101,000
Present value of net working capital (at the end of the estimated useful life of the productive assets considering a required return on investment of 10% per annum)			
Current assets	$37,000		
Less, Temporary cash investments	16,000	$21,000	
Current liabilities		8,000	
Net working capital		$13,000	
Factor 0.2896			3,800
			$104,000
Add, Temporary cash investments			16,000
Total estimated valuation*			$120,800
Per share (5,000 shares)*			$ 24

*If a discount factor of 15% is utilized, total estimated valuation would be reduced to $89,000 and the per share valuation would be reduced to $18.

NOTES TO VALUATION

——— 1. This shortened discounted cash flow analysis assumes that the current level of operation and cash flow will be maintained for the average remaining life of the productive assets. The assumption is based on the presumption that future capital expenditures, which in themselves will generate sufficient cash flow to recover their own cost and appropriate earnings, will constantly extend the average remaining useful life. The analysis gives no recognition to potential growth or technological change.

——— 2. The initial computation in this analysis is a determination of the present value of all future cash which theoretically could be taken out of the company over the estimated life of the productive assets. We start with *Net Income* of $10,000 and add back *Depreciation and Depletion* since these represent book but not cash expenses.

——— 3. *Interest Expense* is also added back since it represents a return on capital rather than an operating expense. The financing used, stock vs. debt, does not affect the intrinsic value of the operating assets, but only the equity in these assets. Consequently, *Interest* payments should not affect operating earnings. As we see, *Long Term Debt* is also removed.

——— 4. Current expenses which benefit future operations —such as *Research & Development*—are also added back since they could be stopped if the business were to be allowed to "run out."

——— 5. *Interest on investments of excess cash* is removed since we will add in the Excess Cash Investments at their full non-discounted value.

——— 6. For example purposes, *10%* is used as the minimum acceptable return on investment. The footnote at the bottom of the valuation summarizes the results if we use an interest factor of 15%.

——— 7. The *estimated useful life* of productive assets is determined by dividing the annual depreciation expense into the undepreciated book cost of the property and equipment.

——— 8. Assuming an interest rate of 10% and a time period of 13 years, we use published present worth tables to find the *Discount Factor.*

——— 9. The result of $139,000 represents the present value of $19,500 payable periodically for 13 years assuming a 10% annual interest rate. After Long Term Debt is removed, the value is $101,000.

———10. Once a business is terminated through consumption of the property and equipment, the remaining net working capital can be converted to cash and withdrawn from the business. Consequently, the present value of the net current assets at the end of 13 years is computed, again using an interest rate of 10%. The excess cash in the form of *Temporary Cash Investments* is valued at its full amount since theoretically it is immediately available for reinvestment.

Much has been written, pro and con, on contingency payouts. In this chapter, the authors do not take sides, but examine the possible ways in which the technique can be used. Their conclusion: it can be made to work to the mutual advantage of both parties.

9

CONTINGENCY PAYOUTS: A POWERFUL TOOL IN ACQUISITIONS

by Thomas A Steele, III and W. Robert Reum,
Executive Assistants, City Investing Company

It may well happen in the course of negotiations that, with the best intentions in the world, the two parties simply cannot come together on price.

If the acquiring company is publicly-owned, there may be a practical limit beyond which it cannot go without suffering undesirable consequences. Typically, the immediate dilution of its earnings may affect the price of its stock, or cause criticism among its shareholders or other members of the financial community.

If the selling company is aware of its true potential value to a particular buyer, it may hold out for a price which, measured solely on the basis of current earnings, may appear unrealistic or exorbitant.

However, if the deal makes sense in other respects, there is a possible solution which is finding increasing favor with both buyers and sellers: the contingency payout, or, as it is sometimes called, the incentive payment arrangement or the "earn-out."

The buyer makes a down payment in cash, stock, debentures, or a combination thereof, with the agreement that he will pay an additional consideration if the seller meets or exceeds agreed-on performance standards for a specified number of years after the acquisition.

Although the technique is not new (the Gillette Company used it to acquire Toni in 1948), it has been employed infrequently until the last few years. Lately its use has grown significantly as more and more companies are finding it difficult to make "good" acquisitions.

According to W.T. Grimm & Company, which keeps track of mergers, the number of deals with contingent payouts announced in 1969 totaled 728, compared with 305 in

---

1968. The 1969 figure constituted 12% of all acquisitions in that year, as against 7% in 1968.

The technique is a seller's tool as well as a buyer's, which accounts partly for its attractiveness. It enables the seller (usually the owner of a closely held company) to receive a larger total payment for his company than he would in an outright acquisition, and at the same time retain significant control over his company's performance. On the other hand, it enables the buyer to align his payment more closely with actual earnings generated, and to use this payment as an incentive to prod the seller into better performance.

LIMITING THE COMMITMENT

Consequently, both parties are required to make only a partial commitment when the deal is consummated. For example, the terms in the acquisition of Jefferies & Company by Investors Diversified Services, Inc., called for the issuance of 400,000 shares of IDS Class A common stock and 50,000 shares of preferred. The preferred stock will be convertible over four years into at least 80,000 and at most 560,000 Class A shares, depending on Jefferies' earnings.

There are disadvantages to the incentive payment method, too. For one, the buyer usually will end up paying out more, if the acquired company performs very well, than he would have in an outright acquisition. We shall discuss the advantages and disadvantages in more detail later, after an examination of the technique.

HOW PAYOUTS ARE USED

The contingent payout is used when some, though not all, of these conditions are present:

The selling company can be operated as a separate division or subsidiary. This is necessary because the earn-out generally requires a measurement of the contribution which the seller has made to the overall performance of the parent for a certain period.

The parent is willing to leave major profit-and-loss responsibility in the seller's hands. Only in this way can the buyer accurately measure how the acquired company's managers have influenced its performance. At the same time, the seller can expect his reward to be based on *his* performance, not on the parent's management skills.

The seller has suffered a recent drop in earnings. Naturally, the buyer will hesitate to accept the seller's likely assurances of higher future earnings. With the contingent payout, the buyer can protect himself against an unreasonable purchase cost if the improvement fails to come. The seller is closely held. The seller may argue that because he owns the business, he has made no attempt to maximize earnings or minimize expenses. For example, if he has been taking the maximum salary that the Internal Revenue Service allows, he may contend that, to obtain a "true" picture of the company's value, certain items should be added to stated earnings. The incentive payment method protects the buyer against the possibility that the seller has not taken as much out of earnings as he alleges.

The selling company does not possess a meaningful history of operations. It may be newly formed but have exciting prospects, such as the patent rights to an unexploited invention or a new product under development. Because the company has no record on which to base meaningful projections, the buyer may be unwilling to pay a significant amount in an outright acquisition.

With a contingent payout, the buyer can participate in the highrisk venture by making a smaller initial commitment. At the same time, the seller will be provided with the funds he needs to realize his potential, plus the chance to receive a larger total payment than he might have otherwise.

BASIC ELEMENTS OF TECHNIQUE

While contingent payout agreements can be varied according to the needs of the buyers and sellers, there are some aspects that are always present when they are negotiated.

The first thing the parties do, of course, is determine the amount of the down payment and the amount to be paid out on a contingent basis. As a rule, the more uncertain future earnings are, the greater the proportion of the total payment the buyer wants to be made subject to a contingent payout. In return for accepting a lower initial payment, however, the seller will generally expect to have the opportunity to earn a total price for his business at or above what he was asking before the earn-out compromise entered the negotiations.

If a tax-free reorganization is desired, negotiations on the amount of the down payment may be constrained by an Internal Revenue Service guideline which requires that at least 50% of the maximum issuable shares must be transferred when the merger is consummated.

Once the down payment has been negotiated, the contingent payment can be based on any criterion. Earn-outs have most commonly been based on earnings or sales, but they can use increases in net worth, cash flow, or return on operating assets. The most important qualities of the standard are its relevance to the interests of the concerned parties and its measurability.

Typically, the payment period extends from three to five years. In a shorter period, the conditions causing the buyer to opt for the incentive payment are not likely to be satisfied. On the other hand, the seller is usually reluctant to settle for too long a delay in receiving his full compensation. Furthermore, to obtain a tax-free merger, the buyer must issue all the stock within five years.

DEFINING THE TERMS

Having agreed on the criteria to be used, the parties must then determine how they will be defined during the life of the contract. For example, if earnings are used, attention must be given not only to the definition of earnings, but also to what costs are "necessary" to produce those earnings. Points of contention here often include:

The practice of capitalizing expenses where direct write-offs might be more appropriate.

The rate at which the amortization of lease-hold improvements is charged to income.

The depreciation policies used for currently owned assets and those acquired during the contract period.

The level of executives' salaries. The buyer normally insists that they will not be reduced in order to prevent "manufactured" additional earnings which, under a contingent payout, would be of greater value to the seller than the additional compensation.

The amounts charged for corporate overhead and services.

The minimum level of discretionary expenditures, such as research and development, and advertising.

The amounts charged for intracompany loans, if their use is contemplated.

One way of handling these items is to insist that "earnings" must be determined by a public accounting firm in a manner consistent with prior periods. Another method is to put members of the parent's management on the subsidiary's board, if it is still functioning after the acquisition. Finally, the parent can insist that the acquired company follow control procedures it sets up, and that the parent's auditors do the accounting.

The objective of these measures is maintenance of necessary expenditures in such areas as discretionary expense, fixed assets, and new product lines. In those cases where the parent insists on disbursements which the subsidiary believes are not required under the contract (for example, for an expansion of facilities), they should be excluded from the incentive payment formula. A good guide as to whether a contested expenditure should be a corporate versus a subsidiary cost is the immediacy of impact on the subsidiary.

ESTABLISHING A FORMULA

Once the measuring criteria have been defined satisfactorily for both sides, the next step is the determination of a method of tying the payment to the fulfillment of the criteria. Innumerable formulas have been devised to accomplish this task, each reflecting the necessities of a particular situation, but three types are used most often.

1. *The set standard*—The performance criterion most commonly selected for this type of formula is earnings or sales, either in the year immediately preceding the start of the contract period or the average over a specified period. Whether the payments are made depends on the seller exceeding the standard, while their *amounts* depend on the extent to which he exceeds the standard.

   Frequently this "excess" is further adjusted, or charged, for the use of the parent's capital or for an equivalent required return on the parent's original investment, before the payment is made.

For example, Company A agrees to purchase Company B for $1,000,000 down, a sum determined by capitalizing B's earnings at 10 times the average earnings for the past five years—$100,000. Company A may also pay up to an additional $200,000 a year over the next five years based on the amount (after a charge for the use of A's capital) by which B surpasses its $100,000 average earnings standard in each of those years.

The allocation multiplier is the critical element here. It is the basis for compensating the seller for exceeding the standard. If he is to be paid in stock, a capitalization factor is generally applied to the excess, and the resulting sum is divided by the per-share market price of the buyer's stock to determine the number of shares he is entitled to.

Some discussions of this method have noted that it affords a higher initial earnings per share than does a straight stock transaction, because of the lesser number of shares originally issued. But since last year, when the Accounting Principles Board of the American Institute of Certified Public Accountants issued its Opinion 15, that is no longer possible. Opinion 15 requires that fully diluted earnings per share account for all such contingent stock issues.

2. *The moving standard*—Under this formula the first standard is the previous year's earnings; then for the rest of the contract it becomes the highest earnings achieved during any year of the contract. The excess is determined as in the set standard formula.

The moving standard prevents a "whiplash" effect, a result of the seller's attempt to make his earnings fluctuate in order to increase his payment. Consequently, this formula demands more of the seller because it rewards only steady growth.

If the seller meets this more stringent standard, he will expect his "bonus" to be greater. The buyer, however, may feel that growth in earnings per share should be expected in the normal course of business, that this is what he initially paid for, and that only growth beyond this "normal" increase should be rewarded with extra payouts. Such is the attitude of one large midwestern corporation, which requires a growth rate of 10% per year before the acquired company becomes eligible for additional payment.

3. *The cumulative standard*—The objective of this formula is to overlook fluctuations in annual earnings during the contract period and focus on aggregate performance. To determine the standard, multiply current earnings by the number of years in the contract period. This total becomes the base against which the aggregate is measured, and any excess is rewarded with an additional payment.

   This variant encourages the seller's management to focus on the entire contract period rather than to concentrate on generating profits from year to year. Management is more motivated to build for the future than it would be under the other two formulas.

While these formulas indicate how contingent payouts can be constructed, the parties frequently modify them to fit their needs. SOS Consolidated, Inc., for example, sometimes enters into a contingent payout agreement in which it splits the profits with the acquired company during the contract period, and then calculates a "balloon" payment based on the total profits over that time.

Another instance is the agreement last year by which Intercontinental Industries, Inc., was to acquire most of the stock of Prebuilt Homes, Inc., from three shareholders. The terms called for the exchange of 925,000 Intercontinental common shares—half initially, and half in 1974 (if an earnings formula is satisfied)—for 81% of Prebuilt's stock.

The formula will be satisfied if 81% of Prebuilt's net earnings, cumulative over the first five years, totals at least $22.75 million. If the company's earnings do not warrant exchange of all 462,500 shares, however, Intercontinental can exercise an option to repurchase up to 412,500 of the initially issued shares, at ten cents a share. This agreement was a revision of original terms, under which the three shareholders would have received cash compensation beginning in 1974, but less Intercontinental stock.

NEGOTIABLE ITEMS

The usual areas for negotiation under contingent payout formulas include:

1. The designation of an appropriate standard. A low one may adversely affect the buyer; a high one may prevent the seller from receiving adequate additional compensation, if any.

2. The size of the allocation multiplier. While the rate of return desired by the buyer dictates the limits of the multiple he is willing to allow, the seller must realize that the buyer is receiving a stock value equilvalent to his current price/earnings multiple for the net earnings contributed by the seller.

3. The multiplier (capitalization factor) tries to put earnings on equal terms with stock value—if stock is the medium of exchange. The higher the multiple, the more advantageous to the seller; the lower the multiple, the more advantageous to the buyer (assuming the same market price per share), for

he is receiving greater value in terms of his stock price for the seller's earnings than he is paying for those earnings.

For example, let us assume that Company X has purchased Company Y according to a formula whereby each $50 of net earnings after taxes will provide Y with one share of X's stock. That stock is selling at $50 at the time of the agreement, and X has guaranteed that Y will always get a minimum of $50 of stock value per $50 of earnings.

This may appear to be a reasonable agreement, but let us take a closer look. Assume that Company X is well established and enjoys a P/E multiple of 20. So for each dollar of after-tax earnings per share X can create $20 of market value in its stock.

If X's P/E ratio does not change as a result of acquiring Y, the $50 in earnings that Y provides in exchange for the one share of X's stock is worth $1,000 (20 times $50) in the market. But Y is getting only $50 of market value from X.

Therefore, when negotiating, the seller should be aware of the leverage that the buyer's P/E multiple gives to his earnings contribution and insist that some "reasonable" capitalization factor be applied to the excess earnings in determining the number of shares he is to receive. The factor should approximate the parent's P/E ratio, though perhaps lower to adjust for uncertainty and the possibility of a negative impact on earnings.

4. The relationship of the formula to the market price of the buyer's stock (assuming the buyer is publicly owned). If the relationship is left undecided, the fluctuations of the market make both the buyer and seller subject to forces that may have nothing to do with their transaction.

But if the buyer negotiates on the basis of the stock value as of a recent date or, better yet, guarantees an equivalent dollar amount of stock, the seller is protected against stock depreciation.

5. The number of shares issuable during any one period.

The buyer will want to protect himself against excessive dilution in any year, or over the whole contract period, by placing a maximum on the issuable number of shares. The seller will want to make sure that the excess over the maximum amount that he can receive in any one year can be carried over to the next period, or in some way preserved for his "use" in future periods.

6. The contingent payout as x number of shares or x dollar value. The seller must realize that if he agrees to receive value in terms of share price, he is electing to take an equivalent dollar amount and so will not share in the buyer's growth.

For example, using the formula we stated before, as the market price of the parent's stock rises, he will receive fewer shares (although the value of his down-payment shares will be increasing). On the other hand, if he agrees to receive a certain number of shares per dollar of excess earnings, he benefits proportionately in this growth.

7. An employment contract for the acquired company's managers. The contract, often a feature of contingent payout agreements, usually covers the earn-out period and includes a "no compete" clause effective after the period.

ADVANTAGES OF TECHNIQUE

For both sides, a checklist such as the one on page 148 may prove useful.

The incentive payment technique has great attractions for both parties, which the outright acquisition does not always have.

An agreement on price can often be reached that would be impossible without the use of a contingent payout. If the buyer cannot agree to a satisfactory immediate consideration for the selling company, on a contingency basis he can offer to pay even more than the seller's initial asking price without taking the risks involved in an outright acquisition.

If the acquiring company possesses limited financial resources, the method is attractive because only proven performance is rewarded. Moreover, the payment can come out of the acquired company's earnings. As the group vice president of a well-known multimarket company pointed out: "Any time that I can borrow money from a seller at advantageous prices, I'll do it."

The earn-out appeals to acquisitive companies which are concerned about goodwill on their balance sheets. Although goodwill is considered an asset, it does not impart additional borrowing power.

Because the acquisition-minded company desires high leverage, anything that will soften the impact of goodwill on its books is very attractive. In an outright purchase all the goodwill of the acquired company is booked immediately, but in a contingent payout the buyer can gradually increase the goodwill account as payments are made over the life of the contract.

With an incentive payment offer in hand, a company can gain an advantage over another in competition for a third. If the selling owner-manager wants to remain autonomous and to retain profit-and-loss responsibility, he will be more attracted to the suitor who can offer him such benefits, plus frequently a larger total payment.

As we have noted, the earn-out is a powerful incentive tool, because the seller is paid only on the basis of performance. Furthermore, since he is on view not only by top management but also by the other subsidiary or division heads, pride will motivate him to perform well.

The contingent payout allows the buyer a "grace" period in which to learn the seller's business. It also gives him time to evaluate the seller's executives and decide if he wants to retain them after the earn-out period.

If the decision is negative, he can use the interval to search for and prepare new management. The parent may even bring the new management into the division before the end of the period to ease the transition.

It is much more difficult for the buyer to assess the accuracy of the financial statements of a closely held company than of a publicly owned company. If the seller has misrepresented his earnings, the use of an earn-out protects the buyer by forcing the seller to use his statements as the standard against which he will be measured later.

The contingent payout also gives the buyer a means of overcoming the most serious obstacle to merger: agreement on price.

For example, one well-known conglomerate decided it would pay no more than 15 times earnings for an acquisition, but many prospective sellers wanted 25 times earnings. If outright purchase had been attempted, these deals would have fallen through. But they were consummated through incentive payment formulas whereby less than 15 times earnings was paid initially but the seller could earn extra payments which made the total consideration greater than 25 times earnings.

In addition to being eligible for a larger total payment for his business, the seller receives certain other significant benefits from a contingent payout.

That an acquired company remains a relatively autonomous unit may be important to the pride of the entrepreneur who has built his company from scratch. It is also important to those managers who get satisfaction from exercising their enterpreneurial instincts. By remaining autonomous they can retain responsibility over profits and losses. They can see the worth of their efforts and have their performance measured against a standard.

If the earn-out formula calls for payment of a specified number of shares when the acquired company achieves a given earnings level, the seller is in a position to benefit from any increase in the value of the parent's stock, thus participating in the latter's growth.

If the seller complies with certain conditions imposed by the Internal Revenue Service, the exchange of stock will remain tax free. These conditions are: (1) all of the stock must be issued within five years, (2) the maximum number of shares that may be issued must be stated, and (3) at least 50% of the total shares must be issued in the initial distribution.

PROBLEMS TO CONSIDER

Although the advantages of contingent payouts are significant, there are also some limitations inherent in this kind of purchase.

While separation of the seller's operation for the life of the contract facilitates performance measurement and enables the parent to avoid paying for performance or benefits it has actually generated, it also precludes the parent from providing assistance to the extent that it might in an outright acquisition, or gaining synergistic benefits from the amalgamation.

(Some flexibility, however, can be preserved through inclusion of a "disaster" clause in the contract. The clause permits the buyer to place his own management in the acquired company if that company fails to perform a standard. One company has gone so far as to insist on a disaster clause that takes effect if the acquired company falls short of the minimum standard in *one month.*)

The autonomy of the acquired company can also reduce flexibility in the event that the parent later acquires another company in the same product area and wants to integrate the operations of the two.

Although the desire to retain the seller's management may justify use of a contingent payout plan, it could backfire if those executives cannot be motivated to perform. On the other hand, they may work so hard to obtain the extra payments that they lose sight of the long-term objectives of the business. This "incentive myopia" could have the effect of causing conflict with the plans of the parent company, and even reducing the value of the acquired company.

Trying to anticipate eventualities like these frequently results in complex contracts, which may deter a seller who prefers a simple deal. Furthermore, complex contracts may generate "loophole negotiating." If the seller and his lawyer are adept at such bargaining, the buyer could find himself faced with unanticipated problems during the earn-out period.

For example, the buyer may be subject to expensive litigation if the seller feels that the acquiring company has not performed in a manner that allows him to maximize his reward under the agreement.

Another disadvantage to the buyer is that he will often pay more for a company than he would have had he bought it outright.

The Internal Revenue Service requirements of a 50% down payment and the fixing of the maximum number of issuable shares to obtain a tax-free exchange may blunt the seller's incentive. Having performed very well in the early part of the incentive period, and aware that he can receive only a specified total number of shares in any event, he may slack off for the duration of the period.

The contract may permit the acquired company's owner-managers to receive a substantial block of the parent's stock. This holding may present control problems for the buyer if there is no maximum placed on the shares potentially issuable.

Finally, the segregation and allocation of general overhead costs is a problem under normal circumstances. When contingent payments are at stake, however, the importance of overhead allocation increases if the seller is rewarded on the basis of annual earnings. Improper overhead allocation could result in overpaying him.

Not all the risks are on the buyer's side. The seller is assuming that he will end up with more money or stock than he would have in an outright sale of his company. But if he does not meet the standard because of poor performance, he will lose out.

Furthermore, his potential compensation in the form of stock is limited if the deal was made according to the tax-free exchange requirements of the IRS. So if the company records unusually high earnings because of an event like the unforeseen large sales of a new product, the former entrepreneur might not be rewarded enough even under the terms of the agreement.

Usually, however, to obtain the total payment the seller is under constant pressure to perform according to formula yardsticks. Many entrepreneurs are not accustomed to this kind of pressure and may be uncomfortable living in glass houses where every action they take can be attributed to them. The contingent payout does not provide the shelter which an outright acquisition might.

At the same time, the seller's management may feel somewhat isolated from that of the buyer. While the degree of isolation will vary, it may adversely affect those managers who want to feel they are part of a "team."

This feeling of isolation may become *actual* isolation at the end of the earn-out period, for there is no certainty that they will be retained. If the acquired company's executives have met or exceeded the parent's projections, they may not want to be severed from their success.

During the contract period the executives may find themselves severely limited as to their managerial discretion.

Their salaries may be restricted, for example, or they may be required to spend a given amount per year—no more, no less—on research and development.

Finally, many sellers dislike the earn-out method because, rather than receiving full payment for an earnings stream at the time of the acquisition, the seller is being paid for a period of years out of his own earnings.

On balance, however, the contingent payout method enables acquisitions and mergers to be consummated that might otherwise have fallen through.

For the buyer it provides a way to tie most of his payment to proven performance, thereby reducing his investment risk and giving him an important incentive tool.

For the seller it provides a means to gain payment for his company above his original asking price and, at the same time, permits him to retain a large measure of autonomy and profit-and-loss responsibility.

NEGOTIATION CHECKLIST

Here is a listing of pertinent questions to consider carefully during the negotiation process.

. . . FOR THE BUYER

——— 1. Is this a situation where a contingent payout would be preferable to an outright acquisition?

——— 2. What form of earn-out would benefit us most?

——— 3. Is it desirable to retain present management?

——— 4. Can the selling group be reduced so that the incentive arrangement will affect only those left in a managerial capacity?

——— 5. Does the percentage of voting stock the seller will acquire under the maximum conditions present us with control problems?

——— 6. Does the amount of the down payment correspond to the uncertainty of the situation? If the seller wants a tax-free exchange, does the 50% down payment requirement afford sufficient downside protection?

——— 7. Does the maximum payment under the contract provide enough incentive for the life of the contract?

——— 8. Is the maximum possible payment a reasonable premium to pay for the protection we get?

——— 9. Will the earn-out motivate the seller's management to operate for our short and long-term benefit?

———10. Can we, and should we, operate the acquisition as an autonomous unit for the period of the contract?

———11. What will be the effect on our EPS under APB Opinion 15?

———12. If it is a purchase, will the arrangement result in an unwanted accumulation of goodwill during the future years of the contract?

———13. Does the contract cover all foreseeable contingencies? That is:

a.) Has the performance standard been properly defined?

b.) Have provisions been made for cost allocation and control?

c.) Has the rate of discretionary expenditures (advertising, R&D, etc.) been agreed to?

d.) Has a decision been made as to treatment of pre- and post-merger financial effects such as liabilities and tax refunds?

e.) Has the maximum payment been set to reflect properly the interests of both sides?

f.) Is the formula satisfactory to both parties?

g.) Have both parties tested the operation of the formula under a variety of assumptions?

h.) Is there a "disaster" clause to protect us?

i.) Is there an acceleration clause to allow us flexibility in the future?

______ 14. Have we explored our legal liability to the seller?

______ 15. Should provision be made for the seller's management after the contract period?

... FOR THE SELLER

______ 1. Is the contingent payout the best alternative?

______ 2. What form of earn-out would benefit us most?

______ 3. Can we work effectively with the buyer's management for the period of the contract?

______ 4. Is the performance standard acceptable? Does our accountant agree with it?

______ 5. Do we accept the possibility that the buyer will be rewarding us out of our own earnings?

______ 6. Have we properly estimated the growth of our company within the framework of the other company? If so, are we tying ourselves to a company that cannot grow as fast as we can?

______ 7. Does the maximum payment provision of the contract sufficiently exceed the amount we would receive in an outright sale?

______ 8. Does the proposed down payment provide enough protection in case we do not earn the incentive payments?

______ 9. Does the contract fairly represent our interests? That is:

a.) Is it unduly restrictive of managerial discretion? Can we live with it for its duration?

b.) Has the allocation of overhead expenses to our operation by the buyer been properly defined?

c.) Are our rights and obligations clearly set down?

d.) Is our contribution to the value of the buyer's

stock adequately recognized in payments?
e.) Has a maximum or minimum price on the buyer's stock been established? What is our exposure to the stock market? Are there antidilution provisions?
f.) If a maximum payment has been set, does it allow sufficient reward for us if we achieve an unforeseen breakthrough in earnings?
g.) Is the buyer prevented from installing unwanted management or requiring unusual expenses?

———10. Are the restrictions of an employment contract compatible with our personal objectives?

———11. Is the buyer's stock a good investment for the near and long term, or should we receive another medium of exchange?

———12. Have we considered the post-contract period?

Generally, it is the seller who controls the timing of negotiations, by simple virtue of his perogative to reject or entertain a tentative offer. In this chapter the author, who has been responsible for his firm's successful diversification and acquisition programs, suggests how the buyer can use effective timing to move negotiations toward successful conclusion.

10

THE EFFECTIVE USE OF TIMING IN ACQUISITIONS

by Stephen F. Snyder, Vice President,
Corporate Development, The Greyhound Corporation

Of the many definitions of timing, one of the most graphic is probably this: "regulating the speed of motion so as to cause it to reach its maximum effectiveness at the correct moment."

Anyone even casually interested in sports would surely have to agree that it applies with some precision to Arnold Palmer and Rod Laver, and pre-eminently to Ted Williams in his prime. The purpose of this chapter is to suggest, and try to demonstrate, that the same definition has application in planning of strategy in negotiation.

Let us start with a premise: the reason a seller will consider the sale of his company is because he feels it will be worth less to him in the future than it is today. This in itself is a question of timing, a modification of present value theory under which a dollar received some time in the future is worth less than a dollar received today.

There are a number of reasons why a company may be worth less in the future to the seller than it is worth today. I say "to the seller" because it does not necessarily follow that it will be worth less to the buyer in the future. The assumption, in fact, is just the contrary. If you understand why it is worth less to the seller in the future, you have a good beginning. If your company can provide the ingredients to make a company worth more in the future, you have a good ending. It is between these points that I suggest you focus negotiations.

TIMING AS A FACTOR FOR THE SELLER

The seller may advance an estate problem as the major reason. This often turns out to be the classic bromide. If you satisfy yourself that this is actually the reason, however, you should have an easy go of it, provided you have an acceptable listed stock with which to trade. Of course, there are interesting wrinkles here. For example, we completed a transaction in Canada where there is no capital gains tax and therefore it was not necessary to structure a tax-free exchange. However, there was a growing probability that one was to be instituted and this served to accelerate the timing of the negotiations.

Another reason may be the seller's knowledge of impending capital requirements. This was the case in our acquisition of Aircraft Service International. The company was in the business of providing ground handling services to commercial airlines in twenty cities throughout the country. Basically, this includes everything that must be done to the plane from the time it touches down until it takes off again—turnarounds, cleaning, pumping in jet fuel. Competitively, Aircraft Service saw some heavy outlays to set up underground fueling systems at various airports, and with the Boeing 747 and its counterparts imminent, the company also saw some heavy capital requirements for the equipment required to service these larger planes. A tow truck alone costs about $125,000, and the total equipment for one 747 for one gate may run as high as $1 million. Therefore, the capital requirements imposed upon the company in its operation set the timing for a major change. Greyhound's financial strength fit the company's needs. Without such major backing, the company may have lost its competitive position.

Another reason that a company may be worth more today to a seller or to its management than it will be in the future could be defensive in nature. A company that suddenly finds itself a take-over candidate through the announced intentions of another firm may choose to ward off an unwanted suitor by going into the arms of another company. The telephone usually brings many such offers to a company president when his dilemma becomes known. Recent examples of this would include Harley Davidson's embrace of American Machine &

Foundry, and Sinclair seeking asylum with Atlantic Richfield. The defensive posture has recently been utilized in a more subtle manner. It has been suggested that University Computing saw an interesting value in Western Union with its $1.40 dividend which is tax-free because by normal tax accounting Western Union probably lost money in 1967, instead of making a reported $17-½ million. The dividend is therefore essentially a distribution of capital, and would have covered the interest rate on borrowed funds.

A company's competitive position may provide another reason why it may be worth more to the seller today than tomorrow. In each of the prior instances, we have assumed that the seller's reasons did not hold for the buyer. That is, the buyer would not have the estate situation, this was the seller's problem; the capital needs were assumed to fit the buyer's ability to finance them; and the defensive situation was again only the seller's problem.

EFFECTS OF TIMING ON BUYERS

However, if the seller knew that he was going to lose a major government contract, or suffer a strike, or have labor problems, or that a competitor had developed a better product or a new competitive ability through perhaps being acquired itself, then the ancient principle of *caveat emptor* must persist. We held discussions with one publicly held company and determined that we did not wish to pursue the situation. The president and majority owner of the company had approached us to acquire his firm. He had been as aggressive in his approach as one can possibly be without overdoing the fact that it was he who had dropped the handkerchief. He had already realized the major portion of his growth through acquisitions within his field, and we felt that he could not continue this approach to growth much longer without running afoul of Washington problems. About one month later, I picked up the newspaper one morning to find that they had attacked over twenty of his acquisitions, going back to 1960. *Caveat emptor.*

The timing of change is another element. In the life insurance industry, for example, the timing of change has contributed to a lengthy list of available acquisition candidates. With full industry recognition that the percentage of the consumer savings dollar going into life insurance has declined from 50% about 20 years ago to 16% today, great attention has been given to the culprit—equity securities. The mutual fund-life insurance combination has been launched in most of the larger companies through the adoption of a holding company, or affiliation with a mutual fund. The banks are also following the department store of finance, or total money management approach, and in defense of the insurance companies' defense, the stock exchanges are considering allowing members to sell insurance to combat the mutual funds. The life insurance companies less able to adapt to this product change are usually those which are available. However, to the buyer they may pose a "Barbie doll" problem. The buyer must also be prepared to meet the change. When you buy the doll, then you might have to buy the dress (the mutual fund), and then the coat, and so on.

WHEN TO BUY

Other timing considerations include the general business environment for transactions. The price earnings ratio of a company's stock will certainly affect its thinking with respect to acquisition. Some of the leading acquisitors must face the dilution problem when using their securities. This, of course, is a cipher which feeds upon itself, because the expectation of an active acquisition program may contribute to a higher

P/E ratio, while a slower acquisition pace lowers this expectation level.

At any rate, a high P/E ratio certainly provides a good medium of exchange for the acquiring company, and a low P/E ratio may preclude the stock alternative. The timing of a drop in an acquirer's stock will affect a deal if he is obliged to use his stock at a price considered too low. On the other hand, a drop in an acquisition candidate's stock can cause renewed interest.

Concerning the company itself, a number of other considerations may affect the seller's timing. The seller's past record of sales and earnings, funds invested and expensed that have not yet begun to pay off in profit results, the company's life cycle and maturity which may be correlated with its growth prospects, the company's size, which will affect its ability to show continual dramatic increases as the overall base of sales and earnings gets larger, alternatives such as going public—all these are key factors.

I have been referring to timing which may affect the seller's reasons for thinking that a company may be worth less in the future to him than at present, and the necessity of the buyer's developing an understanding of this aspect during discussions and before initiating price negotiations. In the course of developing this understanding the buyer will get a sense of the seller's time requirements. Obviously, there will generally be a greater degree of urgency in the defensive take-over previously cited than there would be in the estate liquification situation.

However, again, the sense of timing will depend upon the respondent. I have encountered situations where, after meeting for the first time over dinner, we discussed the relatedness of the companies during the appetizer, the general framework of a transaction during the main course, agreed to visit the plant during dessert, reviewed the financial statements after touring the plant, and entered into serious negotiations of terms after reviewing the statements, all in the same evening! I have also exceeded an elephant's gestation period even getting to the appetizer stage.

THE NEED FOR FLEXIBILITY

As far as setting out a particular sequence of steps is concerned, I do not believe it is realistic to prepare a timetable. One individual will want to spend a lot of time getting to know you, some of your associates, and your philosophy before you get much hard information, or even set foot on the premises. Another individual will attempt to ascertain your parameters for the transaction at the very outset.

This, of course, depends on the degree of the acknowledged availability of the company. I attempt to defer evaluation discussions until there is opportunity to develop the understanding upon which they should be based. This includes financials, markets, managements, and so on. Once such negotiations have begun, these factors may continue to exert their influence within another dimension of timing—the elapsed time between commencement and culmination of negotiations.

In today's marketplace we are seeing an acceleration of timing in all business dealing. This is a function of the age in which we are living. A recent ad in a scientific magazine shows a little boy studying. The copy reads, "He has three times as much to learn as you did. Can he learn three times as fast?"

Today's business developments occurring in one area have an increasingly significant affect on the other areas, as regards market displacement, new market creation, cross production, and so on. Industrial provincialism is as obsolete as political isolation. In our environment, changes are occurring so rapidly that no industry or corporation can be analyzed in a vacuum, yet acquisitions are formulated after one or two meetings in an office.

There are probably more acquisitions being made, and less time taken per transaction, than ever before. As a consequence, we are seeing a higher incidence of broken corporate engagements and unhappy corporate marriages. The elapsed time of negotiations is now also frequently affected by early announcements as a result of the SEC disclosure considerations, and the resultant pressures from outsiders once an announcement is made.

Paradoxically, the controversial SEC disclosure requirement, which has been decried by some corporate executives, has been used by many of the same critics as a negotiating weapon with interesting strategic implications. I know of more than one instance where disclosure requirement has been used as an excuse to announce negotiations after only a preliminary discussion, with the underlying thought that such an announcement would psychologically commit the sought-after company to the acquisition route.

THE DANGER OF MOVING TOO FAST . . .

However, this early announcement gambit is risky if you do not solidify your position quickly. There has been a recent change in accepted business ethics, as far as the "hands off" policy in regard to brides-to-be is concerned, and an announcement may bring several proposals from other suitors. Nevertheless, once an announcement has been made, all parties to the announcement are usually interested in moving things along to some conclusion, and it can thus be an impetus in this regard.

My own preference is to build an understanding on a

softer approach, without the duress, and predicated on the philosophy that a better-knitted fabric will sustain the inevitable stress. To me, the most critical period of timing is the final countdown period before final signing, when a crescendo of emotions, details, trivia, and unexpected influences build up to the point where they tear at this fabric.

This, in my experience, is the time when communications must be constant. Other personalities come into play; accountants, tax experts, and lawyers become involved. I call this the period of doubt—not only because more questions are being raised, but because it is only natural to have doubts about so important a decision just prior to its consummation.

. . . OR TOO SLOWLY

It is important to move quickly before the seller's doubts can crystalize. If possible, now is the time to set a definite time limit, pick a date and set it as a goal. You can always extend it if necessary, but so long as there is an unlimited time to make a decision, it will never be made.

Board meetings, year-end or quarterly reporting periods, a desired effect of pooling-of-interests treatment for a company acquired late in the year—all these and others are real or apparent reasons for a deadline.

In my original premise that the reason the seller will consider the sale of this company is because he feels it will be worth less to him in the future than it is today, I did not mean to imply that he therefore will expect less for it.

The first thought relates to timing, in the sense of readiness or receptiveness. The second thought relates to value. Here too, timing is important, and there are several approaches that can be used to overcome the pie-in-the-sky projection which a seller may advance.

TIME AS A NEGOTIATING TOOL

We have utilized going-forward formulas a number of times to overcome such evaluation gap, and match the timing of a supposedly idyllic future with a reality of actual results. We usually predicate such an approach upon less than the present value of a company at closing, with more than the present value as the carrot, and the actual value in the future as the yardstick.

This offers protection on the downside, and if properly structured, not only provides an important incentive for owner-management to make the company go, but also provides the buyer with an effective pay-out period that need not be any longer than he wishes.

There are a number of interesting ramifications in such a transaction. If you are structuring a tax-free exchange, you may take note of the IRS guidelines for consideration of such an exchange involving a contingent payment. Briefly, they are: that all the stock be issued within a five year period; that there be a valid reason for not issuing all the stock immediately, such as the difficulty in determining value; that the maximum number of shares which may be issued in the exchange be stated; that the reason for the agreement evidencing the right to receive stock in the future must prohibit assignment; that such a right can give rise to the receipt of only additional stock of the acquiring corporation, or a corporation in control thereof, and that at least 50 per cent of the maximum number of shares which may be issued be issued in the initial distribution.

The ability to distribute up to an equal number of shares in the future focuses attention on the price of your stock at some future time. Suppose, for instance, the agreement calls for a fixed payment at closing, with an additional payment contingent on the average earnings over a two or three year period, and with the price of the contingent payment stock to be determined on the basis of an average daily closing price two or three years from now.

To the buyer, this is advantageous if the price of the stock rises during the period. He will distribute fewer shares in the contingent payment. Yet, a significant rise in the stock price can hardly make the seller unhappy. He will enjoy appreciation in his original shares and still receive current market value in two years for the then current earning capacity of his company, plus having two years in the future to grow his company's earnings. Thus, this kind of timing deserves bilateral consideration.

THE VIRTUE OF CONTINUITY

Basic to a relationship between buyer and seller is the concept of a prompt follow-up. Once the seed is planted, it must be nourished to grow. Hopefully, it will be nourished in secrecy until it achieves some substance, and although the secrecy can be overdone in some quarters, it cannot be overemphasized.

My notion of over-secrecy is conditioned somewhat by a situation in which I was involved not long ago. An intermediary called me to say that he had the proverbial "perfect situation" for our company. I asked him whether he would tell me about it without telling me who it was. He replied that it was privately held and gave me the sales level and the earnings level, but that was all. Not even the industry. And, oh yes, the fee was to be paid by the buyer.

He stoutly refused to say anymore, except to say that it was related to our activities. Since he would not tell me anything else, I inquired how he would have us proceed, and he insisted upon an approach that I suspect is unique. He wanted us to select an escrow agent, and deposit with this escrow agent a series of envelopes identified by the different letters of the alphabet, and containing the names of all transactions we might be working on. He would then deposit an envelope, containing the name of the company in question.

The escrow agent was then supposed to open his envelope, and open our envelope beginning with the first letter of the company's name to determine if we were working on this company, and then return all the other unopened envelopes to us. Apparently, this man had had an unpleasant experience with some large company a few years ago, and he had never gotten over it. As far as I know, his secret is still inviolate.

Secrecy of negotiations can best be preserved by having as few parties involved as possible. We work strictly on a need-to-know basis, and minimize any correspondence to the company which could be seen by an uninvolved party, even to the point of hand-delivering communications. We frequently bear the guise of customers, consultants, or tax men, when on the acquisition premises, and when negotiations are under way.

SETTING A CLOSING DATE

Once discussions have survived the period of doubt, you will be faced with the question of timing the closing date. Possibly this question will have come up before the signing of the agreement. In either case, provisions must be made for an examination of financial statements by independent accountants. The timing involved here depends upon the size of the company and the state of its reporting process. I was involved in one acquisition where the seller kept no books at all. The corporation was wholly owned by one man and located in the Bahamas, where there is no tax. Therefore, it was not required that he make up any kind of financial statements.

I have always maintained that finance is nothing more than pieces of paper, but I have never had it so vividly demonstrated to me as in this situation. We literally built financial statements out of piles of paper, and I was very happy to see the certified accountant come in and check us out.

In the event you are applying for a tax-free ruling, you may require several months. Time may be required, too, for stockholder approval and in the preparation of proxy statements. The period of advance notice to stockholders before holding a meeting, as required by your company's by-laws, must be considered. In this regard, under the revisions in the new Delaware law, it is possible to obtain consent from stockholders without a meeting.

If the company is subject to the filing requirement of the SEC, additional time should be allowed for admission of proxy material to this agency for approval, before mailing to stockholders. In a statutory merger of consolidation, or where stockholders in a selling company who are offered capital stock of the acquirer have the right of appraisal under state law, a further delay might be necessary to permit them to submit their demand for appraisal and cash payment.

When new securities are to be issued as a result of business combinations, it may be necessary to file a registration statement under the Securities Act of 1933, and an application for securities under the Securities and Exchange Act of 1934. A listing application may be required to list the securities on the major stock exchange. Time may have to be allowed for clearance by other regulatory bodies such as the FCC, or ICC, and their counterpart state authorities having jurisdiction. These considerations, which depend on external factors, are in essence static timing elements compared with the give-and-take between parties which is dynamic.

Dynamic considerations adhere to no enduring rules. An old expression has it that absence makes the heart grow fonder. Another insists that "Out of sight is out of mind."

Which is correct? Both may hold true under certain given conditions. In this respect, the timing of negotiations becomes less an art and more of a science. For science is the attempt to describe phenomena under certain definite conditions, and the ability to recognize the existence of these conditions is really the essence of timing.

Question: There is considerable controversy over the effectiveness of contingency pay-outs. Why do you advocate them?

Mr. Stephen F. Snyder: I can only reply to the question on the basis of my own personal experience. We have been involved in a couple of situations where we have used them and they have worked very well. The incentive aspect alone has been very effective, especially in areas that were new to us, where we had limited expertise.

I think another way to look at it, is that it protects you on the downside. Also, if you structure the formula correctly, it will still provide a payout within your criterion. If you have a ten-year payout criterion, for example, you can set up a mathematical formula that will allow you to come out within the goals, no matter what happens.

I might add that contingency may be a useful approach if your own price earnings ratio is not as high as you would like it to be, because you can actually give the seller more than you can really justify giving him on the basis of his present earnings.

I also like to use it because most of the sellers I have talked to regard their business as pretty much their baby, and of course, they are emotionally involved. But like anybody's child, to the parent it seems a little bit better than it might seem to somebody else—a little bit more handsome, a little bit better in every respect. This may not necessarily be true to the buyer. You can overcome this difference in valuation, because you can simply say that if in fact you do what you say you can do, this is what will result. I can only say that in my experience, it has worked out pretty well.

Question: Following up on that, how do you convince the seller that he is in fact going to get out of this all that he envisions in the early outset of the discussions? In other words, when you're in control, when you're handling the purse strings and so forth. He doesn't still have the right to call on monies and set policies, and so on, as he would have. How do you suggest getting over this?

Mr. Snyder: There is no way you can fully protect the seller against this hesitation. You must develop a sense of rapport and a sense of trust, which is important anyway, but one of the things we do is we put as much in a contract as possible in this regard. For example, we agree, in a contract, that we will not allocate any corporate overhead to the acquired company during the period of payout, and in fact, quite the reverse happens, because the way we are set up, as a holding company, we have a certain number of experts in the parent corporation.

I refer to people in functions such as tax, and legal, and so on. Their talents are made available to this company, as well as the other benefits that would hopefully accrue, at no charge. This is another way that we try to assist them.

I might also say that we can only agree to advance monies to the new company at whatever the going rate might be if the company were to borrow independently, but what really happens is that a company has assured financing in the future, provided that it can demonstrate that its projects are economically sound and can return the kind of return on investment that we like to see. These are some of the approaches.

Question: Have you ever, in a contract, obligated yourselves to loan a certain amount for capital investment?

Mr. Snyder: No, we have not. We have evidenced in writing, a willingness to do so, provided that the request for funds meets with our return on investment criteria, and in actual practice, I think any of the companies who became associated with us, who wanted funds from the parent, have gotten these funds when they demonstrated that this was the case.

Question: Did you ever have the seller examine your corporate goals and protect himself against future dilutions, and if so, how do you handle it?

Mr. Snyder: We all know that there are many situations where a company has been acquired by another, and the stock has subsequently fallen out of bed, and the seller has not been very happy about this. There is no point in naming names. These things are in the newspapers every day.

We have not ever worked a transaction where we guaranteed the seller an anti-dilutionary effect. We hope that he has the same faith in what we're doing and trying to do as we do and that we share this common thought when we get together. In some cases, I'm aware of situations where companies with very high price earnings ratios have set up guarantees of certain stock prices, because while their earnings could maintain the same level or even increase, a small drop in the price earnings ratio could materially, adversely affect the price of the stock.

We like to argue that both our price earnings level and our earnings are lower than we would like and lower than we anticipate. We ask our sellers, those with whom we've become associated, to come to a like conclusion.

Question: At what point do you bring in the operating people, the people who are going to be responsible for generating the profits that you think will accrue from the acquisition?

Mr. Snyder: We know before we start that we are certainly going to rely very heavily on the people involved, the continuing management element involved in any company that we're going to become associated with and which joins us. We are going to look at them very carefully. In the process of this, we bring in our own operating people a little bit later in the game, but before we really finalize something. I like to have as few people involved as possible in the early stages, to establish a rapport and build up a relationship. Our people are aware, if only off-premise awareness; we discuss the company with them, but physical contact comes later in the game.

Question: How and when do your legal people become involved in negotiations?

Mr. Snyder: Well, that's a good point since things accelerate so fast. They enter about the time there seems to be a general feeling that we have a possible meeting of the minds. When we get down to specific discussions where we are talking about legal aspects, then our legal people come in. I have a very close working relationship with our legal people, and they don't try to negotiate a transaction. They're trying to advise us as to what the legal risks are, and let us make the business decisions.

Question: I have a question with regard to the use of the oral or written proposal. When you're about ready to move into negotiations, do you have a carefully detailed written proposal, or do you outline something verbally at the outset?

Mr. Snyder: I would say, it depends upon the parties involved. I prefer an oral basis. When you work on an oral basis, you've got to be very careful to define the exchange between the parties. It's easier to create a misunderstanding in oral communication than if you put things down in writing. I follow both approaches. I will put something in writing, but to me there's a certain "inscribed in stone" effect about the written word. I would rather try to work on a give and take basis up to the point where we have the feeling that we're hitting on all cylinders. Usually we skip initial writing approaches, although we do provide written information on the company. We reduce our thinking to writing for our own internal use, for our own executive group, and somewhat later, we try to reduce it into writing for the seller.

Question: Do you use the team approach?

Mr. Snyder: No, we don't. We centralize everything at the corporation, the holding company. We do this for a couple of reasons. With various people running around, you can run across each other's tracks and there can be problems. You can run across negotiations that are in process, and I know of more than one situation where a company was involved in a situation quite secretly and a subsidiary was involved in the same situation, each of them for awhile not knowing of the other's presence. There is also a legal liability with respect to finders. There are a lot of people in the field—and I'm not at all deprecating the intermediary role because I think it's an important one—who send you ideas all the time, and you've got to know what the history of contacts or even unsolicited proposals has been on a particular company. We have all this filed very carefully so that on any particular company we know, as far back as the files go, exactly what contact, if any, has been made by anybody in any of our companies. We encourage people to provide us with thoughts, leads, ideas, and analyses, but the actual contact work is all coordinated in the corporation.

Question: When you have developed your strategy and selected several private companies in an area, any of which might be equally desirable or almost desirable, do you pick one and concentrate on it before you develop the others, or would you approach them simultaneously?

Mr. Snyder: We would approach them serially, one at a

time. I had one interesting experience in this regard with one of the companies that I approached on a research basis trying to find out about the industry. This was a privately-held company that had absolutely no inclination to sell. In fact, we talked generally about this, and they were pretty adamant. In the course of our discussions, they realized that it was our intention to become involved in their industry, and that we very likely would become involved with one of their competitors. In that case, the wheel turned a little bit and they suddenly became very interested in the idea of pursuing some discussions with us, and these led to the eventual culmination of a transaction. But to answer the questions in a few words—no, we would only deal with one company at a time in a particular industry.

Any business decision involves the acceptance of risk. It should be possible, however, to recognize and quantify that risk, and therefore make provisions to minimize it. The author, a senior executive of one of the leading financial consulting firms specializing in acquisitions and mergers, describes a number of specific ways in which this can be done, by both buyer and seller.

11

EFFECTIVE HANDLING OF RISK IN ACQUISITIONS

by E.P. Fillion, Jr., Executive Vice President, W.T. Grimm & Company

The personal, or human aspects of corporate acquisition negotiation have in the past two or three years attracted a good deal of attention, yet most merger manuals do little more than raise the question of human factors before launching into a detailed analysis of accounting, legal or tax ramifications. Perhaps the authors find it difficult to do more than generalize about human factors, and so avoid them. These factors can, however, play a vital and sometimes crucial part in the outcome of the negotiation and the future of the merged business.

The art of negotiation is far better developed in Europe and Latin America than in this country. The American's difficulty in negotiating successfully extends far beyond the merger table. Our economic system was not developed on a barter basis, such as the Persian rug market, the outdoor farm produce square, or the Brazilian gem shop. It has only been in the last few years that we have considered offering less than the sticker price on an auto—and who today attempts a negotiation for a pound of tomatoes?

THE NATURE OF THE MERGER MARKET

While list pricing of many products and services is under some pressure, by and large our pricing attitude is still basically a matter of take it or leave it. It is perfectly normal that this same philosophy should carry over to the merger field. But one should take note of an important characteristic. The merger market is not yet broad enough, and certainly not balanced enough, to permit the creation of a competitive base. Furthermore, our emphasis on individualistic capitalism and corporate paternalism frequently cause us to view a business more as a child than an inanimate corporate being. As a result, the seller tends to set a price which includes payment for a "boss franchise," and the buyer works in the opposite direction, giving voice to his own pre-existent "boss franchise." In cases where these emotional characteristics do not exist, or their existence is recognized and controlled, the buyer and seller's valuations of the tangible worth of a business are generally quite close. The problem is therefore first to understand, then to control, the emotional inputs of inquiry and response.

There are many different ways to approach the subject of negotiation. Certain corporate buyers have adopted and polished some rather sophisticated techniques. Only a few sellers have been equally successful. In this regard, however, it is a good idea to remain alert when a prospective seller, by voice or action, conveys the idea that he is just a small town boy who does not know the ways of the world.

It is essential to remember that negotiation begins with the first direct contact between buyer and seller. In fact, actions of the buyer before direct contact, but known to the seller, may shape the subsequent negotiation. We have seen very few deals reach completion where the jointly expressed attitude was—now that we know all about each other's business, let's sit down and negotiate.

KEEPING A DEAL CLOSED

Some time ago, my firm was called in to try to save a corporate marriage in which the president of the seller wished to rescind the contract six weeks after the closing. He had been steadily wooed by the president of the buyer, to the point that a social relationship had developed. There had been many informal golf games—each had been entertained in the other's home, and the two couples had cruised together for ten days. In the six months preceeding the deal, there had been almost daily social contract between the two. In the six weeks after the deal, the seller had heard from the buyer just once—and that was a very businesslike transmission of a criticism. Is it any wonder the seller was disillusioned? The buyer, on the other hand, couldn't understand the problem —after all, he had closed that particular deal, and was hard at work on the next.

In another instance, a buyer was cautioned to emphasize the operational fits of the two businesses, and not be concerned about the possibility of repeated denials of availability by the seller. The face-to-face discussion proceeded smoothly, surprisingly all the way to the point where buyer and seller had worked out a consolidated organization chart. When a lull fell in the conversation, the buyer bluntly asked the seller what his price was—and that was the end of the conversation.

Possibly the greatest cause of broken negotiations is the failure of either or both parties to clearly and completely develop their own objectives. Corporate marriage is not, or should not be, a casual affair—yet very often people seem to enter negotiations with the attitude "Let's see what develops!" Each should know exactly what he hopes to accomplish, set a ranking of importance, and determine in which areas he can legitimately compromise and still realize his acceptable net objective.

THE ASSESSMENT OF RISK

Since there is no perfect company—for if there were, we wouldn't have acquisitions—there is likewise no perfect marriage. Probably the greatest difference we note between companies that do make successful acquisitions and those that are still trying is the seemingly trite recognition that business is a risk. The company that tries to make a riskless acquisition will not be successful.

The main problem in any negotiation is how to learn

enough about the other company in order to be able to answer one question: Can I achieve my objectives and at the same time reduce business risk to an acceptable, realistic level.

SOME RULES FOR BUYERS . . .

Since people are different, so are interactions in negotiation. Meaningful generalizations are difficult, but possibly some do's and don't's may prove helpful. First, from the buyer's side:

1. Do not expect the seller to bare his soul at the first meeting. Skirt the touchy issues—to be taken up at a later meeting after you have had time to reflect on them. Don't be guilty of shooting from the hip. Different sellers will hold back greatly different types of information. What does surprise me, actually, is how readily a seller will admit to burying profits. Fortunately, the IRS doesn't have an ear everywhere.

It is also surprising to discover how few executives properly do their homework before meeting their prospect for the first time. Yet, if they should fall down at this first visit, the chances are slim that they will get a second chance. We all know about acquisition checklists, but how many have you ever seen that require inquiry into the seller's hobbies, his business and personal philosophies, his aspirations—all of which would serve as guides in sizing up the personality of the man you are going to have to ultimately convince.

One of our clients demands that a W.T. Grimm officer first meet personally with each prospect. The client then spends no less than an hour firing personal questions at us—all directed to the subject of the prospect's personality. I have seen this client play roles all the way from a Wall Street attorney to a shirt-sleeves production man. Certainly, he has guessed wrong on occasion, but I would hazard a guess his batting average is better than most.

Considering that, at best, negotiation is a low-yield business, who can sensibly run the risk of sizing up a man in the first 30 seconds?

2. Do expect to have to "sell" yourself, and your company, to the seller. We are currently trying to resurrect a negotiation that had fallen apart because the buyer whizzed off to Europe thinking the seller was his at his own convenience. While the buyer was overseas, the seller held detailed talks with another buyer who is playing up how much he needs the seller's technical know-how.

3. Do structure a team-approach to the seller. In the previous example, the buyer could have had a second-in-command stand in during his absence. In the social relationship mentioned earlier, the buyer would have been well-served to have had a four-way, not two-way, golf game, so there could have been a multiple point of contact.

I can cite one rather unusual application of the team approach. It may not be universally applicable, but it *has* worked well for one particular company that is very active in acquisitions. After a first meeting with the prospective seller, the buyer would invite the seller into the corporate offices and see to it that he met as many of the top executives as possible.

Immediately after that meeting was over, the buyer's team would sit down in an informal brainstorming session and try to rank the order in which their people had appealed to the seller. They would then turn their number two choice loose to do the actual negotiating. More often than not, as most negotiations go, they reached a stumbling point.

At this point, the buyer would bring in the man that they felt had formed the best relationship with the seller, and in essence allowed him to be a third party. He would meet the seller on the seller's own ground, not openly criticize what his colleague had been doing, but at least leave the door open wide enough to let the seller know that "You're now talking to a different guy, and I'm sure the two of us can work out the differences." As I understand it, this saved a lot of deals that might otherwise have fallen through. It was not a question of altering terms so much as altering the human factors involved.

4. Do not assume the seller is yours for the asking. In today's market, each desirable seller has many opportunities to merge. The buyer with the most effectively oriented sales presentation will have the inside track. Again, I mean effective in personal, not financial, terms.

5. Do guide the seller—especially if he is a privately-owned company—in considering the technical aspects of the deal. Many sellers don't know what section #1245 of the 1964 Revenue Act is all about, and may not want to admit this ignorance, or call in an accountant at what they consider to be a premature time. Later, however, the seller may balk at the deal when he finds out the size of the depreciation recapture tax bite.

6. Do what you can to allay post-merger fears. If you have made successful acquisitions—and prior management has been retained—suggest to your current prospect that he talk to the acquired management—and not in your presence. Lay out a full program for the merged operation. Show the seller where he will fit. If you want to change his company and still want him, it is best to cover these changes clearly during negotiation, not spring them on him after the close. Certainly you run the risk of losing the deal, but that may be the lesser of evils—and you will gain the seller's respect.

7. Do attempt to reach substantive agreement before demanding an exhaustive examination. We know of one company that kept an in-house analyst busy full time for eight

months on a prospective merger before even approaching the other company. When the approach was finally made, the buyer was shocked to find the asking price was $12 million, when he had been thinking about offering four.

8. Do constantly try to put yourself in the seller's shoes. Be responsive to his personality and don't let your own ego get in the way.

9. Do not waste time trying to negotiate a bargain. In most cases where a true bargain results, the effect isn't apparent for several years.

10. Do focus your thoughts and presentation on the future, not the past. Your interest should be in what you think you can do with the company—not what the seller has done.

Lastly, do constantly remind yourself that no merger is made in heaven.

. . . AND FOR SELLERS

From the seller's standpoint, there are some other considerations:

1. Do not think every buyer is out to fleece you. After all, he may need you worse than you need him.

2. Do be prepared to tell a complete, concise story about the status, prospects, and problems of the business. Who knows, the buyer may be so caught off guard he will air some of his own dirty linen.

3. Do not try to play it cute. You may find yourself out of your league and end up tripping on your own robes.

4. Do listen to what the buyer doesn't say—as well as what he does.

5. In a merger, as opposed to a cash sale, do recognize that you must evaluate the buyer as closely as he is looking you over.

6. Do get expert counsel at an early date. In all probabil-

ity you will find you don't know all the answers, and trying to shift gears late in a negotiation is difficult.

7. Do make a rational self-appraisal of your sincerity in trying to reach agreement. If you're not serious, don't waste everyone's time.

8. Do not overprice your company—unless you can bail out immediately. If you stay on, you will have to live with trying to improve the operation for the new boss so that he gets a realistic return on his investment.

9. Finally, like the buyer, recognize that no marriage is perfect.

GETTING HELP FROM OUTSIDE

With the growing complexity of corporate consolidation occasioned by the increasingly restrictive requirements of the IRS, SEC, major security exchanges and government regulatory agencies, few companies are capable of effecting a successful deal without outside assistance. From the technical standpoint, there is a greater need than ever before to secure the services of experienced auditors, tax attorneys, general corporate counsel, and attorneys well-versed in regulatory matters. The associated costs are high, but it is a misguided chief executive who thinks he can economize by doing his own legal, accounting or even public relations work. This point has not yet been completely accepted, as the current rash of stockholder suits can attest.

There was a time when one negotiation would suffice; when there was a meeting of minds of the two principals, the deal was in the bag. Today, this negotiation is no less important, but added to it are the negotiations between two auditing firms, two tax counsels, and two corporate counsels. By and large, the accountants, attorneys, and public relations counsel are charged with technical aspects of a transaction, but depending on their personal experience, they may all be of assistance in negotiating the deal. We once witnessed a negotiation where the seller's attorney entered the picture after price had been decided and handled the negotiations for fringe benefits, employment contracts, and other "details" so skillfully that the effective price was increased by some 15%.

WHAT CAN "FINDERS" FIND?

By and large, however, when we think of enabling third parties, we are talking about the finder, business broker, intermediary, or merger specialist. Unfortunately, self-bestowed titles and true capabilities have become quite confused. Some finders are interested in negotiating, and are expert negotiators. Some self-styled merger specialists are nothing more than name droppers. Nor does the cost structure clear the picture. On one hand, an investment banker may be largely responsible for bringing about a $25 million deal at a cost of $100,000. On the other, a finder might expect only to drop a name and stand back, presenting a flat 5% bill after the transaction has been completed.

Part of the problem may be due to the fact that few chief executives have truly answered the question—why is there a middleman in the first place? I am certain that answers to this question would vary widely. I can only give my own, somewhat conditioned view.

We see the intermediary's main purpose as being an experienced sounding board. If he is capable, he can guide both buyer and seller to workable compromises by interpreting what each is really saying, or trying to say, and by playing back what the other is thinking but not saying. In a negotiation, the knowledge of a principal's reaction to a particular point or presentation is necessary before going to the next related step. Otherwise, the talks will proceed along a wrong avenue, inpelled by a false assumption. Furthermore, the merger specialist should have enough broad experience to be able to suggest approach or negotiating techniques to his client, and to be able to suggest alternative structures for a transaction. There are very few places in merger negotiations for the take-it-or-leave-it philosophy. This is generally the last straw—and the need to resort to it suggests that negotiation was not well handled. Of increasingly less importance is the capability to find a prospect. Of steadily more importance is the ability to make a successful approach to a prospect so that the stage is set for a sincere and meaningful negotiation.

In our opinion, a prospective buyer or seller should talk to a reasonable number of middlemen, decide first whether he wants a middleman at all, and if so, to accomplish which goals. With the requirements known, it is then a decision as to who can best perform at what relative cost.

WHAT DO FINDERS COST?

Pricing policies are not as structured as they should be—but this lack of standardization does not justify the loose way in which verbal and some written contracts are drawn. There should be little sympathy for a chief executive who ends up fighting about the size or payment of a finder's or brokerage fee. The problem should have been avoided by settling on the ground rules at the outset. But a super-tight contract is no answer either. What it usually signifies is that the principal does not really want the services in the first place. We have seen middlemen demand compensation out of all proportion to what service was provided. On the other hand, we have seen chief executives encourage middleman efforts, then try to denigrate them.

Fortunately, the trend in the intermediary function is changing. There are still the high-power operators, be they agent or principal, but we see a steady move from an opportunistic to a planned approach in which the intermediary is becoming more of a trusted adviser and less of a promoter.

Since costs still vary widely, the only answer is for principal and agent to talk out in full what is required by both parties, and review what the associated costs or contingent liabilities are likely to be. I do not mean to imply the solution is easy—for negotiation is still an art—and it is hard to set a price on art. In one case, we conducted a negotiation over a two and one-half year period. In another, two phone calls, 30 minutes apart, did the deal. Presuming that the deals were of comparable size and the desired result was accomplished in each— how would you price one relative to the other?

Success in negotiation and success in utilizing third parties both hinge on one factor—how you deal with people. It is possible that you can overpower them with your own dominant personality. It is also possible—and usually more successful—to approach them at their own level, and slowly alter their thinking until you both meet somewhere in the middle of the table.

Complete mergers and acquisitions are always announced in financial terms—so many shares for so much consideration. The road that led to agreement, however, is usually paved with other factors. The author draws on his own experience as a successful negotiator to discuss one of the most important of them: the creative approach to value.

12

A MARKETING APPROACH TO ACQUISITIONS

by Thomas C. O'Connell,
President, Northstar Industries, Inc.

In the internal dynamics of most large companies, the marketing function usually does not have very much to do with acquisition activities. To be sure, marketing management is involved, along with other groups, in evaluating potential acquisitions. In fact, it is often the marketing group that proposes the acquisition in the first place, and works out the reasons why it should be undertaken. But once the decision is made, the tendency is to let the merger and financial specialists take over, with the option of calling in marketing, production or research people as they are needed.

I believe this may be a fundamental strategic mistake.

In suggesting this, I am not trying to create additional duties for marketing managers. Most of those I know are kept fully busy with their problems without taking on additional responsibilities. However, during my association with General Mills, we developed and put into operation an acquisition program that was based directly on a marketing approach. In a little more than five years, this program resulted in more than 20 acquisitions which in terms of investment exceeded one half billion dollars, and in terms of operations diversified the company into such chosen fields as toys, chemicals and jewelry. As of now, these acquisitions have all turned out well, and in fact, represent the fastest growing segment of the corporation. On the record, then, it seems that we were doing something right.

FOUR PRACTICAL RULES

Since we did not follow a highly-structured plan, I cannot provide a step-by-step action program. We did have some preconceptions, however, and we learned a lot along the way. Some of it had to do with fairly simple things that recurred with such frequency that one might begin to think of them as rules. A lot had to do with putting together negotiating teams. This, we found, was central to our whole effort; but first, the rules.

Rule 1. No matter how high or low, the price is never right. You can work very hard and come back home thinking you have developed a tremendous package with a very good company at an attractive price. The next morning you will walk into the office and invariably the first or second remark you hear is: "Well, it could have been better."

As you get involved in acquisitions, you will find that, regardless of what the price is, it's never the right price. I don't think we have ever bought anything at so low a price that someone back at headquarters didn't think we could have done better. I suppose that, like beauty, value is in the eye of the beholder.

Rule 2. The farther the individual is from the bargaining table, the more forcefully he negotiates. As you encounter face-to-face negotiations, most of these hard and firm concepts begin to fall by the wayside. We can sit back in the board room and say we are going to do this, that, and the other thing, and then we sit down and start talking with the principal. He has a very good company, he's an intelligent person, he knows what things sell for, so he says, "This is what I would like," and a lot of preconceived notions go out the window.

Rule 3. The expert negotiator who does nothing but negotiate deals is a myth. You are not sitting down with a labor union to negotiate a contract that must be met; you are sitting down with a businessman who has developed a very good, sound business which is highly attractive. There are very few virgins left; the seller has a fairly good idea of the maximum price you're willing to pay. Therefore, the spread is narrowed very rapidly. As a rule you are not talking across a tremendous range of prices. Based upon our experience, the companies and individuals that I have valued the highest from a business management viewpoint were also the firmest people on a negotiating basis. I do not mean that you must not be a good negotiator—but you must have many attributes, and not only be a negotiator.

Rule 4. The more members involved in the basic meetings, the less will be accomplished. When you meet in Florida with the chairmen of the two boards and ten other specialists, you may as well skip the meeting and enjoy a golf game. Much is accomplished by two people talking and trying to arrive at a mutual interest. Our preference is not to have a third party involved in the serious sessions. A third party can keep the talks progressing, but sooner or later, the principals must deal with each other and get the basic issues resolved.

WHAT IS VALUE?

Underlying these simple rules, the most important input is the knowledge of the specific situation, and the key factors motivating the principals. Values vary among people and are composed of many important factors, one of which is money. In most cases, the total amount of money is not the key concern. Most of the men we deal with are independently wealthy; when someone tells a seller he is making him a millionaire, he is usually wrong. The seller already is a millionaire. The personal factors are very important. Selling a company and merging with someone else is a very trying personal experience. Therefore, we believe the best negotiator is the person who knows the potential customer best. To those who have been in sales, I am sure it comes as no news that every time the national sales manager goes out, he gives some district sales manager heck for cutting prices, then he himself calls on a customer and gives him a lower price than the salesman has ever given anyone in that territory. So we like to have the person who has the greatest acquaintance and understanding of the total situation do the negotiating. We believe he is going to try to do the best job; he knows our interest, he is a hard worker, ambitious, and we feel that we come out much better using him than having an expert at headquarters who never met this person fly out, try to negotiate the deal and go back home. We have tried it that way, and we think we run a high risk of creating animosity. An example might be our acquisition of the Tom Huston Peanut Company, in Columbus, Georgia. It is a fine southern company, and being northerners and more precisely, Yankees, presented us with some problems. However, as we got to know the management, the directors and their families, we were able to generate a good strong relationship. I prefer this approach to having an expert fly in at 1 o'clock in the afternoon for a 2:30 meeting and a 4 o'clock plane to catch. To have used such an approach with Tom Huston would have been bad news for everyone.

Every discussion opens up by saying that money is not the important thing; unfortunately, we spend most of our time talking about it. So, in the last analysis, obviously how much money the company gets is going to be a very important figure. But we like to have the recipient think of the long term value of the money, not the short term value. He is usually disposed to do that anyway. The shares of stock we give him are only pieces of paper, unless we have some real good resources behind them.

KEEPING COMMUNICATIONS OPEN

Breakdowns in negotiations are a problem. We have come very close to completing negotiations and because of a very minor, almost insignificant point, the communications break down. My philosophy is to keep the communications going.

Some people tend to say, "Well, let's go home and think about it for two or three days." Or two or three weeks or a month. Usually things cool off and the law of probability is against you; usually you will go your way and they will go their way. Still thinking in marketing terms, I would like to see a continuity of negotiation, and keep it warm. If a problem arises, try to resolve it on the spot, rather than giving each party time to think about it. That's a good way to lose an order!

The conceptual price is something you must be prepared to handle. I think that a person who has developed a business will usually have a conceptual price in his mind. He believes that his company is worth a set figure, expressed either as fixed value of money, or shares of your stock, or some other consideration. And I have found that this is a very difficult thing to change. He may be right and he may be wrong, but he has it in mind.

Occasionally, time can take care of this. In the case of one acquisition, we agreed to give a fractional share of General Mills at, say, just to make an example, .47 common shares of General Mills for each common share of theirs. But the seller was adamant. He had a value in mind of $50 a share. We wouldn't give him $50 a share at that time, so we went along for three years, talking and maintaining a very good relationship. Finally, the value of our stock reached a point at which we were able to offer him .469 shares. This came out to $50, and that is what he had wanted all the time. Sometimes the conceptual price becomes a very important and perhaps even irrational matter. The man just feels that his company is worth "X" thousands of shares or millions of dollars and that is it.

Buyers too can be stubborn, and *should* be stubborn on certain matters—such as what kind of companies they are seeking for. For instance, we are really looking for people who can run a business very effectively; and not a company hampered by an inept management group. We do not want a problem situation, as we have a scarcity of people. We are not looking for financial manipulations; we are not money men, we like to believe that we are businessmen. We are looking for something that makes sound business sense and we are not looking for a company that basically is "for sale." We would like to believe that most of the companies we have acquired joined us because we worked with their people for a period of time.

The typical company we do acquire is not for sale. I believe this is very important, because the day that someone decides to sell the company is the day that a lot of things in that business are not going to be done—personnel development, new product introduction, quality control, plant improvements—all the things that may not immediately detract from earned profits, but which are essential on a long term basis.

"SELLING" YOUR OWN COMPANY

The approach that we use is to select an area that we are interested in and then do exactly what we would do if we were selling a product. The product that we are selling is the company we represent, the customers we are trying to reach are companies in areas and industries where we have a strong interest. We have very aggressive teams on the road. It visits many, many companies. We talk with many companies and try to find a few companies in an industry that are attractive to us, and then we work with these people over a period of time. Probably the typical company that we have acquired, we have known and talked with for two or three years. Some we have worked with for as long as five years. In a few cases, we were just lucky and contacted a company just at the time when the principal decided to sell the business. But in most instances, we have worked over a period of time to bring the acquisition about.

THE CASE FOR DECENTRALIZATION

I think one of the things that we have done well is to decentralize, if you can describe it that way, the acquisition function.

We have a number of teams, a team in the toy, game and craft area, another in specialty consumer products, a third in corporate acquisition, and a fourth working in the chemical area. In other words, we have not tried to have one man or one expert in the company that can do all these things. We have tried to develop a number of people in different areas and I think we have succeeded. For instance, we started with virtually nothing in international businesses; this year we will have $100 million in sales. We could not have done that if we had not had three people at headquarters responsible for potential international acquisitions.

We have tried to coordinate the teams, but we learned that as you increase the rigidity of the organizational structure, you may lose some creativity. So we have tried to keep a very free-flowing team structure, letting the men in the field come up with the situations. The president of the company, chairman or vice president of the division will make the decision whether we go or we don't go, but they do not have to find the candidates. As a result, we have had a number of people involved in acquisitions.

Obviously we have to be careful not to have two teams going to the same company, so we try to maintain good coordination among the teams, but this is a small premium to pay. In general, given the qualified people, I prefer the separate team approach because it results in parallel efforts and generates more opportunities than would be obtained working through a number of centralized levels of communication.

This is what we have done, and I think it has been very successful for us. We have not used the functionalized approach. We do not use lawyers, accountants or other specialists until we really have an idea of what the situation is, and what the terms are likely to be. We isolate the problems, and then work with the specialists to generate a solution.

Most people who are selling a business have spent their whole lifetime developing it. They are therefore not experts in selling companies. If you, on the other hand, are acquiring a number of new companies, you will develop a certain skill. Nevertheless, you must be careful not to become so sophisticated that you lose rapport with the individual entrepreneur.

As soon as the experts arrive, the first thing they usually say is, "Here is the problem." The people who have been working on the project haven't been looking for problems. They have been trying to figure out how they can get the situation to go. It is important, before focusing on the key problems, to establish the proper climate. I believe such a climate must be a good, sound working relationship. I think, for instance, that the seller should know early in the game what the intentions and evaluations are, even if this means that the talks will stop if a fundamental disagreement arises.

A number of years ago we were working with a company. It was a good company, with a good record. We worked closely with the president, the owner of the business. We kept talking about multiples and the values of companies in the business. We thought we had reached some understanding, but we really did not get down to the price situation. After two or three months of leisurely discussion, the company's president finally said, "Well, I'm convinced. I think

General Mills is a good company. I see some benefits of our association. Let's get down to brass tacks." And all he wanted was 92 times earnings for his latest year, and about 32 times earnings for the last three years. And so we got out very quickly. It makes sense to establish a price range as early as possible.

VALUE VERSUS PRICE

What I try to do now is not to get into the price immediately—you must become acquainted first. In our case, we like to think we are trying to interest the person in selling the business to begin with, and after he accepts this, we try to establish some kind of value that we would be willing to work with. This establishes our ceiling. We try to tell them that people in their business are selling for such and such. And we try to stay away from the multiple whenever we can. Most principals do not think in terms of multiple anyway. It is the stock analyst who thinks in terms of multiples. We feel it is much better to say, "We'll give you $30 million," than to say, "We'll give you 15 times earnings." We want to stay away from trying to match multiples, and $30 million sounds like a lot of money. We try to demonstrate that it is a fair price in that industry, what other people are selling for, what is going on. He has to give a little, we have to give a little, usually we come out with an agreeable price.

Sometimes it doesn't work out that way. We have such a situation right now. We are interested in a company; we feel that we are in the range of a fair and reasonable price—a price which I think we could sell to our Board of Directors. However, with so many companies going public, the owner has had a lot of people coming around and telling him what they could take him public for, which is just more money than we are willing to pay. We do not have to acquire *any* company. We are trying to find a reasonable fit. We think that the value offered was fair. So we had a number of visits, and he kept coming up with high numbers, and he wanted to have another meeting, and meet more people. Finally, he came up with a figure of about 30 to 45 times earnings. And I just said, "I think you have a great company. I think we could work something out, but the kind of money you're talking about is not in the cards. If you should change your mind, let us know."

There are two ways to look at an acquisition program. One is to think of yourself as a buyer, shopping around in the marketplace for companies to buy. The other—and this is really what the marketing approach is all about—is to think of yourself as a seller. You *are* a seller. You are selling your own company to the man whose business you want to acquire.

No salesman in the world ever closed every sale he went after. The last example I cited proves that. But a salesman's rate of success will be greater if he uses all the tools at his disposal. In our case, one of these tools is the reputation of General Mills itself.

We are fortunate in having some familiar products, and of course Betty Crocker herself. I make it a point to send out a lot of packages at Christmas time, and whenever possible, I send it home, not to the office. There's no way to measure the effectiveness of these packages—no accurate way. But presidents and owners of companies do talk to their wives. And I can well visualize a scene in which such a president might say to his wife, "I've got a choice. I can sell to General Mills, or I can sell to XYZ Company." I can also visualize that her answer might be.

Not every company, of course, will have the advantage of

instant familiarity. But I am willing to wager that the XYZ Company could develop some impelling sales tools of its own. And if it has, and has used them effectively, I would no longer be as confident about what that president's final decision will be.

It is possible, in the heat of negotiation, to create pressures on the seller that will cause a good transaction to fall through. The author, who himself has led 17 negotiations to successful conclusions in the past decade, describes how this can be avoided through careful, reasonable planning.

13

CREATING A FAVORABLE CLIMATE FOR NEGOTIATION

by Marshall Butler,
President, Alloys Unlimited

One of the main goals of modern business practice has been the elimination of the old seat-of-the-pants approach to decision-making, and its replacement by rational, systematic techniques. And nowhere have these techniques proved more effective than in the area of mergers and acquisitions.

The wheeler-dealer, let's-forget-about-the-pencil-boys-and-do-this-man-to-man approach has just about vanished, and it is not my intention to make a plea for its restoration.

I do believe, however, that it takes something more than a perfect match-up of numbers to achieve a successful merger. This additional factor—let us call it the creation of a favorable climate—can sometimes play a determining role in the closing of a transaction. More important, it probably *will* play the determining role in the long-term success of a merger, as measured in terms of fruitful collaboration.

By its nature, the creation of a favorable climate does not yield to complete quantification. It can, however, be planned and programmed as an integral part of the negotiation process. How it can be done is the subject of this chapter.

Let us assume that, as a prospective buyer, you have begun the countdown process. You have identified the company you are interested in acquiring. You have made a complete analysis of its products and its balance sheet. You have reviewed its capability in marketing, manufacturing and technology. You have weighed the quality of its people.

If at this point the light is still green, you will continue to the next step, which is to establish a set of parameters. You will determine a price range, and the method of payment. If it turns out to be cash or note, you will want to establish time and terms. If stock is involved, you will want to review what kind of restrictions or conditions you want to place on the stock which you will issue. These conditions will be molded by the objectives you wish to achieve.

If your negotiating team has done its work well, it will be

able to report to you on the particular needs of the seller. These needs may be purely financial; they may also be personal, even emotional in nature. It is important that you know exactly what they are, because it is by accommodating them that you can begin to create the climate which you seek.

You should, for instance, know why the seller is willing to sell. Does he have a health problem, or some other reason that may move him to retire? Does he simply need the money? Does he want to stay on and continue running the business?

Are you about to acquire a company simply because its principals cannot get along together? Is the man sitting across the table from you simply tired of trying to solve his problems and therefore willing to sell them to you?

It is a safe assumption that *any* company which is for sale has problems of some kind, or they would not be for sale. This, however, should not be a deterrent. One man's problem is another man's opportunity.

The seller may have a good manufacturing base and a good marketing organization, but no capability for developing new products. Or he may have the product, but not the capacity to manufacture it.

He may have both, but not the financial resources to put them together. In the case of privately-owned companies in particular, it may often happen that the principals are unwilling to take the personal risk necessary to develop and launch a new product.

Whatever the reason, you are aware of it. You are further convinced, on the basis of your analyis, that the acquisition makes good business sense. You are now ready to go into negotiation.

This is the crucial point, the moment at which you begin to create—intentionally or unwittingly—the climate that will surround both the discussions and, should they be successful, your future relations with the acquired company.

First of all, you must go into this meeting with a feeling of mutual respect. It may be that you—or one of your advisors —have concluded that you are really the Great White Father coming in at the last minute to save a hopeless cause. Perhaps this feeling may even have some justification, but before you let it color your attitude, stop and reflect. However you read the situation at the moment, the people you are going to talk to must have done something right in the past, or chances are that you would not now be going in to talk to them. For this reason, if no other, they deserve to be treated with respect, and with no sign of condescension.

The physical choice of location for this meeting is generally immaterial. You can invite them to your offices, or go to theirs. You can select a neutral ground such as a restaurant, club or other semi-public place. The essential point is that the location be convenient to the seller, or chosen at his preference. In adversary proceedings, there may be some slight psychological edge to meeting an opponent on ground of your choosing. But you are not embarking on a contest, and good sense—if not good manners—should dictate your deferring to the other party.

Timing is important, too. You must be certain that it is convenient for the other party, even if it turns out to be inconvenient for you. If the seller is a small company, it may be necessary to schedule meetings for the week end or during evenings; the man you want to talk to may have a full-time job running his company. In fact, it may very well be that the thinness of his management is a main reason why he is interesting in talking to you about selling in the first place. You, of course, have a large, efficient staff, and can make yourself available at a moment's notice. This makes you more fortunate than he is, but it should not diminish the respect which his efforts should command.

Taking this thought a step farther, the man who is doing the negotiating for you should see to it that he is not interrupted by telephone calls or other diversions while he is engaged with the prospective seller. In this respect, it does not especially matter who your chief negotiator is. It may well be yourself, or one of your division managers, or a senior staff officer specializing in this field. Whoever the man is, the impression he must convey is that at this time, in this place, the most important thing he has on his mind is the successful completion of the negotiations. In fact, it probably would be hugely helpful if he managed not only to convey this impression, but also believed it implicitly himself.

There must, of course, be an atmosphere of total honesty. If, in the course of negotiations you bring up special legal restrictions, complications and procedures, you must present both sides of the picture to the seller. This is based on the assumption that the seller will have his own lawyers and other professional advisors check out such things as tax consequences, SEC restrictions, pooling of interest requirements. His people must confirm the statements that you have made as to what the law is and the pro's and con's. It is much better to have an argument based on the seller trying to have a contract worded in a way that is favorable to him and your refusing to do it than to have him find out that you have misled him on the options that are legally available to him.

Perhaps the simplest way to assure this is for you, the more sophisticated party, to bend over backward in making sure that the seller understands what is being offered, accepted or rejected. One concrete way to achieve this is to keep a set of minutes or memoranda of meetings. These minutes do not have to be signed by the participants—people usually have a natural fear of putting their names to a piece of paper. Their purpose is not to bind anyone to any conditions, but merely to be a record of what has been said. A copy of these minutes should be prepared immediately after the meeting and sent to both parties. As the talks progress, the minutes become doubly useful: they serve the seller as a record and reminder, and they serve the potential purchaser or his staff as a running progress report.

It is frequently useful, in creating the sort of climate I have been describing, to let a potential seller meet the principals of other companies you may have previously acquired. Offer to arrange the meeting, if the seller indicates an interest, and then stay carefully out of the way. Let the men meet and talk face to face. A man *must* have some apprehension over selling his business, or chances are that the business is not worth buying in the first place. Very well, let him meet and talk to someone who has had the same experience he is now contemplating. There will be questions he will want to ask—whether you as a purchaser have lived up to your word, whether unforeseen problems have cropped up, whether it was a good idea to sell. With all the earnestness and sincerity in the world, you will never be as persuasive to a potential seller as someone who has himself undergone the experience.

Early in the negotiation process, it is a good idea to let a potential seller visit some of your plants, or distribution centers, or laboratories. Better yet, let him tell you what aspects of your business he would like to see for himself. At best, you are asking him to enter into a long-term relationship with you; at the very least, you are asking him to make a substantial investment in your business, which is of course what he will do if he takes part or total payment in equity. It would be surprising, and to some degree even alarming, if he did not evince an interest in your business. When he does, give him all necessary opportunity to satisfy his curiosity, unuhrriedly and without pressure. Human nature is predicatable: you may reasonably assume that he will suspect the worst about any aspect of your operations which you try to hide from him. You would do exactly the same if the shoe were on the other foot.

As a matter of procedure, it is better to schedule longer meetings than more frequent ones. Let the pace be unhurried, but not purposeless. Take each point up in order, cover it as fully as possible and in as relaxed a manner as possible. If you or your negotiators cannot answer some specific question, or respond to a point which had not been anticipated, have no fear to table it until the next meeting. That you have not prepared for all eventualities will not reflect unfavorably on your side; that you are willing to entertain the question seriously rather than try to skirt it *will* reflect favorably.

Do not, however, let matters lag, or leave questions unanswered. This will cause the seller to arrive at one of two possible conclusions: that you are not really interested in pursuing the deal, or that you have something to hide. Either conclusion can be fatal, for if the company you are trying to buy is desirable, there are likely to be other possible purchasers waiting in the wings.

No point should be glossed over, and this is why meetings should be paced slowly and allow for full discussion. But there should be a limit to the number of meetings necessary to complete a transaction. In general, it has been my own experience that if negotiations drag on for more than three or four weeks, they are not likely to end up satisfactorily. This is, of course, a rough guide. Certain specific details may take longer to iron out, but the willingness to iron them out —the existence of a cooperative climate—should be evident within this time span.

Another point borne out by my own experience is that the chief negotiator should be sufficiently aware of the legal requirements of the transaction to make the presence of a lawyer unnecessary until the parties are ready to sign a memorandum of agreement. This is not to say that lawyers are not essential in acquisition work. They are essential, on both sides; but it is often helpful if the prospective buyer can be trained by his own legal staff to handle matters up to the point of agreement.

Once that point is reached—once the lawyers begin their work—it is good for the principal of the buying side to stay away from the actual negotiations; and it is better still if he can convince the seller to stay away as well. This is not just a matter of protocol. As the prospective buyer, you do not want the lawyer for the seller to make a stand in front of his client that is indefensible or impossible for you to accept. At worst, you will have reached an impasse. At best, you will be obliged to prove the lawyer's objections ill-founded, and therefore in all likelihood create a sworn enemy.

It is much easier to let the lawyers hammer it out. The position is that you and the seller, as principals, have come to a meeting of the minds, and are merely requiring your staffs to complete their work. If a trouble spot does show up, you will hear about it soon enough. And, if you have stayed out of the conflict, you will be able to approach the other principal directly with a counter-proposal, a compromise, or an explanation of why this particular point is not negotiable. The seller will then take up your point with his lawyer, and make a decision.

This may sound like the complicated way of going about closing a deal. Actually it is not. All you have done is to set up two planes of discussion. One, on which you and your opposite number can remain totally friendly, cooperative and accommodating. The other, where the clause-writing actually takes place, will engage your respective lawyers. That, after all, is their business—to write contracts.

In summary, the creation of a climate favorable to a merger should follow these six basic rules:

1. Investigation of the company to be acquired must be completed before talks start.
2. The parameters of possible agreement must be established by the prospective purchaser.
3. In all his dealings with the seller, the purchaser must treat him as an equal.
4. There is no room for anything except total honesty.
5. The pace should be unhurried, but there should not be long delays, and a time limit should be kept in mind.
6. The lawyers should be kept out of the actual negotiations until the basic terms are set between principals—which is to say, until there is a basic meeting of the minds from a business point of view.

These rules, in my experience, have been effective in closing deals. More important, they are also effective in establishing harmonious working relations for the future.

Question: What has been your experience in negotiations where the seller is represented by an investment banker or a "finder"?

Mr. Marshall Butler: You mentioned two different kinds of people. I do not believe a finder has any place whatever in the negotiations. I have found that when we have allowed them in, the finder has usually ruffled the feathers and gotten the seller more upset than he has the buyer.

Now with an investment banker, this all depends. We have gone through two situations where the principals asked for an investment banker to be their negotiator, and in both of these cases, once it was clear that the investment banker had the authority to concede points and agree to points, he was very helpful. But I think you do not want to have an investment banker who is not going to have authority—the same authority that you as a negotiator have. If you reach a point where the investment banker is only taking notes, then you are in a bad situation. In a selling situation, you want to speak to the man who can sign the purchase order before you make all your concessions, and you do not want to be in that kind of position in this kind of negotiation either.

Question: What do you do if the seller insists on having his lawyer at the negotiations?

Mr. Butler: If the seller insists on having his lawyer as part of the negotiating team, there is nothing you can do; you have to accept it. It is not beneficial, you can try to persuade him, but I think you have to realize, basically, that this man and every individual is different, and there will be some people who want their lawyers. We have usually been able to keep the lawyers out until we have a memorandum of agreement, because it is a very simple thing. The lawyer is not going to tell you how much money you want for the business; the lawyer is not going to tell you what you want; he does not tell you how you are going to accomplish it. Let us agree that we want to give you what you want; *then* you can bring a lawyer in to see that you are actually getting it.

Occasionally—very rarely—we have had a situation where a man felt so unsure of himself that he needed a lawyer there, and again, there is nothing you can do about it. I think one of the points I made was, treat the man as an equal; so you can't just say to him, "I'm sorry, Charlie, you can't have a lawyer;" you are not going to make a deal that way.

Question: In that situation, did you still stick by your rule of not bringing your lawyer in?

Mr. Butler: In that particular case we did, because I felt that we were on sure enough ground that I did not want to have a lawyer fighting a lawyer; he was there as a business advisor, and in that particular case, I felt that we could handle him.

Question: When you use stock in acquiring a company with three or four stockholders, do you necessarily make those owners take an investment letter?

Mr. Butler: We make every company that we ever take sign an investment letter.

Question: My next question follows on this. Where the fellow wants to diversify, how do you cope with that?

Mr. Butler: First of all, we are talking about a closely held company with only one or two stockholders, where they cannot qualify under Rule 133. Rule 133 is the so-called 1 percent rule, where people can sell—even though the stock is unregistered—they can sell a certain amount. How we handle that is by guaranteeing them a registration, or the right to piggy-back. If we have a registration at any certain time, they will do it; and in most cases we also guarantee them that if we do not have a registration within one year or two years or three years, they have the right to call for a registration, and this is how you get them out.

Question: Did you ever come across a situation where, before closing, the acquired company sold off stock?

Mr. Butler: Yes sir.

Question: Well, how do you go about handling that?

Mr. Butler: Well, one of the things they can do in the mechanics of this—they can certainly pass the stock over to the people prior to the exchange. In other words, let us say that you own—you and your brother own 50 percent each in the company, but it is a corporation. You own 50 percent of the stock and he owns 50 percent of the stock. You can sell these people the stock at book value prior to our negotiations, or prior to the signing of the contract, at some price above book value and put some restrictions on the stock, that they cannot sell it for a period of five years tied in with employment, so that the value of it has a very low tax base until their employment period is over. But what we prefer to do is have the company to be acquired make the disposition prior to the closing of the deal.

Question: What about a contingency deal?

Mr. Butler: I do not like contingency deals. We have made, I think, two or three, and I don't like them, because they tend to create management problems. Most of the times that we have made an acquisition, we feel that their being part of us is going to allow them to grow a lot faster. Therefore, we may want to put in new engineering; we may want to increase their expenditures on research and development; we may want to put in a new cost control system which will cause them to complain that it is going to affect earnings. What you are doing is putting in a little piece of sand that is going to grow into an irritation, and if you can avoid that irritation wherever possible, you should. I do not think it is a good way of going; it presents too many problems.

If you are a bigger company and you are going for non-synergistic mergers, you are doing strictly straight financial deals where you do not think that your company is going to have to put a great amount of cash in; where you do not think you are going to be involved with the management, and you are perfectly willing to say: let them operate completely by themselves; we are not going to put marketing inputs, we are not going to put engineering inputs in them for three years or two years, and at the end of that period, then we will move in; you still have the problem of how badly that man is going to bleed the business during the three years. You know, all of a sudden he had 14 men in engineering and he's got 7, and if a man is going to do it, he is surely going to ask for certain rights that he can control the management of this company. Now you have a subsidiary which you are responsible for, but which you cannot control. So I am pretty much against them on that basis.

Question: As you have shaped up your deals, have you consciously tried to limit the number of shares that you have issued to seller companies?

Mr. Butler: The answer to that is yes; but I think the second question to that, or the unasked question, is: have we ever taken a dilution in earnings in a particular year, and the answer to that is yes. In other words, we are conscious of and we always like to—what's the old saying?—buy low and sell high. But there are times when a company has a product or a technology that you think is so great and can add so much to your company that you are perfectly willing to take a dilution for a year; but you then have to have a pretty good investigating team and have some pretty good determinations of where that company is going next year or the year after.

There are common misconceptions concerning mergers which may mislead both buyers and sellers. The author, who has personally been instrumental in consummating transactions which aggregate over $1 billion in principal amount, identifies some of the most important of these misconceptions, and suggests effective remedies.

14

HOW TO MAKE THE "IMPOSSIBLE" MERGER

by John S. R. Shad, Executive Vice President,
E. F. Hutton & Company

This chapter describes the financial fundamentals of mergers and what corporate buyers and sellers should do to obtain the most advantageous transactions to avoid downstream pitfalls. It includes an analysis of 65 representative mergers and acquisitions of medium size publicly owned companies, and an outline of what E.F. Hutton & Company does to assist its corporate clients in consummating such transactions on advantageous terms.

THE THEORY . . .

The most basic financial criteria by which the attractiveness of corporate acquisitions and mergers of publicly owned companies are commonly measured include:

1. The premium over the current market price of shares gained by the stockholders of the selling company.
2. The increase in earnings per share gained by the acquiring company.

The theory is simple. If Company ABC is selling at 20 times earnings and Company XYZ at 10 times, and ABC pays 15 times earnings in market value of its shares for XYZ's shares, both companies' shareholders will benefit. XYZ's will receive shares with a current market value 50% greater than their present shares, and ABC will gain 33% in earnings per share on the additional shares issued to effect the transaction. Such additional earnings can be expected to enhance ABC's market value per share, which will in turn benefit its shareholders.

However, the *relative* benefits actually gained by the shareholders of corporate buyers and sellers vary widely, depending upon market conditions and other considerations.

The rule of thumb throughout the postwar period has been that a corporate buyer should gain at least 20% in earnings on the additional shares to be issued, in order to justify the transaction. However, during periods when many companies are aggressively competing for acquisitions, corporate buyers have actually been willing to dilute their earnings per share in order to effect acquisitions. Such a period was 1968–69. The conclusions drawn from a survey of 65 representative mergers and acquisitions that were in process in the spring of 1969 provide worthwhile bench marks for present corporate buyers and sellers.

. . . AND THE PRACTICE

The 65 representative mergers and acquisitions listed in *Tables A, B,* and *C* were in process in the spring of 1969. The cash and market value of the securities to be issued by the buyers aggregated approximately $10 billion. These transactions had not been consummated, but the terms had been announced. From past experience, I estimate that roughly one quarter of these transactions will not be consummated, another quarter will be consummated on modified terms, and the remainder will be consummated on the terms originally announced. In about half of these transactions, there were no self-evident operating advantages from a horizontal or vertical integration point of view.

Convertible preferreds were being used to effect approximately 46% of these transactions; common stocks, 31%; debt, 19%; and cash or warrant purchases, 4%. In dollars, these transactions involved the payment of $5.3 billion in convertible preferreds, $2.2 billion in common stocks, and $2.3 billion in debt, cash, and warrants, for a total of $9.8 billion.

ON TAX-FREE BASIS

Approximately 77% of the transactions were being effected on a tax-free basis through the use of voting equity securities—that is, convertible preferreds and common stocks. Convertible preferreds were the most popular merger medium; they accounted for 46% of the 65 transactions and for 54% of the $9.8 billion involved.

ATTRACTING THE SELLER

On the basis of the market prices of the buying and selling companies' securities two weeks before announcement of the prospective merger or acquisition, the *sellers'* incentives in tax-free mergers were clear.

1. In the convertible preferred-for-common exchanges, the stockholders of the median seller would *gain* 20% in market value and 56% in dividend yield, and improve the quality of their investment.
2. In the common-for-common exchanges, the median seller would *gain* 21% in market value and 33% in dividend yield.

(Medians—that is, the middle company in each category—rather than averages were used throughout this study because of the infinite percentage increases and decreases in certain categories.)

The sellers would also improve the marketability of their holdings. They were generally being offered the opportunity to upgrade from the over-the-counter market to the American Stock Exchange, or from the American to the New York Stock Exchange, and the securities they were being offered

Table A. Tax-free mergers—common-for-common exchanges

Acquirer	Acquired	Gain in market value to shareholders of acquired company*	Percentage increase (+) or decrease (—) in: Yield to shareholders of acquired company	Acquirer's EPS on shares offered†	Acquirer's book value per share offered‡
American Export	National Equipment Rental	+13%	0%	+11%	— 73%
Baldwin Securities	Beco Industries	+27	+ 17	—19	— 22
Boise Cascade	Aristocrat Travel	+14	§	—33	— 3
Consolidated Natural Gas	West Ohio Gas	+17	+ 68	—34	— 62
Cooper Industries	Dallas Airmotive	+30	+130	—39	— 32
Diamond International	U.S. Playing Card	+23	+ 13	—34	— 49
Diversified Metals	Proler Steel	+ 5	— 88	+ 5	+ 23
Harris-Intertype	R. F. Communications	+12	§	—35	— 39
Hoover	Knapp Monarch	+24	§	§	+140
National Service	Lithonia Lighting	+16	+100	+16	+ 50
Londontown	Originala	+30	— 27	—20	— 51
Nytronics	Eastern Air Devices	+23	0	+ 7	— 71
J. C. Penney	Thrift Drug	+ 9	+125	—24	— 63
Transamerica	Metromedia	+20	+ 50	—17	— 21
U.S. Plywood	American Forest Products	+ 1	+ 43	+40	+ 43
Vanity Fair	H. D. Lee	+22	+ 10	+30	+235
Xerox	Scientific Data	+46	§	—37	— 11
Federal Sign	Breeze Corporations	+31	— 6	+45	+ 13
Pacific Southwest Airlines	Western Air Lines	+45	+ 2	—29	— 18
Sunshine Mining	Anchor Post	+14	+ 22	+18	+385
Median		+21%	+ 33%	—19%	— 19%

*Based on the market prices of both companies' shares two weeks before announcement of the transaction.

†Based on both companies' latest 12 months' reported earnings.

‡Based on both companies' latest available balance sheets.

§Percentage change infinite because of an increase or decrease from zero or a deficit.

were generally more widely held and actively traded than the shares they owned.

SATISFYING THE MERGER

On the basis of the buyers' and sellers' latest 12 months' reported earnings, the *buyers'* incentives were less clear.

1. In the convertible preferred-for-common exchanges, the median buyer would only *gain* 4% in current earnings per common share on the additional shares to be issued on conversion of the preferreds. Under Securities and Exchange Commission regulations, most buyers must report their earnings per common share as if these preferreds had been converted. Thus their earnings per common share would not benefit from the leverage provided by such preferreds. Furthermore, the leverage of the preferred dividends will accelerate declines in the buyers' earnings per common share during periods of declining corporate profits.
2. In the common-for-common exchanges, the median buyer would sustain a 19% *dilution* in both current earnings and book value per share on the additional shares to be issued. For example, assuming a share-for-share exchange, if the median buyer earned $1.00 per share during the latest 12 months, the median seller only earned $0.81 per share. *This 19% reduction in earnings on the additional shares to be issued is the most significant figure in the survey.* It demonstrates the keenly competitive nature of the merger and the acquisition market in the spring of 1969.

While historical data are not available, this 19% median dilution in current earnings per share is believed to have been the greatest in history. It has for years been axiomatic that buyers should avoid dilutionary acquisitions. Historically, a *minimum* objective has been a 20% *gain* in current earnings per share on the additional shares issued. However, only 40% of the surveyed buyers that were effecting mergers through exchanges of common-for-common would gain *any* current earnings on the additional shares to be issued.

HOW TO USE DILUTION

The considerations that justify dilutionary acquisitions in a seller's market include the following. The first is, of course, the competition for acquisitions—the fact that buyers *greatly* outnumbered sellers. The next is the synergistic aspect of some of these transactions. For example:

Continental Telephone has acquired over 500 independent telephone companies during the past six years. On occasion, Continental has paid as much as 40 times earnings in Continental common stock for an acquisition, despite the fact that Continental's stock generally sells at around 20 times earnings.

But Continental has promptly converted these small, independent telephone companies from manual to automatic equipment and from multi-to single-party lines. The improved service has resulted in rate increases and a greater volume of calls. Through centralized maintenance, purchasing, billing, and financing, Continental has also reduced the acquisitions' operating costs.

As a consequence, the prices Continental has paid often work out to less than 10 times earnings a year or two later.

Another reason for making dilutionary acquisitions is that

Table B. Tax-free mergers—convertible preferred-for-common exchanges

Acquirer	Acquired	Gain in market value to shareholders of acquired company*	Percentage increase (+) or decrease (—) in: Yield to shareholders of acquired company	Percentage increase (+) or decrease (—) in: Acquirer's EPS on shares offered†
Arcata National	Kingsport Press	+24%	0%	+ 65%
Bergen Drug	Brunswig Drug	+63	+ 15	+ 77
Broadway-Hale	Neiman Marcus	+34	+163	+ 10
Brooklyn Gas	New Jersey National Gas	+24	+ 70	— 15
Checker Motor	Parmelee Transport	+13	+ 80	‡
Coca-Cola Bottling of Los Angeles	Arrowhead Puritas	+14	+ 79	— 3
Cook Coffee	Gray Drug	+22	+ 53	— 9
Essex International	Transport Motor	+22	+ 58	+ 47
First National City	Chubb	+37	+ 67	— 4
GAC Corp.	Equitable Savings & Loan	+54	+200	+ 4
Hanna Mining	St. Joseph Lead	+ 7	+ 10	+ 21
ITT	Canteen Corp.	+19	+ 25	+ 4
ITT	Grinnell Corp.	+49	+153	+218
ITT	Hartford Fire Insurance	+31	+100	+ 2
Jim Walter	U.S. Pipe & Foundry	+18	+ 33	+ 50
Kidde (Walter)	Crum & Forster	+15	+ 40	— 39
Liberty-SCN Corp.	S. C. National Bank	+20	+ 33	+ 70
Mesa Petroleum	Hugoton Production	+19	+ 10	— 30
North American Rockwell	Miehle-Goss-Dexter	+81	+125	— 24
Pacific Clay	Armstrong Paint	+49	+ 16	+136
Panoil	Dorchester Gas	+ 5	—100	— 51
Pennsalt	Wallace & Tiernan	+20	+ 12	+ 5
Sheller-Globe	Superior Coach	+ 3	+ 65	+ 1
Slick Corp.	Filtrol	+57	+ 25	+114
Talley Industries	General Time	+ 6	+ 25	+ 88
Union Pacific	Chicago Rock Island	+91	‡	§
United Utilities	Carolina Telephone & Telegraph	+13	+ 64	— 33

Westinghouse	MCA	+13	+238	— 5
Woolworth (F. W.)	Richman Bros.	+13	+ 76	— 34
Zale Corp.	Butler's Shoe	+ 3	0	+ 66
Median		+20%	+ 56%	+ 4%

*Based on the market prices of both companies' securities two weeks before announcement of the transaction.

†Assumes immediate conversion of the preferreds, and based on both companies' latest 12 months' reported earnings.

‡Percentage change undefined because of an increase or decrease from zero or a deficit.

§Excluded because merger announced more than one year prior to consumation.

Table C. Taxable mergers—purchases for debt, cash, or warrants

Acquirer	Acquired	Gain in market value to shareholders of acquired company*	Gain in yield to shareholders of acquired company	Reduction in acquirer's return on invested capital
Amfac	Joseph Magnin	+22%	+ 38%	—56%
Athlone Industries	Jessop Steel	+66	+233	—36
Chelsea Industries	Collins & Aikman	+25	+ 93	—81
Daylin	Diana Stores	+22	+425	—74
DWG Corp.	Southeastern Public Service	+ 3	+ 28	†
Eastern Gas & Fuel	Southeastern Public Service	‡	+ 30	—48
Interstate Bakeries	H. D. Lee	+23	+209	—29
Mapco	Tropical Gas	+ 5	— 51	0
Nortek	Rock of Ages	+87	—100	—28
Northwest Industries	B. F. Goodrich	+47	+130	—88
Pepsico	Hardee's Food	+39	—100	—91
Reynolds Tobacco	McLean Industries	+ 9	†	—94
Riker	Standard Kollsman Industries	+21	+567	—53
Standard Prudential	Sterling National Bank	+20	—100	—22
U.S. Smelting	Clevite	+14	+207	—80
Median		+22%	+ 93%	—53%

*Based on the market prices or estimated values of both companies' securities two weeks before announcement of the transaction.

†Percentage change undefined because of an increase or decrease from zero or a deficit.

‡Excluded because Eastern Gas & Fuel "topped" DWG's bid.

the seller's growth prospects may be much more favorable than the buyer's. Such an acquisition can improve the buyer's growth potentialities, image, and price/earnings ratio, and therefore its market price.

Closely-held companies are sometimes motivated to merge because of the potential tax on accumulated earnings. Such companies often have substantial excess cash or other low-return assets that can be liquidated or hypothecated. Thus, even though the transaction is dilutionary on an earnings-per-share basis, the buyer's effective cost may be very low.

If the buyer's debt/equity ratio is larger than the seller's, an exchange of equity securities will improve the buyer's equity base, and thereby permit additional borrowings on better terms than would otherwise be available.

A relatively recent phenomenon has been the number of companies that effect acquisitions, even though dilutionary, in order to place large blocks of their stocks in "friendly hands" and thereby forestall take-over bids. Such transactions, however, can prove to be Trojan horses. Disenchanted block holders have been known to solicit bids from so-called corporate raiders.

Finally, while there are some notable exceptions, most buyers are substantially larger than the companies which they are acquiring. As a consequence, the across-the-board dilution of the buyer's earnings per share is negligible in the vast majority of these transactions.

ON A TAXABLE BASIS

Of the 65 transactions, 23% were being effected on a taxable basis through the use of debt, cash, or warrants. While taxable, installment purchases for cash or notes with down payments of less than 30% permit the seller to spread his capital gains tax over the payment period. The seller's incentives in taxable transactions are again clear; the buyer's are not as self-evident.

EFFECT TO SELLER

The stockholders of the median seller in taxable transactions were being offered a 22% premium over the market price of their stock two weeks before the announcement of the transaction. This is a 5% to 10% greater dollar premium than the median seller was being offered in tax-free transactions. Thus the buyer was "paying" a portion (if not all) of the seller's capital gains tax. It should be noted in this regard that in tax-free transactions the tax is merely being deferred, not avoided.

In taxable transactions, of which 80% were being effected with debt securities, the median seller was not only being offered a 22% premium, but also a 93% increase in yield. For example, if the stockholders of the median seller were receiving $1.00 in dividends per share, they were being offered $1.93 in interest on the debt securities to be received per share.

Buyers can offer such generous yields because interest is tax-deductible, whereas dividends are not. The effective after-federal-and-state-income-tax cost to the buyer of $1.93 in tax-deductible interest is approximately 17% less than $1.00 in nondeductible dividends.

BUYER'S RETURNS

On the basis of the prices to be paid and the two companies' latest 12 months' reported earnings, the median buyer would receive a 53% *lower* current return from the acquisition than the buyer was presently earning on its own invested capital (i.e. its total debt and equity capital). As in the case of dilutionary common-for-common mergers, this figure reflected the keenly competitive nature of the seller's market.

Return on the invested capital has been widely used as a gauge of management's performance. Generally, the higher the return, the better the management. However, return on invested capital is less meaningful in appraising managements of aggressive buyers because the net worth of most companies is significantly less than their market values—which are of course the minimum prices generally paid for acquisitions. Therefore, the return on market value is almost certain to be less than the return on invested capital.

Buyers are willing to reduce the return on their invested capital if they can increase their earnings per share—and therefore increase the market value of their shares. This is of course much more tangible evidence of management's performance than is return on invested capital.

The earnings of the sellers would cover the interest on the debt incurred by the buyers an average of 2.2 times. Thus the buyers were "purchasing" an average of 120% more earnings than required to pay the interest on the debt incurred.

However, in some instances the after-tax cash-flow coverage of the buyers' prospective debt retirement requirements ranged from extremely thin to non-existent. Such buyers must therefore promptly liquidate certain assets in order to reduce their debt, materially improve their cash flow, or refund into longer maturities a portion of their debt.

In looking at the foregoing terms in both taxable and nontaxable transactions, it is evident the spring of 1969 was a keenly competitive seller's market—perhaps the most competitive in history. When the *vast majority* of companies are seeking acquisitions, this is of course the time to be a seller. This suggestion particularly applies to closely held companies.

APPROACHING A PROSPECTIVE BUYER

In this section, I shall examine some of the tactics and approaches that we employ in behalf of our corporate clients in order to obtain the most advantageous transactions.

In order to make an effective presentation to prospective buyers, we begin by reconstructing the seller's five-year operating record, and explain in footnotes any abnormal or nonrecurring expenses and profits.

This includes pointing out the effect on each year's earnings of (a) any major plant moves, fires, strikes, and so forth, and (b) expenses which would not have been incurred by the buyer, such as preferential transactions and leases of family-related interests, in-laws on the payroll, and company-owned hunting lodges, yachts, limousines, airplanes, and so on.

It also includes reviewing the "generally accepted accounting principles" the corporate seller has followed in order to determine what the earnings and net worth would have been if, for example, the company had used straight-line instead of accelerated depreciation, FIFO instead of LIFO inventory accounting, and if it had consolidated any profitable subsidiaries instead of carrying them as investments, and appropriately capitalized various other items instead of expensing them.

The balance sheet should also be reconstructed to reflect the "fair market value" (as distinct from "book value") of the assets and liabilities. Of particular interest are undervalued assets (such as real estate), inventory, "cushions," and excessive contingency, bad debt, and other reserves.

In general, closely held companies are doing everything they can to minimize their taxes. Consequently, they tend to understate their earnings, in contrast to publicly owned companies that attempt to show their earnings in order to increase the market value of their shares.

It should be noted in this regard that the financial statements of two identical companies would be dissimilar if they followed different "generally accepted accounting principles." For instance, one might report profits and significant net worth, and the other, losses and a deficit net worth, even though they were in fact identical companies.

The purpose of setting forth the seller's financial statements on both an "as reported" and an "adjusted" basis is not to deceive, but to illuminate. Such presentations have facilitated transactions that would not otherwise have been of interest to buyers, for they would have been unaware of the seller's methods of reporting earnings and assets unless those methods happened to correspond with their own.

MEASURING TRUE MARKET VALUE

The next step is to prepare detailed financial comparisons of the corporate seller with the most comparable publicly owned companies. This study includes a "comparative pricing schedule," which measures the market value of the seller's securities against those of the most comparable publicly owned companies.

When the seller's stock is closely held, this study is used to test the alternative of "going public" against what might be realized through a merger. In many instances, the investing public will pay a higher price than corporate buyers. Generally, not over 40% of a company's shares are sold on an initial public offering, but the balance might be liquidated within two or three years.

When the seller's stock is already publicly owned, the comparative pricing schedule is used to determine whether its securities are being overvalued or undervalued by the market, relative to comparable investment opportunities. Such relative valuation will determine the premium over the market price that can be realistically sought from a potential buyer.

A similar study is also prepared of all of the most comparable transactions that have been consummated within the past two years. This study includes the parties and terms of each such transaction. The purpose is to determine the prices paid and which buyers have been the most aggressive—that is, those that have paid the highest prices for comparable companies.

COMPLETING THE REVIEW

The selling company's major competitors, customers, and suppliers are also carefully reviewed, for it is generally within these groups that the greatest operating advantages can be realized through a merger. It is also within these groups that potential antitrust problems are encountered. However, small to medium-sized companies sometimes overemphasize the possibility of such problems. Ideal merger prospects should not be lightly dismissed simply because of the possibility of such problems—which are often surmountable.

All other things being equal, the buyer that will enjoy the greatest operating advantages as a result of the consolidation can justify paying the highest price.

A WORD OF CAUTION

As a result of the foregoing studies and reviews, we have a good idea of (a) the maximum price that can be realistically sought, and (b) the most promising prospective buyers. The next step is to initiate conversations with such buyers.

If it becomes generally known that a company is "for sale," it can demoralize employees, be used against the company by its competitors and others, and dampen the interest of prospective buyers. Therefore, we do not disclose the seller's specific identity until a serious indication of interest has been obtained. The prospective buyer is initially provided information sufficient for a "ball park" price reaction, but not sufficient to specifically identify the company.

SELLER'S PROBLEMS

Because of SEC, tax, and market considerations, stockholders of the seller are seldom in a position to immediately liquidate all the buyer's securities they are to receive. Their perspective should therefore not merely be that they are selling their company, but, rather, that they are using their equity to "purchase" the buyer's securities. Thus, in other than cash transactions, it is essential that the seller appraise the buyer.

It is obviously not adequate merely to multiply the number of shares offered by their market price. The future value of the securities will depend on the buyer's future prospects. Therefore, it is necessary to appraise the *quality* of the buyer's management, operations, financial, and other resources, as well as the preferences, quality, and marketability of the securities offered.

There are often SEC or other limitations on the ability of the seller's stockholders to sell to the investing public the securities they receive. Unsophisticated sellers have been shocked when they discovered that their "letter stock" or restricted shares typically sell at a 20% or larger discount from the free market price of such securities. It is therefore essential that the sellers insist that the buyer grant them the right to register, under certain circumstances, any restricted securities they are to receive.

In the absence of an exemption, one must register with the SEC the shares he intends to sell, and he must make available to the purchasers a prospectus which is intended to make full disclosure of all the material negative facts concerning the corporation whose shares are being sold.

There are essentially three situations in which one may sell to the public-at-large shares that would otherwise be restricted:

1. *The "1% rule."* One may be able to sell on the open market within six months shares equal to the less of (a) 1% of the total outstanding issue of such securities, or (b) if the stock is listed on a national exchange, the largest volume of such shares that traded within one week during the four weeks preceding commencement of such sales.
2. *"Piggyback" registrations.* If one wishes to include his shares in registration statements subsequently filed by the buyer, he should obtain an explicit agreement to this effect as a term of the merger.
3. *Demand registrations.* The buyer may also be willing to give the seller's former shareholders the right to register "on demand" the shares they receive from the buyer.

The legal, accounting, and printing costs of preparing the foregoing registration statements and prospectuses typically range from $25,000 to over $100,000. An agreement can generally be obtained to the effect that the buyer will bear all but the brokerage costs and the transfer fees of all "piggyback" and one "on demand" registration.

An additional important consideration is whether the registrations are for "shelf" or "spot" offerings. A shelf registration is one in which the selling stockholders are permitted to feed their shares into the market over a period of time. A spot offering is one in which all the shares are sold at one time at a single price through an investment banking firm.

The advantage of a shelf offering is that one may sell from time to time and at the prevailing market prices. Also, the brokerage commissions on shelf offerings of listed stocks typically amount to only 1% to 2%, as compared with 3.5% to 7% for spot offerings.

The disadvantage of shelf offerings is that brokers throughout the country are put on notice that a block of stock is overhanging the market. They are therefore reluctant to recommend purchases until the shelf offering has been completed. In addition, the multiple sellers under a shelf offering are competing with one another. Their respective sales reduce the prices that others can obtain.

Buyers usually wish to limit registration rights because of the time and expenses involved, the liabilities incurred if full disclosure has not been made, the limitations imposed on a company while it is in registration, and the fact that sales tend to depress the market price of the buyer's stock. If registration rights are granted, it is in the buyer's interest to limit them to spot instead of shelf offerings, and to piggy-back rather than on-demand registrations.

BUYERS' ADVANTAGES

Before incurring the expense and diversion of management's time, prospective buyers should realistically analyze their ability to compete for acquistions. An ideal prospective buyer is a company with a strong balance sheet (i.e., a strong working capital position, excess cash, and nominal debt and preferred securities outstanding), and a New York Stock Exchange listed stock that is trading at a high price/earnings ratio (over 20 times) which is justified by above-average past and prospective growth.

The ideal buyer enjoys unique operating advantages, such as strong production, purchasing, marketing, and/or research and development capabilities. For example, a buyer with a strong marketing organization might dramatically increase the sales and earnings of a smaller company that produces a complementary product. Such a buyer can justify paying a higher price than companies that do not enjoy similar operating advantages.

A sound acquisition program should maximize the buyer's strengths or minimize its weaknesses. Buyers attempting to maximize their strengths are generally in a better position to compete for attractive acquisitions than companies that are attempting to minimize their weaknesses.

Acquisitions made for the purpose of diversification are generally defensive in nature. The buyer is typically attempting to minimize its dependency on a slow-growth, declining, or highly cyclical industry. Conversely, horizontal and vertical integrations (through the acquisition of competitors, customers, or suppliers) are generally intended to maximize the buyer's strengths.

Once the buyer's operational and financial strengths and weaknesses have been analyzed, and its acquisition objectives and criteria—namely, the size, nature, and price range of optimum acquisitions—have been clearly defined, it is necessary to conduct an exhaustive search for suitable acquisitions.

When a worthwhile prospect has been uncovered, an early determination should be made as to where effective control resides and whether the holders thereof will be receptive to an offer. From this point of view, the ideal acquisition prospect is a closely held company in which the controlling stockholder has reached retirement age and does not have younger members of his family coming along in the business.

It is exceedingly difficult to acquire widely held companies in which the managements hold only a modest equity interest. Professional executives typically want greater autonomy and less accountability. The prospect of stockholders receiving a high price for their stock is no great inducement to a managment that holds a nominal interest in the company. However, it is among such companies that bargains are often found—i.e., companies whose securities are selling at low prices relative to their earnings, cash flows, and/or underlying assets.

If effective control resides with the investing public-at-large, one should appraise at the outset the probability, time, and cost of acquiring the company (a) through a merger with management's cooperation, or (b) through open market accumulation, the purchase of large blocks from institutional investors and/or a public tender or exchange offer to the company's shareholders. This requires an analysis of:

——The holdings of the officers, directors, and over-10% stockholders listed in the company's proxy statements.

——The published holdings of institutional investors.

——The volume of trading in the stock.

——The terms and conditions of all the outstanding classes of securities (particularly the voting stock and issues convertible into it, and warrants and options to purchase it).

——The voting rights—whether cumulative or noncumulative.

——The method of electing the directors—whether annually or on a staggered basis for a term of years.

The average premium over market price typically paid by buyers, in mergers approved by both companies' managements, is approximately 20%. An additional 3% to 4% should be added to cover brokerage commissions, legal, accounting, printing, advertising, and other costs. This does not take into account the significant diversion of management's time from its normal operating responsibilities.

In the case of tender and exchange offers opposed by management, it is typically necessary to offer *at least* a 25% premium and to set aside an additional 5% to 10% for expenses. If litigation results, as it often does, it escalates the cost and protracts the time.

The odds of effecting a contested acquisition at a reasonable premium are not favorable. Management has the corporate treasury with which to defend itself. Unsuccessful offerers have occasionally realized substantial profits on the shares accumulated at lower levels prior to a tender offer, but few have felt adequately compensated for the time, expenses, and bruises they have incurred in their losing battle for control.

ADDED FACTORS

In appraising the probability, time, and cost to effect an acquisition, there are certain important considerations that may reduce the effective cost or justify "paying the price."

If the prospect has substantial depletion or depreciation charges, the price may be a low multiple of cash flow, even though it is a high multiple of earnings. There are a number of companies with large cash flows that have been acquired largely with loans against the acquisition itself.

The balance sheet may disclose undervalued or low-earning assets that might be liquidated or hypothecated. The age of a company is sometimes significant. It may have on its balance sheet real estate acquired in, say 1890—at 1890 costs.

The prospect's accounting principles should be reviewed to determine whether its assets are undervalued and its earnings understated, relative to companies which utilize less conservative accounting principles.

Through a spin-off or outright sale of all or a portion of the equity of a growing subsidiary, buyers have recovered a substantial portion of the cost to acquire the parent company.

Companies with low debt/equity ratios are often attractive, for it is sometimes possible to finance a substantial portion of the purchase price against the acquisition itself.

Companies with fully funded pension plans are obviously more attractive than those with substantial past service liabilities. If the prospect's pension program is overfunded (as a result of successful investments or a reduction in the prospect's labor force), it may be possible to include the buyer's employees in the fund and thus to reduce the buyer's own pension fund expenses.

FIRST CHECKPOINT

If the decision is to enter into direct negotiations with those in effective control, it is desirable to attempt to obtain an early agreement in principle on the key terms of the contemplated transaction. If an agreement cannot be reached on such terms as the price, the type of securities to be used, the tax consequences of the transaction, the continuity of management, and the name of the surviving company, neither party is warranted in engaging in the exhaustive analyses required prior to consummation of the transaction.

In order to obtain such an agreement, it is necessary for both parties to provide at the outset realistic projections and candid disclosures of any material negatives or other potential obstacles to the transaction. Because of the substantial sum involved, each party is going to thoroughly appraise the other before the transaction is consummated. Therefore, it is in the interest of both parties to candidly discuss potential problems at the outset, rather than to wait until they are discovered after extended negotiations and appraisals.

SECOND CHECKPOINT

Depending on the complexity of the transaction and the parties' experience in consummating such transactions, preparation of the definitive contracts will typically take from 30 to 90 days, which is generally more than adequate time for the parties to carefully appraise each other.

If the buyer is significantly larger than the seller, the buyer will conduct a more exhaustive appraisal than the seller. Under such circumstances, the seller's appraisal of the buyer is usually limited to publicly available data.

While the seller can take comfort in the premium its shareholders are being offered over the current market price of their shares, it must also be satisfied that the shares being offered, compared with the shares now held, afford at least as favorable appreciation potentiality and/or greater "downside" protection.

THIRD CHECKPOINT

Certain aspects of the seller should be carefully appraised by the buyer (and vice versa, depending on the relative size of the two companies and whether the transaction is for cash or securities).

There are many things companies can do to increase their earnings in anticipation of a merger or acquisition, with a view to obtaining a maximum price. These include the reduction or temporary deferment of various expenses, such as maintenance, advertising, insurance, research, and development. Sales and net income can also be increased by accelerating shipments to customers, with the understanding that payment will be due in accordance with usual delivery schedules.

If a company has been enjoying unusually wide profit

margins and a high rate of return on its invested capital, it may be due to a strong proprietary position in its field, technological leadership, outstanding management, or unusually favorable long-term leases, raw material, or other contracts—which may expire in the near future. Further, abnormally wide margins and high returns are invitations to prospective competitors.

A comparative analysis should be prepared of the company's key ratios with those of the most comparable companies. All anomalous comparisons (particularly those which are unusually favorable) require further inquiry and analysis. The key ratios include the gross and pretax profit margins, return on invested capital, pretax cash flow coverages of fixed charges (chiefly debt services and rent), current ratios, working capital, inventory and receivable turnovers, debt/equity ratios, tax rates, compound annual sales and earnings growth rates, price/earnings and price/book value ratios, and yields on all outstanding short- and long-term debt and equity securities.

A breakdown of the company's sales and gross profits by major product and customer categories will provide (a) an indication of its product mix, and (b) the sources of its profits by major product and customer categories. A similar breakdown of the backlog figures facilitates appraisal of the business in immediate prospect.

A schedule of the company's major customers, suppliers, and competitors, with indications of the volume of business done by and with each, and the company's relationship with each, is used to make trade checks and to appraise the company's competitive position and its dependency on any single customer or supplier or group of customers or suppliers. Depending on the nature of the business, it is generally desirable for no single customer to account for more than 5% of sales and earnings.

The reasons for recent and planned changes in marketing, production, distribution, personnel, and other operations and policies provide clues to areas of strength and weakness. A comparison of research and development expenditures with current sales and earnings accounted for by products introduced within the past five years provides an indication of the success, relative to cost, of the R&D program.

FOURTH CHECKPOINT

The major physical facilities should be examined from the point of view of location (relative to sources of supply, markets, and labor costs), and whether the plants are modern and well laid out, utilize the latest production equipment and techniques, and are well maintained.

A company's strike history, its wage scales, and whether it is unionized are other material considerations. Nonunionized companies often point out that their hourly wages are at or above the union scale; however, analysis often discloses that they are not paying full fringe benefits such as employee pensions, health and accident insurance, vacations, and so forth. Thus their actual labor costs are appreciably lower than their unionized competitors'. Usually wide wage scale differentials cannot be expected to persist indefinitely. If a company is unionized, the terms and termination date of its contract are important considerations.

FIFTH CHECKPOINT

Disclosure should be requested of all material contingent liabilities that are not carried on the company's balance sheet or covered by insurance in the ordinary course of its business. Such liabilties include legal actions and state and federal agency proceedings that are threatening, pending, or in process; guarantees and warranties; contract termination penalties and renegotiation provisions; and potential tax claims. The year through which a company has been audited by the Internal Revenue Service and its record of past tax deficiencies are material considerations.

By selling and leasing back its plant, a company can remove mortgages from its balance sheet and improve its debt/equity ratio and working capital position. These are desirable objectives; however, the satisfaction of such lease obligations is of course just as fundamental to a company's survival as its debt obligations. Leases should therefore be capitalized when appraising the leverage in a company's capitalization and the return on its "adjusted invested capital."

A description should be requested of all inter-corporate transactions and situations where officers, directors, major stockholders, corporate affiliates, or others have guaranteed or endorsed any of the company's obligations or vice versa. This includes so-called "solvency agreements" and "stockholder undertakings," which are often not disclosed in a company's financial statements. If a company's credit or profit reflects such arrangements, this must be taken into account, for they typically do not survive the closing.

LOOKING AHEAD

Projections should be requested of the company's operating statements and balance sheets for the current and at least the next fiscal year, along with explanations of any nonrecurring or unusual items, and the facts and assumptions on which the projections are based. The accuracy of past projections provided to banks, security analysts, and others should also be reviewed.

Potential problem areas should be candidly discussed, including possible actions by customers, competitors, suppliers, labor unions, key personnel, company lenders, and others. Copies should be requested of all studies, reports, and analyses of the company and material aspects of its operations which have been prepared within the past two years.

Biographical sketches should be requested for each officer, director, and key executive. Such data would normally include his age, title, compensation, equity and stock option interests in the company, past positions and associations, outside business and other interests, educational background, and any family connections or other close relationships with other officers, directors, large stockholders, customers, suppliers, or landlords.

Difficult acquisitions to appraise are those in which substantially all of the owner-manager's capital has been invested in the company and where the company's present management will continue. Following the merger, they will receive several million dollars in cash or marketable securities—and they may discover latent penchants for yachts and the Riviera.

Such situations have to be appraised in the light of the possibility that the former owner-managers may not continue to direct the company with the same determination and enthusiasm as they have previously evidenced. The depth and ability of middle management, which is always an important consideration, takes on added significance in such situations.

SEEKING OUT NEGATIVES

The next step is to make trade checks with the company's major customers, suppliers, and competitors, its banks and institutional lenders, and executives who have left the company. Competitors and former employees are often the best sources of "material negatives."

Few, if any, companies are without problems of some

sort. Sometimes there are incipient problems that management may not be aware of, such as the impending departure of one or more key executives, a material shift in the buying policies of a major customer, a prospective price increase or a serious shortage of an essential raw material, or the imminent introduction of major new lines or other moves by important competitors.

QUESTIONS TO ASK

After completing the foregoing studies and trade checks, one has a better idea of the things to look for and the questions to ask when inspecting a company's facilities and interviewing its management. For example, high labor costs are generally self-evident from the plant layout and the lack of adequate materials handling and automatic production equipment. Low maintenance expenditures may be supported by makeshift repairs and jury rigs on the equipment. A low inventory turnover suggests the possibility of obsolete and damaged items being carried in current inventories.

WHAT ABOUT MANAGEMENT?

So much for the appraisal of the quality of a company's assets and earnings. Now we come to the most difficult area of corporate appraisals—that of evaluating management's ability to direct the company's future growth. Clues are provided by a company's relative performance within its industry, the speed of its adaptation to changing conditions, its sales and earnings record, margins, and return on invested capital.

However, companies have momentum. Recent success may be the product of policies and actions initiated by individuals who are no longer with the company. Also, managements grow old, and sometimes ultraconservative. Their early dynamic leadership, enthusiasm, and long hours sometimes give way to indecision, committee action, golf, and early cocktails. Therefore, a primary area of inquiry is the age, ability, and depth of a company's management.

Some say, "I can size a man up pretty fast—just give me ten minutes alone with him." Personal interviews are useful in appraising a company's management, but they are far from foolproof. There is impressive support for the conclusion that appraisals of individuals based solely on personal interviews result in little better than random selections.

Three common characteristics of able executives are an unusually high degree of motivation, energy, and intelligence. A 10% differential in any of these qualities can make an infinite difference in performance. Unfortunately, all three are difficult, if not impossible, to gauge with precision in the course of an interview.

For example, a high degree of motivation is fundamental, but it is often the result of complex psychological factors which would take a psychiatrist a year to discover and quantify. Nervousness is commonly confused with energy, and a glib wit with intelligence. Not to mention the difficulty of assessing character, integrity, imagination, foresight, persistency, loyalty, and the host of other qualities one looks for in able executives. Only appearance and personality are self-evident.

While far from infallible, various highly regarded psychological testing organizations have evolved appraisal techniques which produce results superior to those attainable by executives who lack the professional qualifications and facilities to objectively evaluate such qualities. In the least, such appraisals provide indications of areas requiring further inquiry.

In general, considerable reliance has to be placed on the

best available objective data on the executives of a company. Such information would cover their past associations and accomplishments, rates of advancement, training and academic backgrounds, and the opinions of responsible individuals who have had an opportunity to observe their performance over an extended period of time.

A final and most difficult area of appraisal is the "chemistry" between the two companies' managements. Some friction and attrition must be anticipated. The most merciful and prudent solution is sometimes to terminate excess personnel at the outset and to assist them in obtaining other positions.

If the corporate appraisal develops negative considerations or facts contrary to prior representations, it may be necessary to terminate negotiations. However, in the majority of cases such considerations can be "equated out" in the terms of the transaction. It is in part for this reason that only about half of such transactions are ultimately consummated on the terms originally announced.

There are two categories of specialists who, by the nature of their profession, play an essential role in acquisitions and mergers. Speaking for the first category, the author, a practising attorney, describes four roles which a lawyer can play in helping to expedite negotiations, and possibly make their result more favorable.

15

INTELLIGENT USE OF LAWYERS IN ACQUISITIONS

by Warren G. Haskin, Partner,
Bell, Boyd, Lloyd, Haddad and Burns.

The next chapter will make—and defend—the point that accountants are virtually unavoidable in acquisition negotiation. At the risk of sounding baleful, I must add that this holds true for lawyers as well.

The question is not—or should not be—"Do we need that fellow?," but "How can we make the best use of him?"

Being a lawyer, I would answer, "By putting him to work at as early a stage as possible."

There are horror stories about buyers making deals that have turned out to be impossible because of an overlooked covenant, binding on the seller and prohibiting merger or acquisition; about deals that hinged on the issuance of unregistered stock that should have been registered; about deals that contemplated approval by the Board of Directors alone, when in fact shareholder approval was also required; about deals that fell apart because of the necessity of complying with requirements of the Securities and Exchange Commission or of stock exchanges.

Granted, these cases are not frequent. But to the parties involved, one is more than enough for a lifetime.

Bringing a lawyer in early enough should insure against all these and similar complications. But his function need not be exclusively negative. Used properly, there are a number of things he can do to expedite negotiations, and quite possibly to make their result more favorable.

Since it would require an extensive law library to cover the subject, I will try to sketch out only the principal functions which a lawyer can perform for a client engaged on either side of acquisition negotiations. In my mind, there are four such functions, and I will take what I consider to be the least important one first.

THE LAWYER AS NEGOTIATOR

This is the function of the lawyer as a negotiator. In general, this is done more successfully by another member of the team—certainly those aspects of negotiation that deal with price or with policy.

There are occasions, however, when a lawyer can help you by being a negotiator. One of these might occur if you are the chief executive officer of a company and you want to acquire another company (presumably this situation would be for cash), but don't want the other company to know your identity. You might go to an investment banker, you might go to a business broker or you might go to your lawyer, just because you want the negotiating done without disclosure of the company who wants to acquire.

Or, you may be the head of a company and want someone to talk to an acquisition candidate, but without his having the authority to make a binding commitment. You are not sure just what terms you will accept, but the company that you are talking to knows that you are the chief executive officer, and that you have the authority to agree to any terms. In this case, you may prefer to use someone who doesn't have that authority. This is a familiar function of the lawyer in litigation. Cases are settled by the lawyers, and frequently one of them will say, "Well, I can't do that without checking back with my principal." It gives the parties a chance to catch their breath and decide whether they want to accept the offer or not. The lawyer can say in this instance that he doesn't have the authority to agree upon the terms of the deal. The chief executive officer of a company is not in that position.

Occasionally you may find that the company will make a deal which it later decides it wants to alter. But terms have already been settled, and there is no obvious good reason for going back and saying "Let's change this and let's change that." Sometimes, a lawyer can come up with good reasons for doing just that, and can thereby actually improve the deal.

THE LAWYER AS INVESTIGATOR

The second function of a lawyer is the investigative function—the lawyer as investigator. Naturally there will be a thorough investigation by you and your people, if you're the acquiring company, of the business of the candidate you want to acquire. Your accountants will make an investigation of the accounting records and financial statements.

A lawyer's investigation is somewhat more limited. He is there to review and evaluate the legal implications of the merger. The kind of investigation he makes will depend upon the form of the acquisition. If you are acquiring assets, the lawyer will check to see what liabilities you may be assuming that you had not intended to assume, and he will make sure that you know about them. He will check to see whether there are facts that may make you liable for the debts of the acquired company, even though you did not intend to be liable. If the acquisition is stock-for-stock and will require your acquiring stock of the other company, the lawyer will concern himself with whether or not the stock that you are acquiring is fully paid and non-assessable, and whether the stockholders from whom you are acquiring it have good title to it.

In either case, there will be an investigation of the law on the merger. The lawyer will have to check the law and make sure that the merger is possible under the laws of the two states in which the two companies are incorporated. No matter what type of transaction is involved, the lawyer will be making an investigation of the material contracts of the company that is being acquired to make sure that his client understands just what contractual and legal obligations he will be assuming as a result of the acquisition. He will check these contracts to see whether they are assignable, because if you have a contract which is an important part of the deal, you want to be certain that it can, in fact, be assigned to you as the acquiring company. If it is a stock deal, he will also have to investigate the blue-sky laws, the state securities laws in the various jurisdictions that are involved, and the status of the stock under the Securities Act of 1933.

THE LAWYER AS ADVISER

The third function of the lawyer is his function as an adviser. This is his most important role, and his advice to you will have an effect on many of the aspects of the acquisition, including its timing, the kind of notice which is required to shareholders, and what you can expect from the SEC, if the deal has to go through that agency. His advice may affect the form of the acquisition. If your lawyer is also the person you go to for tax advice, his judgement will affect how the merger agreement is structured. His advice will affect the mechanics of the acquisition—what form the contract will take, how many contracts there will be. His advice will also affect the timing and nature of the publicity that you give to the acquisition.

THE LAWYER AS TECHNICIAN

Finally, the fourth function of the lawyer—probably his most familiar one—is his function as a draftsman and technician. He is the one who writes or reviews the contract that is ultimately signed; the registration statement if you are registering stock which is publicly traded; a proxy statement if you are involved in a merger or acquisition which requires shareholder approval. He must write any supplementary contracts. The lawyer writes the listing application, if you are a listed company and are required to list additional shares which are going to be issued in the acquisition. He takes care of blue-sky applications which may be required. If he is also your tax adviser he can handle the request for a tax ruling if you need one. And he is the one who writes the charter provisions if you have in mind the creation of a new class of stock that may be called for by the terms of the merger agreement.

I have covered what I consider to be the four functional roles played by the lawyer—negotiator, investigator, adviser and draftsman. I want to add a few words about the substantive areas of law which the lawyer will deal with in representing a company—whether it is the one that is going to survive the merger or the one that is going to go out of existence or become a subsidiary of the acquiring company.

TAXES AND POSSIBLE ANTI-TRUST PROBLEMS

The first of these areas is concerned with taxes. This is one of the most important factors of all; it can make or break a deal. The company being acquired wants the exchange to be tax-free and accomplished in a tax-free reorganization. The acquiring company is concerned about whether there will be any unknown tax liabilities that it will assume in connection with the acquisition. There are almost always a lot of problems in the tax area.

The second area involves anti-trust law. The first consideration which comes to mind, usually, is section 7 of the Clayton Act. Would the merger itself violate the anti-trust laws? In most acquisitions, there are no problems. In some, there may be a problem, and in those cases the lawyer will have to evaluate the likelihood that the government will challenge the acquisition and, if the challenge is made, whether it will be pursued seriously. Most companies, at that point, will decide that it is wiser to retreat, because it can take years to get the matter straightened out.

The lawyer will also advise you if you get an inquiry from the Department of Justice or the Federal Trade Commission. Typically, these inquiries start with a request for information on the part of the government, and the lawyer will assist you in preparing responses to this request. In addition to section 7 and section 1 of the Sherman Act, which can also be used to attack acquisitions, there may be other aspects of the transaction that invite attention from the anti-trust people. One might be the possibility that the acquisition will be used for reciprocity. This is a fairly new concept in anti-trust law. If invoked and sustained, it can invalidate mergers that are really quite small in terms of market share. The theory behind it is that either the acquired company or the acquiring company may gain a competitive advantage because of relationships between the other party and suppliers or customers. For example, suppliers of the acquired company may be potential customers of the acquiring company.

Finally, the company that you are acquiring may have some liability for past violations which is not reflected in the balance sheet—something you do not intend to assume. Or, the acquired company may be subject to a consent decree, which the acquiring company may or may not become subject to if the acquisition is completed.

WHAT KIND OF SECURITIES

Another relevant area of the law pertains to securities problems. These problems used to arise only in cases where an acquisition was made for stock, but there has now been legislation and rule-making by the SEC which subjects cash tender offers to regulation. These tender offer rules are similar to proxy rules which apply when you solicit proxies from shareholders in connection with an acquisition, and the new law requires an offeror to file with the SEC and furnish to the offeree certain minimum information. This includes the identity and background of the offeror, the source of the amount of funds, any plans that the offeror may have to liquidate the business or merge the business or make any other major change which the offeree should know about. In addition, information must be provided on the value of securities of the company that is sought to be acquired which are already owned by the offeror.

COMPLYING WITH DISCLOSURE

The lawyer will also be concerned about publicity, especially in view of the Texas Gulf Sulphur case and the implications of rule 10b–5. This is a very delicate area. You can get into trouble by announcing too fast and you can get into trouble by not announcing soon enough.

The Texas Gulf case involved a question of fact as to whether a certain ore discovery was material, at what time did it become material, and when should it have been announced. It is easy to see the same concept in its application to an important merger, particularly in the case of the company that is being acquired. I am now assuming that the company is at that time publicly owned and that the exchange ratio puts a considerably higher value on the stock of that company than the public is placing on it in the open market. A lot of people are going to lose money if they sell their stock without knowing that a merger is in the air. At the same time, it would be misleading to announce the merger before a firm agreement has been reached. I'm not talking about the formal, "definitive" agreement, but just a firm agreement to merge. At that time an announcement should go out. Prior to that time you will probably need a lawyer's advice if you are an insider, and are trading in the securities of either company. It is true that an announcement would be premature, but at the same time you have information which the public doesn't have, and which could be considered material inside information. Insiders can be held accountable for any profit they may have realized in transactions in stock that were made on the basis of that information.

PROXY STATEMENTS AND REGISTRATION

If the acquisition involves a sufficient number of stockholders, you will have to rely on your lawyer to prepare the proxy statement, and to give you an idea of what kind of timing you should have in mind in view of possible problems with the SEC. How long will it take for an SEC review if the acquired company is publicly-owned and the transaction is a merger or a purchase of assets? In the case of the merger, both the acquiring company and the acquired company must go to shareholders, subject to certain exceptions.

If the acquisition is a purchase of assets, the acquiring company ordinarily does not have to solicit proxies but the acquired company does. But stock exchange requirements may require submission to the shareholders of the acquiring company, depending upon the size of the company that is being acquired. If you have a stock-for-stock exchange, there is no corporate action, and nothing to submit to shareholders, but you have no exemption from the Securities Act of 1933 for the issuance of stock. In this case, instead of a proxy statement, you must have a registration statement to register the shares that you have used to make the exchange.

If you are dealing with a company that is not publicly

owned there will presumably be an exemption if those shareholders who receive stock on distribution after the assets are acquired furnish an investment letter representing and warranting that they are taking the stock for investment and not for distribution. This may or may not be coupled with a commitment on the part of the issuing company to register the shares at the request of the recipients.

If you have a publicly-owned company with a lot of shareholders, you can usually rely on Rule 133, providing the transaction takes the form of a merger or an acquisition of assets. This is the so-called "no sale" rule, and it says that there is no sale involved for purposes of the registration requirements of the Securities Act of 1933. Everybody knows there is, of course. The shareholders of one company are giving up their stock and getting stock in the other company, but the SEC says it is not a sale for the purposes of the registration requirements. The rule then goes on to restrict affiliated persons of the acquired company, major shareholders, officers and directors, and sets forth limits on the amount of stock that they may later sell without registration. The acquiring company may be asked to make a commitment to register the shares at a later date and at a request of a specified percentage of the recipients. This may be true in the case of a private placement, and it may also be true in the case of a Rule 133 transaction, if the affiliated persons do not want or are unwilling to comply with or limit themselves to the 1% rule that is part of Rule 133.

A lawyer will also become involved in stock exchange rules and regulations. If you are a listed company, your agreement stipulates that you will not issue shares unless they are first listed. When you plan to acquire a company, therefore, you will require a listing application before you can complete the transaction.

There are also aspects of substantive corporation law that

must be considered. Does the contemplated transaction need to be submitted to shareholders? What is the vote required? What kind of notice is necessary? If the kind of security you have in mind is something other than common stock—convertible debentures, preferred stock, debt securities, with warrants attached—can it be issued by a company incorporated under the laws of a particular state?

PREPARING THE CONTRACTS

Then there is the question of the acquisition contract itself. Whether you are being acquired or doing the acquiring, you are always better off if it is your lawyer who writes the first draft of the contract. He will draft it in a way that is satisfactory to you. A lot of changes may be negotiated, but a lot of things may stay the same. Typically, the lawyer for the company doing the acquiring—the surviving company in the case of a merger—will do the first draft of the contract. But this is not always so, and if you have the opportunity to have your lawyer do the first draft, I would advise you to do it that way.

The actual contract will vary according to the form of the transaction. In a merger, the first agreement is usually quite short, and there will be a supplementary agreement, various representations and warranties and the conditions under which the merger can be abandoned by either side. If two large public corporations are merging, the transaction may be regarded somewhat as a marriage rather than as an acquisition, and neither side is expected to give a great deal in representations and warranties. On the other hand, if a large company is acquiring a much smaller one and issuing its own stock for the purchase, the company being acquired will generally make a great many representations and warranties.

Typically the provisions of the acquisition contract will

contain a section on representations and warranties, the most important one being that the financial statements furnished by both parties are accurate. Another is that both sides have disclosed their material contracts to the other. The company being acquired warrants it has good title to its real and personal property, and it warrants that there is no litigation that has not been disclosed to the acquiring company. Ordinarily representations and warranties survive the closing and sometimes part of the consideration is placed in escrow as security against subsequent discovery that a warranty is inaccurate.

There will be a section setting forth the conditions to the closing, and the conditions under which one side can call the deal off. Frequently deals are made based on financial statements furnished by one side or the other, which are represented to be true and correct. One of the common conditions in such an instance is that if they are found to be untrue or incorrect before the closing, the other side has the right to abandon the deal. One of the conditions may be that there not be any material adverse change in the business or affairs of the company being acquired between the time of the signing and the time of the closing. Another condition may be that all regulatory agencies whose approval is necessary have given such approval. Receipt of a favorable tax ruling may be a condition.

There may or may not be employment contracts, binding the key employees of the acquired company to stay in the business. There will ordinarily be an agreement to continue the business as it is until such time as the transaction is closed, and not to enter into any contracts out of the ordinary course of business without the approval of the acquired company. There may or may not be a commitment on the part of the acquiring company to register its shares at a later date for resale by the sellers. And there will ordinarily be an agreement on the part of the principals of the acquired company to use their best efforts to see to it that a favorable vote of shareholders is obtained, if such approval is required.

These are the more or less conventional provisions found in the agreement. A company will also have to set forth when the closing is to take place, what papers are to be delivered back and forth, and a number of other mechanical details. In addition, there are a few provisions which are not typical, because they appear in some contracts but not in all of them.

SPECIAL CONSIDERATIONS

One is a holdback of part of the purchase price, whether that price is in cash or shares. It can take the form of either a holdback where the seller agrees to deliver at a later date, or the balance of the purchase price can be delivered immediately to some third party in escrow. A holdback can be used to protect a buyer in case the acquired company does not achieve a certain level of earnings. If the acquired company says, "Well, our earnings are only $1 a share today, but next year we're going to earn $2 a share," the deal might well be, "Fine, if you earn $2 a share there'll be some more stock. Let's wait until you earn it."

Occasionally, contracts call for additional stock payment if the market price of the stock of the acquiring company does not reach or maintain a certain level during a certain period. This is a device that can be useful for a buyer who feels that he has a growth company, and that his stock is going to keep going up over the years. In effect, the agreement says, "Okay, we'll pay $10 million worth of stock, but we feel that our stock is going to be at $40 a share rather than $25 a share two years from now, so we'll pay you $10 million worth of stock based on what the price of our stock is two years from now. We'll pay you so much now, and if our stock doesn't reach $40 a share, then we will give you such number of additional shares as is necessary to make up the $10 million package." At the same time, such an agreement protects the seller in the event the stock of the buyer, instead of going to $40 a share, declines to $15.

These are some of the pitfalls and some of the possibilities. There are obviously many, many others. And it is just because they do exist that a good lawyer, well-informed as to your plans and objectives, can be of material help to you.

Question: One of the questions that seems to come up from time to time is the business of non-competitive agreements with individuals. Are they enforceable?

Mr. Warren C. Haskin: Yes and no. It depends on the degree to which they are reasonable. Obviously if you're buying a retail laundry business, you can't restrict a man throughout the United States, or even Illinois, if the business has only been operated in Chicago. A lot of lawyers make exceptions for certain geographic areas because they feel that if you make the covenant not to compete worldwide or national, it would be of doubtful validity. I have seen contracts, which always look a little silly to me, saying "won't compete except in states of Nevada, Montana and South Dakota." I think if those contracts go beyond what is legitimate, they're going to fail whether you exclude those states or not.

Question: Many companies do not reveal the terms of an acquisition until the deal is closed, if the acquired company is privately held. How do you react to that? Is that the time for disclosure?

Mr. Haskin: I would say this: if the company being acquired is not publicly-owned, you have to evaluate the timing of the publicity on the basis of what effect it is likely to have on your stock. If you have a company with sales of $50 million which is going to acquire another company with sales of $50 million, and the second company just happens to be privately owned and you are publicly owned, this is going to have an impact on your stock. You cannot just shrug it off and say this is immaterial because that company isn't publicly owned.

The other category, of course, consists of accountants. They too can be enormously helpful. Through example, the author argues that the extent of this helpfulness depends in large measure on the principals.

16

INTELLIGENT USE OF ACCOUNTANTS IN ACQUISITIONS

by Warren G. Wintrub, Partner,
Lybrand, Ross Bros. and Montgomery

Somewhere along the way in every negotiation—however firm the handshake, however clear the intent of the two main parties—technical questions must arise.

When this stage is reached, it is a signal for the participants to turn to their technical advisers and ask, sometimes with thinly-veiled impatience, "Okay, the deal is wrapped up. How long will it take you boys to come up with the answers so we can close?"

ASKING THE RIGHT QUESTIONS

Very often, however, the real problem is not to come up with the right answers, but to ask the right question in the first place. There are always a number of correct or potentially acceptable answers to the solution of nearly any problem. Different people will use different approaches and may readily accept one answer as correct but not another which is just as correct. The objectives and the participants' idiosyncracies must be known in order for the adviser to eliminate correct but unacceptable solutions from his recommendations.

WHAT DOES THE SELLER KNOW?

One difference of approach that needs to be resolved early in the course of negotiation is the question of whether or not to assume that the other party knows what he is doing. For example, should one talk lightly and indiscriminately about buying or selling stock or assets, under the assumption that the other party has never heard of depreciation recapture? It is difficult to visualize that the other party would not know that it can greatly affect the value of the consideration that he is receiving when he is selling his business. Yet in my own experience there have been many situations where the other party just did not know—until it came time to iron out a few remaining wrinkles.

A more subtle question is whether the other party realizes that your $1000, 6%, subordinated debenture is worth no more than $750, if that much. An equivalent kind of question is whether the other party realizes that your stock, which may be listed on a national exchange and which may carry a current price tag of, say, $50, is worth no more than $45 if somebody tries to sell more than 1000 shares, and may be worth no more than $20 if the recipient is sitting with that stock under an investment letter and is forced to look at the long-term, intrinsic value of the company rather than the current published market price which appears in the daily newspaper.

I cannot really answer the question of how much one should assume that the other party knows when you are negotiating a transaction. There is always the danger of your being considered too sharp. All that can be said is that one should never mislead the other party when you are sure you are going to get caught. Other than that, it just depends on an individual's approach to the question of negotiation.

GETTING THE ANSWERS EARLY

In any case, it is absolutely essential that competent advisers be employed, and be employed when appropriate. In preparing a merger agreement, there is always a tremendous amount of apparent nit-picking which takes place. Most of this meticulousness is essential if the attorneys are doing a competent job of protecting the interests of their respective clients. But it can also ruin a reasonable and desirable transaction.

I have seen many transactions break down in this phase of what should normally be, basically, a mechanical operation. It would not have happened, I believe, if everybody had previously done his full job.

For example, in a debenture situation, when the terms of the debenture are being arrived at, the seemingly technical question of security or collateral, sinking funds, maturity date, capital restrictions, default provisions, are really not technical questions in and of themselves. They go to the heart of the matter because they all relate to the question of value. The drafters of the agreement may think that they are protecting the interests of their clients when they start discussing these terms, but in reality they are renegotiating the value if they renegotiate the terms; depending upon how much emphasis is placed on what the rights are under each of these various elements, the value of the consideration given will be affected.

It is recognized that interest rates affect value and are a negotiable item, but I am not so certain that the other categories are recognized for what they really are—value-oriented questions—and not merely elements in legal protection arising under a contract.

Another wrinkle that may suddenly be blown out of proportion is the matter that has never even been brought up because one of the parties simply took it for granted. I am sure you have all met someone who will make a flat statement like "I have never written a merger agreement without an escrow provision, and I don't intend to start now." That kind of approach is not uncommon, but I would suggest that prospective buyers who insist on it have a much higher percentage of unsigned merger agreements in their files than does the average purchaser.

Escrows are always desirable, but they are not always required. One has to consider the facts and circumstances before a flat decision, based upon principle, is made. Many prospective parties to a transaction would be severely offended if they were asked to post a portion of the sales proceeds in order to insure their capability of carrying out their financial responsibilities.

PROBLEMS TO LOOK FOR: PRICE

Let us run through the provisions generally found in a merger agreement. First provision is price. One would expect to find this covered, but even details here are occasionally missed. Is the consideration cash or securities? Are the terms of the securities adequately defined? Are variations in general market value covered? Is the contingent stock to be issued adequately explained? Is the form of the transaction desired—that is, taxfree, taxable, installment sale—accomplished? Do the securities produce the desired accounting result—that is, the purchase or pooling treatment? What about the question of residual securities?

ACCOUNTING RULES

Accounting rules are constantly changing, and distinct variations exist. All poolings are not tax free, and all taxable transactions are not treated as purchases for accounting purposes. You can, for instance, have tax-free poolings, taxable poolings, taxable purchases, and tax-free purchases. As long as more than 50% stock is being given to acquire a company, there are ways of working out a tax-free acquisition. If you want to pay cash and stock, it has to be a statutory merger —the so-called A-type of reorganization—where the companies are merged in accordance with state law. A B-type reorganization consists of a stock-for-stock exchange. In order to qualify as tax-free, it must be based solely on stock. You must make an offer for the stock, and pick up at least 80% of the outstanding stock. A C-type reorganization is, in effect, a bargain and sale. You issue your securities to the company to be acquired in exchange for the assets of that company, which then turns around and distributes the shares received to its shareholders.

Purchases and poolings are strictly accounting concepts. If you meet certain tests, you qualify. The requirements are similar to the tax requirements, but not identical. You really cannot safely generalize that a transaction resulting in a pooling will be tax-free. It just might be taxable.

A change in market value of the stock can cause variations in the accounting treatment accorded to the transaction, as well as changing the apparent price of the acquisition at the date of closing. In cases where convertible securities are issued, the question may be whether those convertible securities are treated as being non equity securities for accounting purposes, or whether they are treated as outstanding common stock for the purposes of computing the earnings per share. The Accounting Principles Board has issued an opinion providing that convertible securities are to be treated as common shares for the purposes of computing earnings per share under certain circumstances.

Price of the acquisition is affected by whether the securities received are truly tradable, or are taken under an investment letter. Generally the buyer will insist on an investment letter, as a disposition of too much stock within a short period of time may preclude him from using a pooling treatment for the transaction.

If contingent shares are to be issued, the question arises as to whether imputed interest has been considered. In many cases, the existence of imputed interest (which requires a portion of deferred delivery stock to be treated as ordinary income) does not arise until the transaction is all but signed. Then, when the issue is recognized, the parties are obliged to scurry around to try and correct the situation.

WHAT ARE YOU REALLY BUYING?

After the determination of price comes the definition of the commodity itself. What is being acquired, stock or assets? Who bears the burden of depreciation recapture if it does exist? Also, what happens to the earnings from the date of the agreement on the price to the actual closing of the transaction? Do these belong to the seller or buyer? Does the buyer acquire *all* the assets including key employees?

Another asset that is often overlooked—or it may be a liability in some cases—is the pension plan of the company to be acquired. A number of companies assume that the appropriate numbers appear in the financial statement. Let me say that they do not. Accounting principles have changed in this area, and the amount of unfunded, vested liability may be picked up from the financials. However there is no certainty that it has been computed under actuarial assumptions satisfactory to the buyer. Interest rates, turnover of employees, unrealized appreciation, are all factors left to the discretion of the actuary, and the buyer might well have differences of opinion with that actuary. An overfunded plan may be merged with the buyer's own plan, and permit him to cut his subsequent pension contributions. This is clearly one portion of the commodity being acquired which is often not accorded sufficient weight in negotiating, and in determining values of a potential acquisition.

ARE YOU REALLY PROTECTED?

Another element that always gets voluminous coverage and raised eyebrows in any merger agreement is the list of representations and warranties. They are designed to smoke out problems. By requiring a warranty, the purchaser is protected if the facts are not as stated. If the seller refuses to warrant, then the purchaser knows that he has found an area which he must examine more carefully.

However, warranties often become an issue over which the seller refuses, on principle, to sign. In that case, the buyer must assess his risk and act accordingly. Among topics to check at this point—and they could be important or not—are: the organization of the subsidiaries of the company to be acquired; the fact that the corporation is in good standing; a listing of the amounts and the authorizations of outstanding stock; the fact that the stock is fully paid; that there are no liens against the stock; that the merger transaction is authorized; that the financial statements have been prepared in accordance with generally accepted accounting principles; that there are no undisclosed liabilities; that there have been no adverse changes in the business from the date of the statement until the current time; that tax returns have been filed and accepted by the various tax bureaus; that the receivables are collectible; that the accounting methods are acceptable; that the company holds good title to its properties; that it lists all its leases; that it owns certain patents and it lists them; that it has proper interest in its trademarks, if any exist. The representations may include statements relating to material contracts that exist, capital projects that are on the drawing board or under way, and outstanding stock options.

They may include such matters as the fact that insurance coverage exists, and is adequate on the facilities of the company; that there is no litigation. They should state whether there is a broker in the transaction. Unusual contracts should be disclosed. Relationships with employees and unions, and any recent changes in compensation scale should be listed. The size of the list, and the work involved in going through it, tends to frighten many businessmen, but the well-advised purchaser is definitely going to want to know about these areas.

The next section in the merger agreement generally consists of covenants—affirmative and negative. Essentially, they are the seller's promises to run the business properly, to cooperate in the process of the merger, and not to take any action which reduces the value of the company—such as paying out large dividends, increasing salaries, or signing new contracts not approved by the buyer.

After covenants appear conditions. These are the "outs" which everybody always leaves himself. They include the idea of material misrepresentation; adverse changes in the business of the buyer or of the seller, or of the stock market itself; the obtaining of shareholder approval; the possible limitation of the number of shareholders that extends to the transaction; the correctness of the warranties; the affirmative covenants having been complied with; an accountant's unqualified opinion of the financial statement; the attorney's opinion as to standing in litigation; a tax ruling being received that is favorable to the transaction; consent of the lenders if they could interfere with the merger agreement; absence of stockholder suits or government restraining action.

ACHIEVING YOUR REAL OBJECTIVES

There are a number of considerations that are present in any acquisition. The buyer will generally receive a much better performance from his advisers if he can let them in on his objectives in making an acquisition. It is much easier to draft papers if the adviser knows what you are trying to accomplish. When I say "what," I don't mean how you are trying to accomplish it. That is mechanical. I mean why are you trying to do something. Don't just say "tax free," because the seller says he wants a tax-free transaction. Possibly a taxable transaction would actually be worth his consideration—I can't see how he would object to that, if he received an additional amount equal to his taxes.

A high percentage of questions that come up in the important phases of negotiation actually turn out to be the wrong questions, because they are framed by people who are not familiar with all the possible options that are available.

Give your adviser a crack at helping you to find the right question. As an example, let's refer back to the merger agreement. One provision that is often put into this agreement is that the auditor will review the tax provision to determine if it is adequate in accordance with generally accepted accounting principles. Well, this may be absolutely wrong if you are trying to accomplish what I think you are trying to accomplish.

There are two concepts of deferred tax accounting; the deferred benefit approach and the liability approach. The liability approach is the one which sets forth the amount of taxes which would be payable if all the differences between financial reporting and tax reporting were eliminated. This is probably the number you are thinking you are getting. The generally accepted accounting principle employed, however, is the deferred benefit approach. This represents the amount of taxes that were not paid in prior years because of differences between financial and tax reporting. It has no necessary relationship to the amount of taxes that will be payable in the future. It is however the number you will probably receive if you ask for a check of the number determined in accordance with generally accepted accounting principles.

The reason for this difference as well as many others is that the current aim, the objective, of the financial statements is to match revenues and expenses appropriately—not to set forth values on the balance sheet, but to have an appropriate matching on the income statement. Using the historical approach to the determination of taxes presents a more accurate income statement, but it can distort the deferred liability account on the balance sheet. Thus, when you want the accountant to give you the number, don't ask him for what it is under generally accepted accounting principles.

There are a number of other areas where generally accepted accounting principles are not the numbers you are looking for in analyzing an acquisition. The financials of the company to be acquired may have been properly prepared, but still the principle may be different from the one you yourself are employing. The mere fact that your accountant agrees that the financial statement of the seller is correct does not mean that those same numbers will flow through to your statements in the same manner they flowed through the seller's statements. Once the company is acquired, its accounting methods must be changed to conform to your own methods, and different results can occur.

I suspect this is not sufficiently understood, and numerous problems arise because of the confusion. The statements of the acquired company may be completely correct, and the representations and warranties will say that they are prepared in accordance with generally accepted accounting principles. Yet you may be extremely disappointed, after acquiring the company, to see what those assets really are.

These have been just a few examples. I am not suggesting that every negotiation is doomed to founder on some last-minute snag, nor am I saying that the most accomplished of accounts or attorneys can guarantee a successful conclusion. Greater recognition of their contribution to successful strategy is not needed. What is needed, if more successful acquisitions are to be made, is a recognition of the types of problems that exist and an understanding of the role of the specialist. An advisor can be no more helpful than you permit him to be.

If there is a single point at which more agreement-bound mergers founder than any other, it is probably the closing. The author, a well-known specialist in corporate law, suggests that the reason may lie in misunderstandings or ambiguities which have been allowed to stand. His proposed solution: have the closing in mind when you start negotiating.

17

THE ANATOMY OF A SUCCESSFUL CLOSING

by Charles A. Scharf,
Partner, Ide & Haigney

It has been made fairly clear by now that there is no consistent, reliable pattern to acquisitions. Because there are intangible factors involved—judgment and, on the seller's side, emotion—each transaction responds to its own system of inner logic.

But it is possible to sketch a very generalized pattern for most negotiations. In my experience, it would go something like this:

The first meeting will produce a "no-go, tentative-go" signal. Subsequent meetings will modify the "tentative-go." If the numbers and the rationale fit, and if the personal chemistry is right, the "tentative" will be jettisoned and negotiations will proceed. There will be ups and downs, but the thrust will be toward final agreement. Then, inevitably, the moment will come when a definitive merger agreement has to be structured and signed.

It is at this point in many cases that the light suddenly changes from green to red. One or the other side pulls up short. Sometimes, it is possible to go back and re-structure. More often, however, the parties discover that there has been some lack of mutual understanding all along and that only now, when everything is reduced to precise writing, does it loom up stark and clear.

I think it safe to say that more acquisitions founder at this point than at any other. I also think that in most instances it need not happen. The purpose of this chapter is to suggest how to avoid it.

In my opinion, that red light should not exist in the first place. In well-planned negotiations, there should be no fixed moment at which the structuring of the merger agreement begins as a formal undertaking. That agreement informally begins to take shape as soon as the parties hold their first meeting, and continues to evolve as an integral part of the negotiating process.

If both parties keep this in mind, the closing itself loses most of its traumatic overtones. It is merely the next logical step in a logical progression of events.

THE MERGER AGREEMENT

The merger agreement is an essential document. It contains all of the terms of the transaction. Of course, there may also be other elements involved in a transaction which are important. For instance, you may apply for a tax ruling or for a no-action letter from the Securities and Exchange Commission. You may also be required to obtain a pooling of interest opinion from your accountants. These are all incidental issues, sometimes very difficult to accomplish and sometimes requiring a great deal of skill, but it is the merger agreement itself which defines the deal because it fixes the rights of the parties to one another.

Once this agreement is signed, your legal rights are fixed, and you cannot change them. The merger agreement also determines what is to occur at the closing—the specific title documents to be transferred, the obligations to be assumed, the stock to be issued, and the numerous certificates and opinions usually required to be exchanged in merger transactions. And the merger agreement starts fixing these closing requirements at the first moment you meet the buyer or seller, since the structuring of the merger agreement has its informal beginnings at that time.

FROM AGREEMENT TO CLOSING

In the usual transaction, the parties proceed to the closing after the agreement is signed. The closing itself may well occur months beyond the date the formal contract is signed because closing preparations often require both time and skill. It is at the closing that the documents passing legal title in accordance with the terms of the contract are exchanged and the ownership of the business changes hands.

The foregoing analysis of the nature of the acquisition strongly suggests the conclusion that the party with the knowledge of what should go into the contract, and how the acquisition will close, is best equipped to negotiate the structure of the transaction. Therefore, it is also my opinion, even though I am an attorney, that contrary to opinions which are sometimes expressed, a knowledgeable attorney with experience in this field ought to be brought into the negotiations at the beginning.

His presence may not be required at the first meeting between the buyer and seller, but he should take part in the negotiations as soon as practicable.

WHEN TO START CLOSING?

If you start structuring your transaction properly right from the beginning, you are going to reach your objectives. If you don't, you may not.

Let me give an example of what can happen. Sometime ago I was called into a transaction in which a very complete and well-written memorandum of intent had already been signed. The memorandum of intent was well done, and contained all the major elements of this transaction. However, the purchaser had inadvertently misinformed the seller as to the effect of one element contained in it.

The purchaser was acquiring stock for stock. He did not want to register this stock with the Securities and Exchange Commission. He had informed the seller in the course of negotiations that upon receipt of the purchaser's stock, the seller would be able to sell up to one percent of the purchaser's outstanding stock, without a registration statement having been filed with the Securities and Exchange Commission and without such a statement being in effect.

In this transaction, the purchaser mistakenly believed that he would qualify under Rule 133 promulgated under the Securities Act of 1933 (in accordance with the provisions of the rule prior to the changes suggested in the Wheat Report). Generally speaking, a registration statement filed with the Securities and Exchange Commission must be effective to permit sale of stock to the public. Rule 133 provided an exception to the rule, and permitted stock to be sold within the limits prescribed in the rule, even though no registration statement was in effect with respect to the stock.

In the course of the negotiations and in preparing the letter of intent, the seller had failed to realize that a stock-for-stock transaction, which is how this acquisition had been structured, did not qualify under Rule 133. If the transaction closed as a stock-for-stock transaction, the seller could not legally have sold the buyer's stock on the open market unless a registration statement was in effect with respect to the stock. The buyer was not willing to register its stock, and the sellers did not want to take stock they could not sell.

This carefully negotiated transaction therefore came to a standstill, illustrating the importance of knowing or obtaining advice on the details of the transaction from the time you start to structure your merger agreement—from the beginning.

PROBLEMS THAT CAN BE AVOIDED

From experience, there are problems which arise with a certain degree of regularity in structuring merger agreements, and I would like to mention some of them briefly, and also point out ways to cope with them by knowing the rules.

The first of these areas concerns taxes. Essentially there

are three types of transactions that result in tax-free acquisitions: (1) the statutory merger or consolidation, (2) the stock-for-stock acquisition, and (3) the assets-for-stock acquisition. But each of these types of tax-free acquisition contains requirements which, if not met, may convert a tax-free acquisition into a taxable transaction.

For instance, not long ago I became collaterally involved in a transaction which involved two prospective acquirers. One was making a tender offer for stock. The other was attempting to buy the business with the management's approval.

The second company was offering its stock for the assets and business of the seller, and the seller was to hold a shareholders' meeting in order to approve the sale of assets, as is required under state law. Customarily, state law requires a stockholder vote to sell the assets of a corporation other than in the normal course of business.

The transaction was structured as a tax-free transaction, falling under Section 368(a)(1)(C) of the Internal Revenue Code, which provides that the buyer must obtain substantially all the assets of the seller in exchange for solely voting stock of the buyer. The transaction appeared to comply with 368(a)(1)(C), because the buyer was offering solely voting stock for all the assets and business of the seller.

But as it turned out, the competing acquirer, which had made the tender offer, was acquiring stock of the seller through its offer and would unquestionably vote the stock it acquired against this particular merger. As a result, under the state law involved, the competing acquirer would be a dissenting shareholder, and would be entitled to require the selling company to purchase its stock held by the competing acquirer for cash equal to the fair market value of the seller's stock, as determined by appraisal or a court.

In order for the acquisition to retain its tax-free character, a buyer must acquire substantially all the assets of a seller. If, let us say, the competing acquirer owns 25% of the stock of the selling company, and must be paid in cash by the seller because of dissent against the acquisition, the seller's assets would be reduced by 25%. Then a substantial question arises under the tax law as to whether or not the buyer is acquiring substantially all the assets of the seller.

Here then is a situation where those structuring the proposed acquisition must look ahead to determine whether or not the proposed acquisition will still qualify as a tax-free transaction if the dissenting shares amount to as much as 25% of the outstanding stock, because the acquirer might not obtain substantially all the assets as required under the tax law. This is what I mean by looking forward—attempting to anticipate the turn of events and their prospective effect on the technical aspects of an acquisition. In the specific situation mentioned, the tax problem was solved by converting the structure of the transaction to a statutory merger, a section 368(a)(1)(A) transaction, from an acquisition of assets, the section 368(a)(1)(C) transaction originally proposed.

THE "POOLING" CONCEPT

Much has been said about "pooling of interests." Pooling of interests is an accounting concept. Whether or not a transaction may qualify as a pooling of interests is determined, as a last resort, by the accounting firm representing the acquirer. Unfortunately, accounting firms do not always agree upon all of the specifics which will qualify a specific acquisition for pooling of interests accounting treatment.

Because of these differences in requirements imposed by different accounting firms, if it appears that pooling of interests will be important to a particular acquisition—and in many current transactions it is an important concept—it is a good idea to approach the accountants of the acquiring company in the early stages of structuring the acquisition, and attempt to determine the requirements of the accounting firm to approve a pooling of interests. You may as well know in advance—if pooling is important in the particular situation. What the accountants will require to treat the acquisition as a pooling may be different from what was required by the same accounting firm in a previous transaction, or from the requirements of a different accounting firm in a concurrent transaction.

SEC requirements also become involved in these transactions. The law states simply that a sale of stock is unlawful unless there is a registration statement in effect with regard to the stock.

THE QUESTION OF REGISTRATION

As you know, many companies do not wish to register stock in connection with acquisitions. Registration is a time-consuming process which limits the operation of the registrant's business during the period the registration statement takes effect. It also entails substantial expense. Therefore, if a purchaser does not wish to register his stock, he must cast the transaction in such a form that the stock need not be registered in order to make its sale lawful.

There are two basic exceptions to the registration requirements which are often utilized in stock transactions. Either the selling shareholders, who are comparatively few in number, may take the buyer's stock for "investment" purposes only in a so-called "non-public" offering, or the transaction may be structured to qualify under the Rule 133 exemption (in effect before the changes suggested by the Wheat Report). Either approach will permit the consummation of the acquisition without a registration statement being effective.

However, any shareholder who signs an investment letter in a "non-public" offering transaction should fully appreciate the legal effect of signing such a letter. Essentially, such a shareholder will not be free to sell the stock without registration unless he has a so-called change in circumstances. The Securities and Exchange Commission's attitude is that a change in circumstances must involve more than a drop in market value of a stock. The seller should therefore receive competent advice on what the legal effect may be when he signs an investment letter, or he may find that he is unable to legally dispose of stock which he may have received as the result of the sale of his business.

The second method of freeing stock for sale without a registration statement is the so-called Rule 133, a rule which the SEC promulgated under the Securities Act of 1933. It applies—speaking very generally—only to situations involving a sale of assets or a statutory merger or a consolidation. If the transaction meets the requirements of Rule 133 (in the form it was promulgated prior to the changes suggested in the Wheat Report), the Rule provides that no "sale" is deemed to be involved for the purposes of Section 5 of the Securities Act of 1933, which makes a sale of securities unlawful unless a registration statement is in effect with respect to such securities.

In a Rule 133 transaction, the buyer may give the buyer's stock to the selling corporation in exchange for the seller's assets; the selling corporation may distribute the buyer's stock to the selling corporation's shareholders; and finally, subject to certain limitations, the selling corporation's shareholders may lawfully sell the buyer's stock in the open market—all without any registration statement being in effect.

Rule 133 limitations on the amount of stock which may be sold by the shareholders of the selling company are based upon mathematical formulas. If the selling company's shares are widely held, the smaller non-control stockholders of the selling corporation may, generally speaking, sell all the shares they receive immediately, and they will not be in violation of any SEC law or rules. However, the controlling stockholders of the selling corporation are limited as to the number of shares they may lawfully sell without a registration statement being in effect with respect to the shares.

Under the rule, the mathematical formulas differ, depending upon whether the buyer whose stock is received is (1) a listed company or (2) traded over the counter. In a situation involving a listed security, a controlling shareholder of a selling company may sell the *lesser* of one of two different numbers of shares of a buyer's stock during any six-month period. He may sell in any six-month period (1) either one percent of the outstanding stock of the listed company whose stock he has received, or (2) the total of the highest week's trading in the stock on all exchanges on which the stock is listed in the four weeks preceding the week in which he put in his sell order.

In addition, under the rule, the controlling shareholder may sell only through regular brokerage transactions. As complicated as the rule may appear, it functions well when a buying corporation is acquiring a smaller corporation whose shares are fairly widely held. A more difficult situation arises when the larger company is acquiring a smaller corporation which is very closely held, with perhaps two or three shareholders. In such a situation the SEC has established an internal policy that such a transaction may be treated as a "negotiated" transaction, which does not come under Rule 133 at all. This is an area in which lawyers may find it difficult to advise, and where expert advice is of greater importance than usual.

There are other areas in the merger agreement which

may cause difficulties and which should be borne in mind right from the outset of negotiations.

REPRESENTATIONS AND WARRANTIES

One such area involves the survival of the representations and warranties made by the seller. Should the representations of a seller in the contract survive the closing, or should they terminate with the closing?

The question may pose a very knotty problem in some acquisition negotiations; but often a compromise solution is reached in which the representations and warranties may survive for a limited period of time after the closing. Thereafter, their survival terminates and any breach of the representations or warranties discovered after the termination of the survival period no longer entitles the buyer to sue under the acquisition contract.

ANTI-TRUST CONSIDERATIONS

Libraries of books have been written on the anti-trust aspects which may be involved in any one of these merger transactions. Section 7 of the Clayton Act deals directly with the anti-trust aspects of mergers and acquisitions. The section has been interpreted and expanded in its coverage by the courts, until it may apply to many situations where one would not expect it to apply. The statute is concise. It provides that a corporation may not legally acquire the whole or any part of the stock or assets of another corporation where the effect of such acquisition in any line of commerce, in any section of the country, may be substantially to lessen competition or to tend to create a monopoly.

These words have been so construed that a "section of the

country" may be a small area around the tip of Lake Erie. A "line of commerce" may be narrowly construed to mean not a line of paints in general, but rather specialized automotive paints. This is how the court construed the statute in the Dupont-General Motors case. The federal authorities will present to the courts the interpretation of a "line of commerce" and "section of the country" which are most likely to bring about the prohibited substantial lessening of competition, or tendency to create a monopoly.

COORDINATING THE INVESTIGATION

Let us turn to conducting and coordinating the investigation of the proposed acquisition. There are three essential areas in every acquisition which must be investigated carefully. They are (1) the business areas, (2) the accounting areas, and (3) the legal areas. In many acquisitions in which I have been involved, the acquirer conducts investigations in these three separate areas at considerable expense and in some detail.

But I have found that sometimes these investigations do not achieve the desired result, because the investigation often is not properly coordinated. The investigation is conducted in three separate areas of endeavor, and, unfortunately, the coordination of the investigation and the results of the three separate investigations is not accomplished as well as it should be in many transactions. The results may be unfortunate.

In my opinion, it is the attorney's responsibility to coordinate the results of the investigation and to highlight problem areas. It is the attorney's responsibility to draft the contract, and he cannot do an effective job unless he is able to coordinate the information involved. However, try as he might, the attorney is not always successful in convincing the businessman and the accountant that he requires full cooperation and detailed information in drafting the acquisition contract. The attitude too often persists among businessmen and accountants that the acquisition contract is primarily a "boiler plate" agreement. It very seldom is.

In most situations, the closing takes place some time after the acquisition contract is signed. This is necessary because, generally, a contract will require that certain conditions be met before the closing takes place. The buyer or seller—usually the seller—may require that a favorable tax ruling be obtained from the Internal Revenue Service. This, obviously, takes time. In fact, it may take three or four months to obtain a favorable ruling that a transaction is "tax-free."

Therefore, in a situation where a ruling of an administrative body is required prior to closing, the acquisition contract should provide a sufficient time period between the signing of the contract and the closing to obtain the ruling. The closing, as I use the term, means the transfer of legal titles by the transfer of title documents and/or stock certificates.

In other situations, it may be possible to arrange matters in such a way that the transaction can be negotiated down to a signing of a contract and a closing which may take place simultaneously. This approach is taken on occasion, but usually only in situations where no administrative rulings are required and general circumstances permit such approach.

THE FUNCTION OF CLOSING IN NEGOTIATIONS

The basic subject of this book concerns strategy in the conduct of negotiations, and the closing may appear remote from the negotiations. But in fact the closing *does* have a direct relationship to the negotiation process. The conditions of the closing and closing documents are being fixed at the very moment the negotiations start. As a consequence, in conducting the negotiations, the negotiator should bear in mind that he not fix impossible conditions for closing—conditions which may not be possible of fulfillment.

In a recent transaction, during three or four months of concerted effort and negotiations, one of the basic problems faced by the seller was whether or not it should apply for a tax ruling. The transaction was complicated; it involved a number of entities which were to be merged, and other complications which caused the seller to consider in more than customary detail the problems inherent in applying for a tax ruling. The seller finally decided not to apply for the ruling. Although it was satisfied with the tax results of the proposed acquisition, it concluded that the Internal Revenue Service would not rule favorably because of the technicalities involved in the situation.

As mentioned, the question of whether or not to apply for a tax ruling had its beginnings three or four months before the contract was signed. It arose when the contract was first being negotiated. If the contract was conditioned upon obtaining a favorable tax ruling prior to closing, the transaction would not have closed unless the requirement for a favorable ruling was waived, because I do not think the seller would have obtained the ruling. The general lesson to be learned is not to negotiate closing conditions into a transaction which are impossible of fulfillment.

The same comment may be made concerning a no-action letter from the SEC. If you condition your contract on a no-action letter from the SEC, where the selling company is closely held, the SEC may refuse to give you the letter under its present interpretation of the Securities Act of 1933. If the negotiations and contract are conditioned on receipt of the no-action letter, you may not be able to close unless one of the parties waives the condition. The same is true of pooling of interests accounting treatment.

Closing requirements should be borne in mind from the beginning of the negotiation and throughout the negotiation, not considered as an afterthought after you have signed the contract. They are in fact an integral part of negotiating strategy, and should be treated as such.

Question: How does Rule 133 apply to over-the-counter securities?

Mr. Charles A. Scharf: In an over-the-counter company, a constituent corporation or affiliated person as described in paragraph (e) of Rule 133, may sell, in any six-month period, up to one percent of the outstanding stock of the issuer. There is no additional limitation involving the number of shares traded in any of the four weeks preceding the sell order, as there is in the rule applicable to listed companies.

Question: What if the proceeds of that disposition go to one hundred shareholders? They don't know what one percent is.

Mr. Scharf: The one hundred shareholders are not affected; the limitation on the number of shares which may be sold applies only to controlling shareholders.

Question: If an over-the-counter company acquires stock in exchange for its business from an unlisted company, does Rule 133 still apply?

Mr. Scharf: Yes, if the transaction meets the requirements of Rule 133. Generally speaking, to be applicable, the rule requires that the transaction be of a type which requires a vote of the shareholders of a corporation which is binding as to the other shareholders, except dissenters. Normally, the types of transactions which meet the requirements are a sale of the assets and business of a corporation for stock or a statutory merger. Whether or not the companies involved are listed on stock exchanges or are traded in the over-the-counter market is not an element which has any effect on the applicability of Rule 133 to a particular situation.

Question: What is the period of time covered by an investment letter? And is an investment letter effective for SEC, pooling of interests, or income tax purposes, or all three?

Mr. Scharf: There is no time limit on an investment letter. An investment letter means that you are taking stock for investment purposes only, and that you have no present intention of selling it. You will hear that one year, two years, or three years will terminate these investment requirements. Actually, there is no fixed time limit. An investment letter relates primarily to SEC requirements, and is often required of selling shareholders to give an issuer greater assurance that the transaction will be exempt from the requirements of registration.

However, many accountants have insisted upon the signing of investment letters in order to treat the transaction as a pooling of interests, although the type of investment letter they may require the recipients of the stock to sign may provide a right to sell certain percentages of stock in the first year and second year without regard to Rule 133, or other SEC considerations. It is a different type of investment letter from that requested for SEC purposes.

Generally, investment letters have no relevancy insofar as the income tax consequences of a transaction are concerned.

Question: What is a no-action letter?

Mr. Scharf: A no-action letter is a letter from the Securities and Exchange Commission. It is analogous to a tax ruling. The circumstances of a proposed transaction are submitted to the SEC, including the fact that applicant would like to sell stock without it being registered. If the SEC believes registration is not required, in its letter of reply it does not say, "We approve of the sale of the stock without a registration being in effect." If favorably disposed, the SEC says, "We will not take any action against you if you sell under the circumstances indicated."

One of the most difficult aspects of acquisition work is to present a complex proposal, complete with alternative courses of action, in simple, understandable form. The author proposes a method for accomplishing this, and suggests how it can be useful to prospective buyer and seller alike.

18

AN ANALYTICAL APPROACH TO MERGER NEGOTIATIONS

by Gary E. MacDougal, Chairman and Chief Executive Officer, Clayton Mark & Company, and
Fred V. Malek, Special Assistant to President Richard M. Nixon

In this chapter, we will attempt to outline an over-all analytical approach which should enable a potential buyer to stand apart from the crowd, and which will endow his offer with a real competitive edge.

In the general area of acquisition work, it is safe to say that much effort goes into screening long lists of industries and companies, and into gathering published data of possible acquisition candidates. While this is important, and must be done at some stage, it is also necessary to develop an analytical approach to merger negotiations which can be understood and communicated effectively.

The lack of such approach may typically result in two kinds of consequences: a) through failure to "sell the seller" on some aspect of the acquisition, management may find itself unable to "close" or complete anything of consequence. Or, worse yet, b) faulty analysis may lead management to acquire a poor company, or to pay so much for a good one that it cannot hope to earn an acceptable return on the investment.

The approach to acquisition negotiations outlined in this chapter is designed to enhance the chances of success in merger negotiations. It shows negotiating executives, too often perplexed by the maze of technical, legal, and financial details surrounding a prospective acquisition, how to handle three critical aspects of the negotiating process:

1. Laying the groundwork for successful negotiations by understanding the financial relationships that underlie any agreement between the two companies.
2. Developing the seller's interest in the non-financial aspects of the proposition.

---

3. Resolving the financial facts in a way that will make possible an early and realistic agreement on terms.

THE TRUE MEANING OF FINANCIAL RELATIONSHIPS

As the first step toward successful acquisition negotiations, the acquiring company should lay the groundwork in two areas: (a) it needs to think out carefully and express in specific terms its own corporate objectives and acquisition criteria; and (b) it needs to study and understand the basic financial relationships between itself and its potential acquisition.

At a minimum, for acquisition evaluation purposes, corporate objectives should include such financial standards as earnings per share, growth rate and annual return on investment. Without these yardsticks, there is no way of knowing whether a given acquisition would act as a spur or a brake on overall corporate performance. Consider:

An acquisition candidate that is showing an earnings per share growth rate of 9% a year compounded will look very good to a company that is currently growing at 5.5% a year compounded and aiming for an 8% growth rate.

However, that same acquisition candidate will (or should) hold little attraction for a would-be acquirer that is growing at 10% a year, and has set its sights on 14%.

The earnings growth rate and return on investment an acquirer should set as its goals depend on many factors that will emerge only from a thoughtful evaluation of internal corporate potential combined with a sound assessment of the business environment. Some companies regularly measure themselves on two counts: First, against their own industry, then against a cross section of all manufacturing companies, such as that provided by *Fortune*'s "500."

For example, an earnings per share growth rate of 12.5%

a year compounded would equal the performance of companies at the bottom of the top quartile of *Fortune*'s "500" during the past decade. A 15% return on shareholders' equity would also place a company at the bottom of the top quartile during this period. The end result should be performance goals that are challenging but attainable.

SOME USEFUL YARDSTICKS

Criteria for the evaluation of investments should include, in addition to the type and size of business and other appropriate screening factors, a return on investment (ROI) target that takes present-value considerations into account. The discounted cash flow method provides a good measurement of the return on investment. A typical company, then, might develop these yardsticks against which to measure prospective acquisitions:

1. Annual compound earnings per share (EPS) growth rate.
2. Annual return on shareholders' equity.
3. Prospective return on the investment, calculated on a discounted cash flow basis.

The buying company can then proceed to examine the financial characteristics of the acquisition candidate, evalute them in the light of the corporate objectives and acquisition criteria it has established, and begin to define the range of feasible purchase prices and terms.

SETTING A PRICE RANGE

Once the buying company has spotted a promising acquisition candidate, has become acquainted with its principal characteristics, and is preparing for the first approach, the time has come to examine certain key relationships in order to determine what price can be paid—and in what form—without undermining corporate objectives. Management should at this point determine:

———The relationships of various selling-company EPS growth rates and new capital requirements to possible purchase prices and discounted cash flow ROI.

———The impact that various earnings-growth rates of the acquisition candidate and various purchase prices and forms of payment will have on the parent company's earnings per share and annual ROI.

———The maximum percentage of control the acquired company would retain at various purchase prices and under alternative forms of payment.

To determine these relationships, we recommend an analytical approach that has proven effective in practice, is relatively easy to use, and can be displayed graphically.

THE VALUE OF A GRAPHIC APPROACH

The graphs make it simpler for negotiating executives to grasp the essentials before talks begin. They provide a sound understanding of the true trade-offs involved and the limitations on purchase price and terms.

Management can thus proceed into negotiations with greater confidence, since the graphs can be used for a quick assessment of the potential impact of changes in terms of prices. This increased flexibility helps to eliminate unnecessary roadblocks and prevent mistakes.

Finally, as we shall see, the graphs themselves become persuasive tools for the acquiring company's negotiating team: when shown to the seller, they help in moving talks on the crucial financial details from an emotional or intuitive level to a more objective plane where the facts convincingly speak for themselves.

We have devised an example to illustrate both the financial analysis which management of the acquiring company should undertake and the graphic guides it could use as tools.

CASE STUDY: SYNERGISTICS CORPORATION

Synergetics Corporation, a publicly owned (NYSE) company with $125 million in sales, is preparing to commence negotiations with Historic Family Enterprise (HFE), a $12-million company closely held by the chairman of the board and his family. To provide a framework for its acquisition program, Synergetics' board of directors has approved these corporate financial objectives and acquisition criteria:

1. All new capital investments, including acquisitions, must provide a discounted cash flow ROI of 12% or better after taxes.
2. The objective for Synergetics' earnings per share growth is 10% per year.
3. The target for Synergetics' annual return on shareholders' investment is 14%.
4. Dilution of earnings per share should be minimized, and any dilution which does result should be eliminated by the third year after acquisition.

The basic financial characteristics of Synergetics and of HFE look like this (HFE's earnings per share are not known, and there is no established market value for HFE's stock):

	Synergetics Corporation	Historic Family Enterprise
Profits after taxes	$5,000,000	$1,000,000
Earnings per share	$5	—
Past growth rate	6%	10%
Management growth projection	6%	12%
P/E ratio	12	—

In preparing for negotiations, Synergetics' management has two purposes in mind: (a) to understand the financial relationships that will exist between the two companies so that it will know what prices are reasonable under varying conditions—and why—and (b) to improve its ability to communicate purchase-price limits which the HFE negotiators will understand and consider reasonable.

At this point, Synergetics' executives must clarify the basic financial issues. Because HFE is not publicly owned, there is no established market price, nor has HFE management indicated a preference for any particular exchange instrument. In addition, Synergetics is uncertain what rate of earnings growth to expect from HFE. Therefore, Synergetics is interested in analyzing these financial aspects:

1. The relationship among probable HFE earnings per share growth rates, purchase-price levels, and Synergetics' discounted cash flow return (e.g., with an HFE annual growth rate of 15%, what is the maximum feasible purchase price if the discounted cash flow ROI is to equal 12% or better?)

2. The year-by-year impact on Synergetics' earnings per share of various HFE growth rates and purchase prices (e.g., at what growth rate is dilution overcome within three years if HFE is purchased for $20 million in common stock?)

3. At a given price, the year-by-year effect on earnings per share of alternate combinations of cash, common stock, and preferred stock (e.g., if the purchase price is $20 million, what is the effect on dilution of increasing the cash portion from 5% to 20%?)

4. The relationship of purchase price and type of exchange instrument to the resulting degree of HFE control (e.g., if the price is $20 million and the terms are 25% cash and 75% common stock, what percentage of the new, combined enterprise will be represented by former HFE shareholders?)

Discounted cash flow return analysis (see page 121), now in use by a number of sophisticated companies, offers several important advantages. For one thing, it provides a means of determining value that is independent of the financial terms involved. If only earnings per share impact is evaluated, an all-cash acquisition of a slowly growing company, for example, can be made to look good on a straight earnings per share basis because the effect of leveraging the company, through the use of cash, is intermixed with the acquisition evaluation.

For another thing, the present-value ROI approach also gives full recognition to the fact that earnings received in, say, ten years are less valuable than those received in two, three, or four years. In addition, management can easily decide by assessing the ROI in terms of present value whether acquiring a given company is preferable to using the same capital for internal projects or for other acquisitions.

The essence of this discounted cash flow ROI approach is to estimate cash inflows for each year of a given period (often a ten-year period is appropriate). These inflows include the capitalized increases in earnings per share. In addition, cash outflows are estimated for the same period—outflows which include the initial purchase price of the acquisition and the amount by which capital investment exceeds depreciation. The initial value of the company acquired is then treated as a cash inflow in the final year of the period under consideration.

In the case of the Synergetics Corporation, assume that management's calculations show that investing new capital at a discounted cash flow ROI rate of 12% or better will produce an annual return on shareholders' equity of 14% or better—thus meeting two of the goals approved by Synergetics' board of directors. (Note that the 12% discounted cash flow is on total capital, whereas the 14% return on shareholders' equity covers only the equity portion.)

Exhibit I. Synergetics' ROI at various growth rates and purchase prices

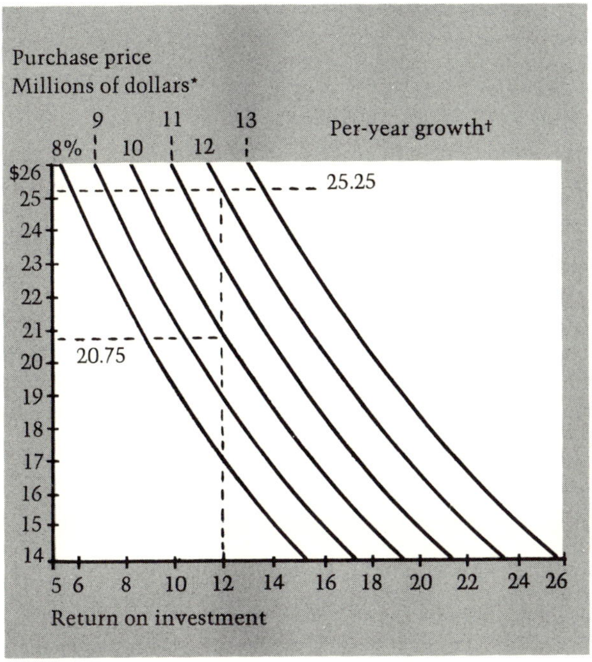

*Cash or stock equivalent.
†Compound annual growth rate.
Note: Discounted cash flow ROI over a ten-year period, based on an average industry P/E of 18.
Source of all exhibits: Wolfgang Krug, research analyst, McKinsey & Company, Inc., Los Angeles.

Therefore, in contemplating the purchase of HFE, the first task for Synergetics' executives is to project a range of possible compound aftertax earnings per share growth rates for HFE, and then to ask:

What is the maximum price we can pay at each of the various HFE growth levels if we are going to meet our 12% discounted cash flow ROI target?

Exhibit I shows graphically this relationship between purchase price, projected HFE growth rate, and Synergetics' return on investment.

If an annual HFE growth rate of 10% seems probable, then Synergetics can pay $20.75 million for the company and get a 12% return on investment. However, if HFE is expected to grow at a rate of 12% annually, a price as high as $25.25 million can be paid without falling below the ROI criterion set by Synergetics' board of directors.

Synergetics' management, therefore, knows that negotiations on the purchase price should stay within a range of $20 million to $25 million, and that the critical factor is the HFE projected earnings per share growth rate.

A second question now confronts Synergetics' executives:

If we are to overcome dilution within three years, as our acquisition criteria specify, what is the appropriate purchase price, and should it be in cash, common stock, preferred stock, or some combination of these?

Using the range of estimated HFE growth rates, Synergetics' executives decide to test the effect of offering a $20 million exchange of Synergetics common stock for HFE common stock to determine both the impact on combined earnings per share and the year in which dilution can be replaced by appreciation.

It is immediately apparent from *Exhibit II* that even if HFE were to grow at a rate of 15% annually, Synergetics' earnings would be diluted through the sixth year after acquisition with a $20 million common-for-common exchange. Lower HFE growth rates continue the dilution even longer. In other words, a common-for-common exchange at this price rules out hope of meeting Synergetics' acquisition criteria.

Synergetics' management then must work out purchase terms and a price that will allow dilution to be overcome by the third year. Again, various HFE projected growth rates—of 10%, 12%, and 15% per year—are evaluated.

As *Exhibit III* indicates, if dilution beyond the third year

Exhibit II. Impact of various HFE growth rates on Synergetics' earnings

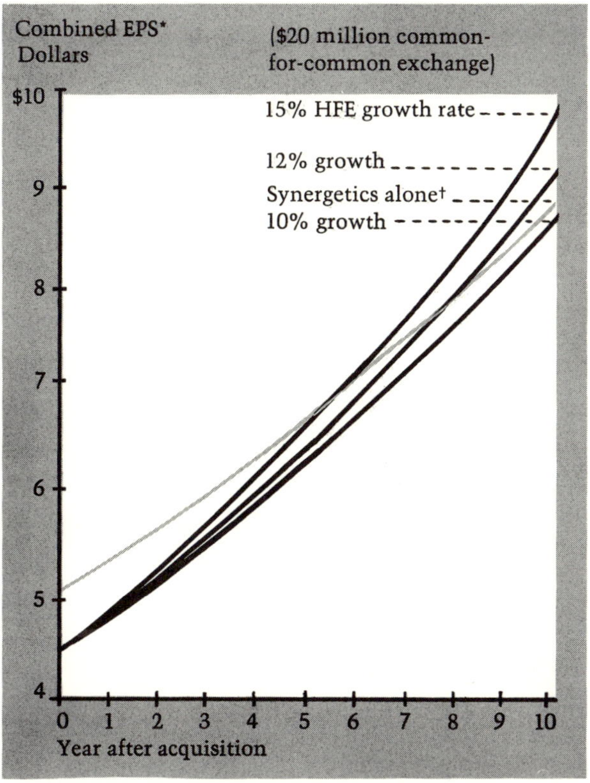

*Assumes projected 6% after-tax growth rate.
†Compound annual growth rates in HFE after-tax earnings.

is to be avoided, the top price Synergetics can offer HFE in a common-for-common exchange, assuming a projected HFE growth rate of 15% a year, is $15.32 million. With a more probable 12% growth rate, no more than $14.16 million in common stock can be paid.

Synergetics knows that the owners of HFE would consider a $15.32 million offer quite unrealistic. It would represent only slightly over 15 times HFE's annual $1 million after-tax earnings, and comparable companies in HFE's industry have been selling for 18 times earnings—which suggests what

Exhibit III. Relationship of purchase prices and HFE growth rates to year in which dilution is replaced by appreciation

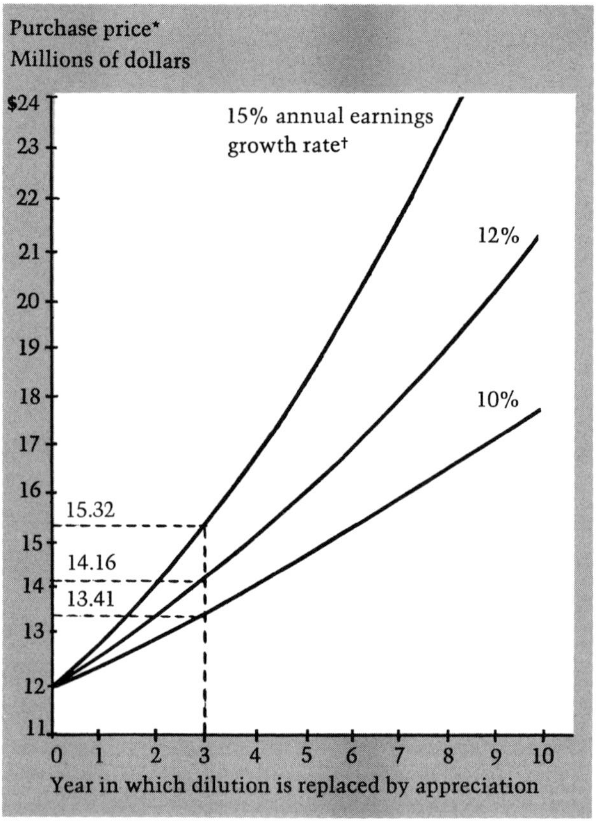

*Assumes common-for-common exchange.
†Compound annual growth in HFE after-tax earnings.

HFE's expectations might be. The average price for all companies acquired in the past few years has been in the range of 23 to 25 times earnings.

With a modest 6% annual growth rate, Synergetics itself commands a price-earnings ratio of 12: HFE's growth rate is expected to be nearly twice that of Synergetics. Thus, if the negotiations are to succeed, it is apparent that Synergetics will have to put forth a better offer. The key question at this point then becomes:

Is there any combination of exchange instruments that will make a $20 million purchase price consistent with Synergetics' own objectives?

As *Exhibit IV* shows, the introduction of cash into the

Exhibit IV. Impact on Synergetics' earnings of alternate combinations of cash and common stock

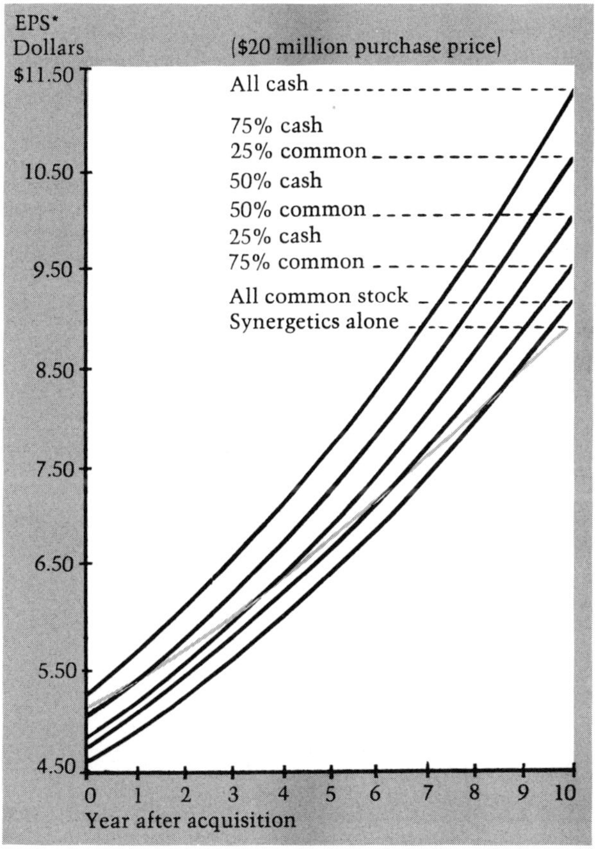

*Assumes (a) Synergetics' EPS growth, 6%, and HFE EPS growth, 12%; (b) 8% interest expense on cash portion; and (c) no goodwill amortization.

acquisition package substantially affects the impact of the acquisition on Synergetics' earnings per share. Assuming that the 12% projected growth rate for HFE is most likely, paying about 50% of a $20 million purchase price in cash will produce neither dilution nor appreciation within three years.

Exhibit V, which covers a broader range, indicates the

Exhibit V. Relationship of cash and common stock combinations at various purchase prices to year in which dilution is replaced by appreciation

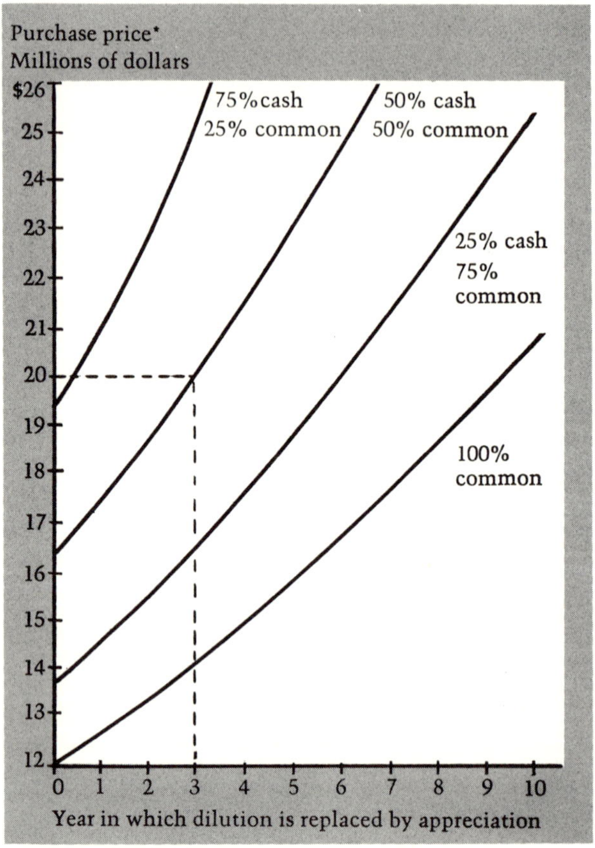

*Assumes (a) Synergetics' EPS growth, 6%, and HFE EPS growth, 12%; (b) 8% interest expense on cash portion; and (c) no goodwill amortization.

various purchase prices and the various mixes of cash and common stock that could result in earnings per share appreciation after the third year. This exhibit shows that if Synergetics wants to keep the cash input of the package below 50% for tax purposes, then its offer cannot go above $20 million.

Exhibit VI illustrates a similar family of curves, developed

Exhibit VI. Relationship of preferred stock and cash combinations at various purchase prices to year in which dilution is replaced by appreciation

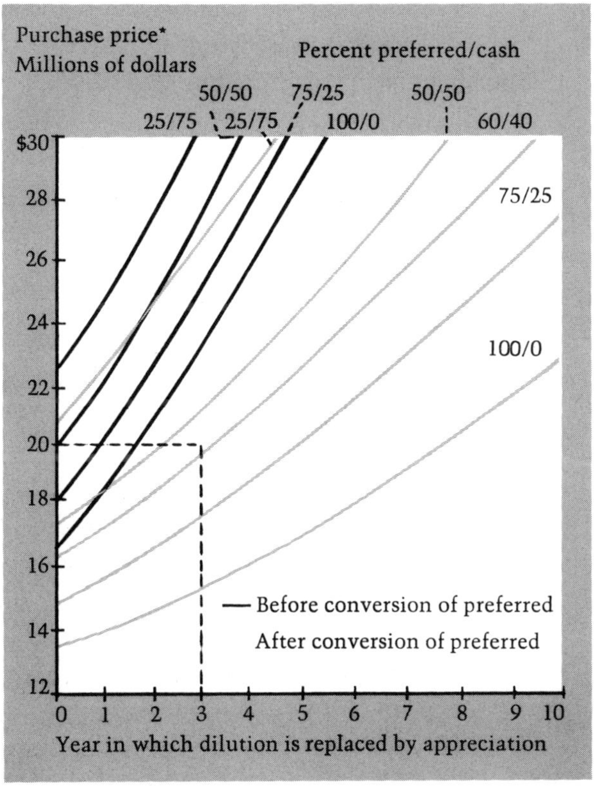

*Assumes (a) Synergetics' EPS growth, 6%, and HFE EPS growth, 12%; (b) 8% before-tax interest expense on cash portion; (c) no goodwill amortization; and (d) terms of preferred: 6% yield, priced 10% over underlying conversion value.

to show the results of various combinations of cash and preferred stock. Given a $20 million purchase price of 40% cash and 60% convertible preferred, EPS appreciation will begin in the fourth year, after conversion of the preferred.

By this time, Synergetics' management realizes that it must use a fairly high percentage of cash and/or preferred stock to effect a deal that meets its criteria for acquisitions. During the negotiations ahead, the charts will help its team to move quickly from discussion of one financial instrument and one purchase price to an alternative, keeping a clear view of what the effect of each would be on corporate objectives.

Since HFE is a closely held company, the degree of control that HFE shareholders can exert after the transaction becomes especially important. Hence the natural question for Synergetics' management is:

What combinations of cash and stock would give HFE shareholders too much control of Synergetics and at what purchase price would this occur?

Exhibit VII illustrates how Synergetics improves its own control as the purchase price is reduced and the percentage of cash or of preferred stock in the package is increased. This is the only exhibit of the series which Synergetics' management would do well to keep to itself.

As we shall subsequently see in the final section of this article, *Exhibits I* through *VI* can—and should—be shown to HFE's management when discussion of the financial terms begins. Actual experience has shown that charts such as these become a useful negotiating tool which help to guide both parties toward a reasonable and satisfactory agreement.

Having established the basic financial relationships which underlie the acquisition, Synergetics' management must now turn its attention to other aspects of the coming discussions, with an eye toward the errors that so often result in unsuccessful negotiations.

Exhibit VII. Relationship of cash, common, and preferred stock combinations and various purchase prices to degree of ownership by former HFE shareholders

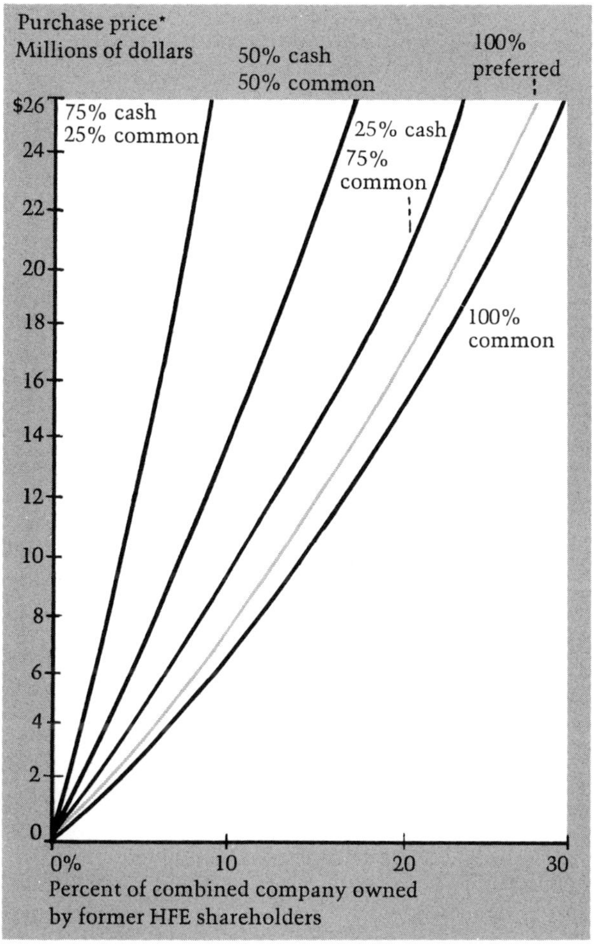

*Assumes preferred stock is priced 10% over conversion value.

It is not unusual to see a would-be buyer approach a company he knows is for sale—often with his investment banker in tow—and devote most of his time to discussing purchase prices, terms, and the financial advantages that selling shareholders can expect. By doing this, he implicitly overlooks a major fact of life in today's merger-conscious business world: any attractive company known to be interested in selling (and most that are not interested) will have four or five—perhaps even dozens—of offers. Most of these will be reasonably attractive financially, with several offering to exchange securities which promise comparably attractive growth prospects.

In a situation like this, the prize often goes to the company that can offer the seller something more than money: a sound future for the business to which he has devoted years of hard work and personal commitment.

Both owners and managers of a selling company are normally extremely concerned about the future of their enterprise, *whether or not they retain a continuing stock interest.* Even if management does not hold substantial shares, the owners will feel a personal obligation to their employees, and will usually want their support in any merger or sale.

In most cases, the buying company itself will hope to keep on the acquired company's management after the deal is closed. The would-be buyer who can arouse the seller's interest in the nonfinancial aspects of the acquisition has won an advantage that sets his company apart from the crowd of aspirants. This entails considerable work even before the negotiations commence.

To begin with, management of the acquiring company should gain a thorough understanding of the seller's business and industry. Elementary as this point may seem, executives of a would-be purchaser often enter negotiations armed with only the sketchiest knowledge of conditions in the business their company is seeking to enter. In such cases, it is not unusual for the seller to call off discussions before they really gets started.

Once the negotiatiors have familiarized themselves with the selling company's background, they must work out a streategy to activate the seller's strong, though sometimes latent, interest in the nonfinancial aspects of the merger. They key tasks at this point are:

———To identify, and then communicate, specific business advantages from which the selling company can benefit after the acquisition.

———To map out a thoughtful and stimulating growth plan for the new combined enterprise.

———To develop sound and continuing personal relationships.

Each of these factors will vary in importance according to the situation, but all of them should be completely thought through during the initial planning for negotiations and refined as discussions progress.

There is no "cookbook" approach to help the buyer spot business advantages that will interest the selling company. The characteristics of the selling company itself and of the field in which it operates are all-important. For example, a highly fragmented industry in which there are numerous single-product manufacturers serving the same market offers the chance to present telling sales economies.

Industries and companies that have been historically slow in adopting new technologies present another example, if the would-be buyer has advanced technology which the seller could not economically develop on its own.

These are two examples of the business advantages a buying company should seek to develop. The essential thing to remember is that in most good companies top management is vitally interested in such goals as improving competitive position, capitalizing on new market opportunities, and investigating other major growth possibilities. A merger is likely to make substantially more sense to these men, regardless of purchase price, if it means they can achieve one or more of their primary objectives.

In each case, executives of the buying company should do their homework, thoroughly exploring the advantages they can offer, and then, early in the negotiations, begin to work with the potential seller to determine their value. Discussing such opportunities in itself helps to form a strong link between the two companies during the period when they are getting to know one another.

Before negotiations begin, management of the buying company should develop a preliminary growth plan for the new, combined enterprise based on careful research into the seller's business and industry. Nothing will cause the selling company to lose interest faster than a naive, superficial growth plan that overlooks important industry factors.

What should be presented—again, early in the negotiations—is a thoughtful, fact-founded plan, in writing, which is considered a *preliminary* suggestion. Executives of the acquisition candidate should be asked to contribute their ideas. Participation in further development of the plan will strengthen their interest in seeing that the negotiations succeed. A combined growth plan might include:

1. *A statement of corporate goals for the new enterprise*—to convince the seller that the combined company is really going to move ahead and achieve something that would not be possible for either company alone. (As these goals are considered, the discussion focuses on the months and years ahead. Small current differences in specific financial terms then tend to become less important.)
2. *A joint marketing program*—to capitalize on existing economic trends. (The emphasis should be on using

the combined resources, financial and otherwise, of the two companies.)

3. *A tentative program for further acquisitions in the same or allied fields*—to utilize the selling company as the building block.
4. *A thoughtful organization philosophy*—to include the reporting relationship of the selling company, compensation arrangements for its top executives, employment contracts, and director representation.

The acquiring company's management should think through these organizational questions prior to the negotiations and raise them early in the sessions. They are matters of great concern to the selling company's owners and managers, but are often awkward for them to bring up without appearing more interested in the acquisition than they would like to admit.

An exciting growth plan demonstrates the potential for increased earnings per share and the creation of added value. This is particularly meaningful where an exchange of stock is contemplated. Equally significant, in almost all cases, the plan can offer a more stimulating environment and broader horizons to the sellers' executives.

Advancing an explicit growth plan can be especially important when the company in question is "not for sale" and therefore no financial pressures can be applied. In such a case, an imaginative, strong growth plan may be the *only* reason for it even to consider a merger.

Even when all business interests interlock and the financial terms are acceptable, a surprising number of acquisitions fail to mature because the buying company overlooks the importance of the "personal touch." Particularly when large corporations are involved, it is easy to think that the financial terms, the compelling logic of a sound plan, and the business advantages are all that count. Yet there are enough examples from recent years when the success or failure of the negotiations depended on personal relationships for even the most rigidly analytical manager to take them into account.

Not surprisingly, the chief executive officer of the acquiring company plays the most vital role in developing effective personal contact with the seller. Many people who own, or who are in a position to influence the sale of, a company are already independently wealthy. A feeling for "their kind of people" can be the determining factor when they come to decide on a long-term relationship.

It is particularly important that the acquiring company's chief executive officer participates in the initial discussions and maintains close contact with the principals as the negotiations proceed, not only to demonstrate his sincere intentions but also to offer concrete evidence of the seller's importance to the buying company's plans. For example:

Not long ago, a senior vice president and director of a large West Coast company approached the president and chief executive officer of an East Coast capital goods manufacturer. The aspiring buyer's vice president was startled when the president of the company he had contacted failed to return his phone calls; surely the president of the acquisition candidate had an obligation to shareholders to consider any offers made in good faith. Serious discussions never began, and communications between the two companies were both rare and unusually awkward.

Several months later, through an investment banker, the senior vice president discovered that the president of the East Coast company had, in fact, been talking about selling with a number of other large corporations. Why had he spurned the advances of the West Coast company? In his own words,

"If the chairman or the president does not think it worth his while to come and talk to me, then I can't see any future in our trying to work together."

If discussions between the companies take place in large, formal sessions with a rigid agenda, it is impossible to develop any kind of personal rapport. Informal contacts should be encouraged—even though they may involve nothing more profound than a common interest in fresh-water fishing.

Once negotiations are under way, no week should pass without some casual discussion—by phone or in person—between the two chief executive officers. This regular contact can act as a sort of safety valve which prevents misunderstandings from building up to the point where a serious disruption in negotiations could occur. Although this strategy may seem obvious, it is frequently overlooked and serious misunderstandings often develop during the long, silent periods.

Although the chief executive officer of the acquiring company should keep in close touch with his counterpart, this does not mean that another competent senior executive cannot take over the major role in actual negotiations. What is important is that the seller feel free to contact the buyer's chief executive officer as often as he pleases. It is also vital that the senior executive in charge of day-to-day talks be given adequate authority, since nothing can cool negotiations more quickly than to send a representative who must continually obtain his chief executive officer's approval before he makes a commitment.

By the time discussions begin to evolve into true negotiations, there should be an atmosphere of warm goodwill between the executives of the buying and selling companies. The problem then is to be able to resolve financial terms in a way that allows the economic considerations to be communicated without diminishing this goodwill.

It is at this point that charts such as those used to illustrate the Synergetics-HFE case history (Exhibits I through VI) can be shown to the seller and become effective negotiating tools. The buyer can use them to elicit initial reactions without actually proposing a price, knowing that they are concrete evidence of the acquiring company's thoughtful approach to the future. As such, they inspire a sense of respect for management's preparation and thoroughness.

The acquisition prospect can readily accept the logic of the buyer's need to obtain a return on investment equivalent to its target rate. The desire to avoid earnings dilution is equally understandable. In thus introducing a discussion of such basic financial relationships at an early stage in the talks, the acquiring company tends to appeal to the candidate's common sense and good judgment. In this way, the discussions can be based on objective considerations, and emotions cannot so easily enter.

Perhaps even more important—as actual experience has shown—is that by demonstrating clearly the financial relationships, and thus "opening the book" to the candidate, the acquiring company creates a feeling of mutual trust and understanding. Again, the focus is on the future and on the success of the new, combined enterprise which, by now, both the buying company and the seller can begin to see as a reality.

Behind the confusion that has grown up around the term "disclosure," there is a common-sense intent. The author, formerly chief communications officer for Litton Industries and currently head of his own financial public relations firm, suggests that a common-sense approach will readily solve whatever problems disclosure may seem to entail.

19

DISCLOSURE: A COMMON-SENSE APPROACH

by Crosby M. Kelly, President,
Crosby M. Kelly Associates, Ltd.

Anyone who devotes any time at all to pondering the ways and means of communication—and this covers a growing portion of mankind—must eventually concede the almighty power of a cliché whose time has come.

In the acquisition world, the time came—and happily in some cases is waning—for terms such as functional interface, multiform managements, complementary capabilities.

Another term which runs the danger of falling into the cliché well, and which I would like for the next few pages to rescue and examine more closely is "disclosure."

Clichés tend, by nature, to be monolithic. I would like to suggest that disclosure—the concept as well as the act—is far from monolithic. It involves obligations, but also opportunities; duress of sorts, but desirability as well.

Let's go back just a little bit. The recent cases in the last few years which have involved the word disclosure may have tended to panic a lot of people. They may even have caused many good firms to refuse to talk with anybody, because they were fearful of their liabilities regarding "disclosure." Some of those cases really found their substance, their excuse for being, in the Securities and Exchange Commission regulations.

THE INTENT OF DISCLOSURE

The SEC regulations go back first to the Securities Act of 1933, and then to the following Act of 1934, and then to the revision of the Act in 1964, and that is where "disclosure" came from. If we look at those acts in their entirety, we find that the meaning behind the law, the intent behind the law, was not in the negative sense of disclosure, but in the positive context of dissemination of information. The law intended to put all the horses in the gate evenly weighted and then to pull up the gate to let them all start to race at the same time. The horses in this instance being the stock owning public. The basic reason for the existence of the Securities Act was to give stockholders of all levels of sophistication an even chance at the information that would contribute to their decision-making.

In this respect, the Securities Acts and subsequent rules and regulations were really "communications" acts. It was a news dissemination act. It was an act about information which of course contained some sophisticated clauses, because it had to deal with sophisticated situations. Being law, it was written in legalese, and it became a little complicated at some points. Also, as time passed, it developed a few teeth. Opinions had to be rendered regarding the law, and so it became more and more complex. But in truth, the fundamental thought was that the lawmakers wanted to see to it that adequate news or adequate information is disseminated about a company before a company can take money away from innocent people.

That is the idea. It isn't an attempt to block the dissemination of the news. It isn't an attempt to withdraw from disclosure. And if one does not yield to indignation or panic, there is a lot of common sense in what all the authorities are saying about disclosure.

POSITIVE AND NEGATIVE ATTITUDES

Some companies will continue to take the attitude, "No, we won't talk to anyone." Others are saying, "We have an open door. We'll talk."

I think the distinction is not so much in intent as it is in execution. The trick, or the technique, lies in the discriminating character of the talking. Companies, if they are smart, are not confining their talking to their own, or what is generally called insiders. They are not just sharing among "the boys" the fact that they discovered oil in the North Slope, and letting all the boys feather the nest before they tell anybody else. They are simply recognizing that at this point in time, this is inside information, and it must be treated as inside information, and that insiders had better comport themselves as they ought to, with a sense of responsibility to the stockholders.

WHAT—AND HOW—TO DISCLOSE

There is no great mystery about *what* you would disclose in terms of a press release, but I think there is a judgment factor there. In my own mind, and I've not had this disputed, I have believed that if I honestly felt a given piece of information could affect a buy, sell or hold decision regarding the securities of a company, I ought to release that information and hopefully, simultaneously, so that everybody has an even chance at it. Actually, the news-release duty begins when there's a risk of leaks. Corporate needs may easily take priority until this leakage risk exists.

If you disclose what in your best judgment you think would materially influence a security buy, sell or hold decision and you distribute it impartially to everybody, you have little to worry about. It is when you go from insider information to that broad disclosure that the problems come in.

Other than that, it just isn't all that difficult, even in registration periods. I have known a number of companies that have said they would not appear before the analysts society because they were in registration, even though they made the date six months ago. In itself, that is not a valid reason to cancel; there is nothing that says you can't appear before an analysts society even though you are in registration. Being in registration simply limits you to discussing reported history plus the facts that are in the registration statement, which, of course, might reduce the interest level, for lack of news, of the presentation. Similarly, when in registration, continue to get out your press releases. Of course, do it fairly with everybody.

If somebody asks you a question, answer it with this one thought in mind: that you would be willing to, and you would, and you would intend to, answer it the same way for any other person that might ask you. If no one else bothers to ask you, you are in the clear because they didn't ask you. If you are fearful because you don't want to write 27 pages in a press release or stockholders letter to tell them everything, every nut and bolt item in every division of the company, that is all right, don't. Nobody is going to read it anyway. It isn't material, and certainly the press isn't going to print it.

But, if somebody asks you a question, answer it. If you feel that it wouldn't affect you negatively from a competitive standpoint or if it isn't military security consideration or it isn't insider information still unreleased, answer it and you are in no trouble.

LAWYERS AND DISCLOSURE

I would caution you always, if the area of disclosure pertains to mergers and acquisitions, to consult your legal counsel with your own reservations. He may often be inclined to tell you what you cannot do. That is fine, but also he will tend to protect himself and save himself potential trouble by suggesting that if you don't do anything, you can't get in too much trouble. It is at that stage that he and I part company.

I do not believe silence is golden in the world of communications; when in doubt, I am inclined to communicate. I am more inclined to say, "Mr. Lawyer, prove to me that I am going to get into trouble by doing this. When my heart is in the right place and my intentions are good, prove to me that I am going to damage somebody and that there is legal liability by my communicating." When in doubt, communicate. The lawyer may well say, when in doubt, don't communicate. How can you get in trouble not doing anything? As a matter of fact, it's often easier to get into trouble by *not* talking than by talking.

DISCLOSURE AS OPPORTUNITY

Laying aside that cliché of disclosure which I think is a big ogre, I would like to suggest that you look at the *opportunities* involved in news dissemination—in the sharing of information at the time of merger and acquisition, or during the course of a merger or acquisition.

There is the opportunity, for example, to protect yourself against competitive buyers by a well-thought-out communication policy and program. There is the opportunity to communicate with the stockholders of the firm you are buying, to add them to your stockholder body and add that much more public opinion on your side. There is the opportunity to communicate with your own stockholders—to have them more enthusiastic about your company; the opportunity through proper and adequate communication to have impact on a Government regulatory body and their decisions, opinions, attitudes about your merger and acquisition.

I do not suggest that in all these instances wholesale, broadside communications will help. A program must be reasoned out and used with skill and discretion. It will include the opportunity to do a lot with your employees—yours and those of the company to be acquired.

You have not only an opportunity but a responsibility here. The management of your company is wondering how much more competition there is going to be for their jobs.

You are going to have two controllers. Who is going to survive? And the other management says, "It was great when we used to work for our boss, but now, you know, we are going to be working for another outfit. Who is going to be our boss and how do we know it will work out?"

WHEN TO DISCLOSE

There are all kinds of opportunities to get added values from the act of merger and acquisition by proper dissemination of news and information during the procedures of merger and acquisition. When I say "during the procedures," let me arbitrarily divide a merger and acquisition activity into six stages.

1. The very preliminary discussions that might be held between the president of your firm and the president of the other firm.
2. The serious yet personal and informal discussions between two presidents; the time when they and/or other company representatives actually negotiate toward the writing of some sort of a contract.
3. The signing of that contract.
4. The period between that signing and the closing.
5. The closing.
6. The post-closing period.

Before discussing what to do in these various stages and in regard to various audiences, it is helpful to take a look at what is the news, or as a journalist might say, what is the news peg. What is it in the action that is news or that is new information?

One has to match content with audience, because a customer is going to see this merger/acquisition through one pair of glasses; employees through another, management through another; the government through another. Each audience is going to see things differently, and you are going to want to describe or disseminate news in a different language to these different people at different times.

In essence, a sort of guideline thought might be to try to answer for everybody whenever you can his constant human question, "What does it mean to me?," or in many instances, "What's in it for me?" If you can have that frame of mind as you address yourself to these various audiences, it can be helpful. "Well, what's in it for me?" is answered by this kind of information:

1. For a number of people there will be an interest in information of a financial character—the details as they affect each stockholder. Are the earnings on his stock going to be diluted or the opposite, appreciated? This often pertains to management and employees of both companies. It pertains to the analyst and the banking world. It pertains to the commercial bankers. What are the financial aspects of the deal as it goes along?
   The more you withhold in that regard, the greater you expose yourself to the risk of false and unjustified conclusions. Sooner or later the details will come out, and you may be in trouble if, for lack of accurate details, someone made a wrong, and financially significant decision.
2. Another kind of information that you may want to look at would be plans for the future—because when they ask, "What's in it for me?", employees, management, customers, financial people are gen-

erally thinking of tomorrow. By tomorrow, I may mean Friday, the fifth day of December or I may mean next year or the year after, but plans for the future give you an opportunity for getting out good news and being meaningful.

There are the short-term plans for the integration of the two entities, if you are bringing them together, or for the management structures if you are leaving them apart. In the immediate sense of the word, questions need to be answered as to the plan for the management of the new company and the policies of that company, the insurance programs of that company, the annual bonuses and whatever else is it that people are concerned about. What is going to happen short-term?

Secondly, comes the question what is going to happen long-term? Is the merging of these two going to provide for the new entity, a greater financial plan, or a greater credit line? Is there going to be an integration in products, in markets, in services? What about the long-term opportunities?

This re-introduces our friendly cliché, "synergy." Are you going to have synergy in manufacturing capabilities? Are you going to make greater plant utilizations or are you going to add manufacturing skills by virtue of these two merging? In the product area, will you be broadening a product line? In marketing, will you be economizing or expanding the marketing capability of both firms? In outside services, will you be able to tap greater talent in advertising, legal counsel, and all kinds of specialized services by virtue of the larger entity?

Much newsworthy information is generated in the course of merger and acquisition negotiations and procedures.

I think generally, to be consistent with the spirit of disclosure, we have to say that when boss meets boss, or when two principals first talk, or when the finder first makes his overture, there really is not much to talk about and chances are that the rumor channels would elaborate undesirably on premature, inconclusive information.

REACTING TO RUMORS

I do not think that when we are only *thinking* of talking seriously with somebody else, it is quite news. But I think we have to be prepared, even at that stage, for rumors to start. One point which the New York Stock Exchange does state very clearly, is the need to come out with some kind of a statement to put to rest rumors if they appear with impact on stock trading.

You can be just as guilty of bad communications if you let an untruth persist—just as guilty as if you fail to tell the truth.

When serious discussions begin between the parties, I think one has to give some serious consideration to how tight the insider control is. Currently, an insider has been interpreted as being anybody who is privy to inside information, that does not mean that he must be an employee of the company. In fact, recent interpretations are that if someone gets this news from an insider and is aware that his source is an insider, he has himself *ipso facto* become an insider to the extent of that knowledge.

If you are an officer of the company and you go home and talk to your next-door neighbor, your next-door neighbor has a legal responsibility and liability. He is an insider. So is your secretary and anyone she may confide in. In this great day of affluence, with over 30 million people—approximately one out of every seven men, women and children in the United States of America—owning publicly-held securities, we have a lot of secretaries who own stock.

It is important that you know how tight your insider controls are. Chances are you have rules, established by the company as to how employees will comport themselves as insiders; but when those serious discussions start, it is a good idea to look at your insider network and see if there is any risk.

During the negotiation stage, one reaches the point where he had better start talking because the insider network can no longer be controlled. Outside counsel, tax advisor, accounting firms, and others are involved and are insiders. They have secretaries, and they ride in public elevators. Therefore, at the negotiation stage one should start thinking about releasing information.

A SOPHISTICATED AUDIENCE

One of the great common concerns is that people say, "Yes, but if I announce the word that we are negotiating with a company and are working towards an agreement then if we don't get an agreement, won't I have mud in my face when I say we broke off the negotiations?" I don't think so. I ascribe much more intelligence to the reading audience, particularly the reading audience that might be among your stockholders, customers and the financial community at large. Of course, the issuing company must be very sure the wording is plain as to where things stand.

They know there are negotiations going on all the time. Anybody that has ever sold anything knows he doesn't make 100% of the sales he attempts. He negotiates and sometimes he sells, and sometimes he doesn't. I do not think there is anything disgraceful about losing a sale, or that you can be considered touting if you make an announcement. Hopefully, you try to develop a good batting average. On the other hand if you announce negotiations frequently and every one of them fails, you had better look at your negotiating strategy, not your communication policy.

As to specific techniques, I question whether there should ever be a press release that is written, approved by management and released in only one version. If you have two plants, one in Rockford, and one in Springfield, Illinois, you ought to have one make some mention of Rockford and the other one make some mention of Springfield. How many times do we labor over press releases, get the lawyer's approval, the financial department's approval, this department's and that department's approval only to emerge with a release which is such a compromise that isn't *really* meaningful to anybody. It isn't what you want to tell your customers, and it isn't the way you want to put it to other people. I seldom have found —I say seldom only to hedge, I don't know that I have ever found—a case where one version of the press release would truly serve all the communicating opportunities that are there. The facts are the same, of course, but the areas of self-interest are not. Therefore, they cannot be served by an omnibus version.

What I have tried to suggest is that disclosure, far from being some alien concept rammed down the throat of the business community by inherently hostile forces, merely involves the communications aspects of the over-all business of managing an enterprise. It has its special aspects, but so do accounting, corporate law, personnel administration and the design and construction of a new manufacturing plant or an adveritising campaign.

All these activities—considered "normal" business practices—deserve and receive proper planning, programming, supervision and evaluation. "Disclosure" deserves the same, and can pay back in ways which are both intangible and tangible.

Furthermore, there is a positive aspect to disclosure as part of a company's continuing relationship with the financial community. The author, who was himself an analyst and portfolio manager before starting a financial relations firm, suggests specific ways in which these positive aspects can be realized.

20

DISCLOSURE: A POSITIVE APPROACH

by John P. Kehoe, President,
Shareholder Perspectives, Inc.

Any fairly constant reader of business pages must have been struck, during the past year or so, by a recurring phenomenon.

In news stories and announcements about mergers and acquisitions, terminations seem to be running about three to one in relation to closings.

There are undoubtedly many reasons for this unhappy ratio. The action of the stock market itself does not, however, seem to be one of them. A tabulation made in October, 1968, showed the ratio to be two and one half to one in favor of cancellations. And the *total* number of "Company X and Y announced jointly today that they had broken off negotiations . . ." stories in 1968 was almost double that in 1967.

In view of this time-table, there seems good reason to suggest that one of the major causes for the increase in "no-go" decisions is simply extreme caution on the part of companies, and their legal counsel, in handling the disclosure problem.

TOO MUCH DISCLOSURE?

It almost seems as if the word has spread from board room to board room and law library to law library: "When in doubt, talk." If there is any chance that even a casual conversation or a tentative feeler between two companies may possibly some day result in the chance of a merger, let's tell the world fast.

I don't think this makes much sense for business as a whole, nor for individual companies. Furthermore, I would hazard the thought that this kind of wholesale public airing was not what the regulatory agencies had in mind when they began circling in on the problem of disclosure.

The desire of legal counsel to be cautious is completely

understandable. It is hard to get into trouble by being over-cautious, especially in a period of uncertainty. And, not to take anything away from counsel, their principal concern, generally, is to keep their clients out of trouble.

However, it is possible that the mass effect of over-caution has been to confuse the investor, to say nothing of the potential buyer or seller. If most deals seem to be falling through, there must be something wrong somewhere. Perhaps the whole concept of acquisitions has had it, and we may as well look to other business strategies.

This conclusion is, of course, unfounded,—and unintended.

The New York Stock Exchange statement on disclosure in matters of mergers and acquisitions reads as follows:

"Where it is possible to confine formal or informal discussions to a small group of the top management of the company or companies involved and their individual confidential advisors, where adequate security can be maintained, premature public announcements may be properly avoided.

"In this regard, the market action of a company's securities should be closely watched at a time when consideration is being given to important corporate matters. If unusual market activity should arise, the company should be prepared to make an immediate public announcement of the matter."

"INSIDERS" AND "OUTSIDERS"

The policy statement goes on to point out that at some time it usually becomes necessary to involve other persons in the conduct of preliminary studies or to assist in other preparations for contemplated transactions. These preparations may, typically, include: business appraisals, tentative financial arrangements, attitude of large outside holders, availability of major blocks of stock, engineering studies, market analyses and surveys.

The Exchange's experience has shown that maintaining security in the face of this kind of activity is virtually impossible. Accordingly, it states that fairness requires that the company make an immediate public announcement as soon as confidential disclosures relating to such important matters are made to any outsiders.

There can be no reasonable quarrel with the Exchange's position. Merger negotiations *are* material information to a reasonable investor, and he is, therefore, under the doctorine of fairness entitled to have access to that information.

The operative word in the Exchange's statement, however, is "outsiders," and the safest way to define it is by exception.

Outsiders are those persons other than corporate officers and directors, legal counsel, investment bankers and other counsel who are willing to adopt an insider attitude toward confidential information, and be bound by the rule governing insiders' behavior.

This rule is clear enough: information received by insiders is not to be used to their own advantage or to that of a select group or groups, and therefore to the disadvantage of the investing public at large in the marketplace.

The Texas Gulf Sulfur, Merrill Lynch and other recent cases may have dramatized the significance and intent of the law, but it did not change it. In 1934, the Senate Committee of Banking and Currency made the following observation in its report on stock exchange practices:

> "It is universally conceded that adequate information as to the financial structure and condition of a corporation is indispensible to an intelligent determination of the

quality of its securities. The concept of a free and open market for securities necessarily implies that the buyer and the seller are acting in the exercise of enlightened judgement as to what constitutes a fair price. Insofar as the judgement is warped by false, inaccurate or incomplete information regarding the corporation, the market price fails to reflect the normal operation of supply and demand. One of the prime concerns of the exchanges should be to make available to the public honest, complete and accurate information regarding the securities listed."

A PRACTICAL APPROACH

This paragraph can still stand as a fair statement of the philosophic, or moral, spirit behind the theory of full disclosure. Its intent is not hard to perceive. In practice, however, doubts may arise.

Some of them were voiced during a recent conference of the Financial Analysts Federation. The guest speaker was Philip A. Loomis, Jr., general counsel of the Securities and Exchange Commission, and this was one of the questions put to him:

"Announcements of merger discussions between Company A and a privately owned company for an undisclosed amount of stock are being made with increasing frequency. At what point is it incumbent on the company to make such information available publicly?"

In other words, when do we disclose? This was Mr. Loomis's reply:

"I think that when a proposed acquisition reaches a stage where it is fairly definite, the company would be called on by the Stock Exchange to make some sort of announcement.

"In any event, insiders might be prohibited from trading on the basis of their knowledge that this is going to be what the deal is going to be. We—meaning the SEC— have a case pending in the District Court which raises precisely this point.

"On the other hand, just to make life difficult for all of us, there are some companies which like to stir up a little excitement by announcing a contemplated acquisition which somehow never occurs. It is not an easy question and really requires an analysis of the facts in each case."

Surely, at a distance of 35 years, this statement underlines the original spirit of compliance which guided the framers of the still-existing legislation.

Recent SEC and court opinions have broadened the technical definition of "insiders" to include anyone at all who hears confidential information from someone else who, to his best knowledge, received that information directly from the company.

This has become one of the perplexing aspects of the whole problem. It leaves a burden of proof on someone—and it is not yet clear just on whom—that trading done on the basis of a rumor was or was not insider trading. This would depend not only on the source of the rumor, but also on the route by which the rumor reached the trader. And, further, it would depend on whether the trader did or did not believe that the information was indeed first-hand.

A man overhearing two secretaries chatting in an elevator; a waiter or shoe-shine boy; a type-setter evincing more than cursory interest in a piece of copy; anyone of them could be an insider. And so could their mothers, fathers, girl friends, golfing companions and conceivably even psychiatrists. Given the natural communicativeness of the human animal, the list is endless.

Dogged diligence in disclosure would therefore create a new Babel, to say nothing of hopelessly drowning all available financial news media.

A NEED FOR GUIDELINES

Some sort of guidelines are needed. Based on experience on both ends of the news ticker, I would like to suggest the following. They are designed to comply with both the recent decision of the Court of Appeals for the Second Circuit in the Texas Gulf Sulphur case, and the recent suggestions proposed by the New York Stock Exchange. Companies not listed on that exchange are, of course, not bound by these proposals, but they nevertheless suggest an intelligent approach to the problem of timing significant news releases.

These are the guidelines:

1. Both the NYSE proposals and the *Texas Gulf Sulphur* decision emphasize the importance of promptly making public announcements of material developments, if feasible and practicable from a business point of view and not adverse to the interests of the company.
2. Both the NYSE proposals and the *Texas Gulf Sulphur* decision, however, recognize that business reasons might necessitate the withholding of a public announcement for reasonable periods of time. Indeed, a premature announcement can prove to be as misleading and troublesome as an overly delayed announcement. If material information is being kept confidential:

   (a) the confidential matter, to the extent possible should be confined to small groups of top management personnel and their confidential advisers. Lower echelon personnel should be brought into confidence only to the extent absolutely necessary. Further, the fact that the particular information is confidential and non-public should be made explicit;

(b) if sources outside the company, e.g. bankers, financial and technical advisers, underwriters, etc. are advised of the confidential matter, it should be recognized that continued secrecy becomes increasingly difficult and the necessity of a public announcement becomes more acute;

(c) the company should be alert to unusual market fluctuations in the value of its stock and to the possibility of rumors. If either rumors or unusual market activity is perceived, the company should be prepared to make an immediate public announcement;

(d) the company should not issue any press release or other public announcement which in any way relates to the confidential matter *or* which could in any way be deemed false or misleading in light of the withheld information;

(e) all persons having knowledge of the confidential matter including officers, directors and employees of the company, as well as any outsiders (including members of the immediate family of the foregoing) should be advised neither to purchase or sell stock of the company, including puts, calls and warrants, nor accept stock options of the company if granted by a committee that may not be advised of the development; and

(f) all persons having knowledge of the confidential matter should be advised to maintain complete secrecy. Disclosure of the confidential information to anyone could result in liability to the person releasing the information as well as to the company.

3. The decision in the *Texas Gulf Sulphur* case has defined a material development as one "which in reasonable and objective contemplation might affect the value of the corporation's stocks or securities." While this general definition cannot be easily applied in all situations, it is reasonably likely that, as suggested by the NYSE, the following would be material developments:
   (a) negotiations leading to acquisitions and mergers;
   (b) stock splits or unscheduled stock dividends;
   (c) arrangements preparatory for an exchange or a tender offer either by the company for the stock of another company or by another company for the stock of the company;
   (d) changes in the rate of dividends or earnings;
   (e) calls for redemption; and
   (f) significant new contracts, products or discoveries.
4. Other examples of corporate developments which might be considered material would include:
   (a) arrangements to sell off substantial portions of the assets of the corporation;
   (b) discovery of the fact that certain inventories had a substantially greater value than that carried on the books of the corporation;
   (c) plans to purchase substantial quantities of the company's stock;
   (d) knowledge of pending or threatened adverse civil litigation or government investigations or dis-

position of substantial existing favorable or adverse litigation; and

(e) major management changes.

5. If the material confidential information relates to or involves another public company, the officers, directors and employees of the company and other persons who are privy to the confidential information should not purchase, sell or deal in the securities of that other company and the persons having knowledge of the material confidential matter would be under a duty to maintain secrecy to the same extent as if the development related solely to their own company.
6. When a decision is made to make a public announcement concerning a material development, the announcement should be made on an Immediate Release basis. To the extent possible, the release should be factual, concise and definite as to price, ratio, timing and/or any other pertinent information necessary to permit a reasonable evaluation of the matter. The draftsman should be careful to exercise reasonable business judgment under the circumstances in writing a release based on the facts as known at the time. It is also incumbent upon the draftsman to exercise "due diligence" in ascertaining the truth of the facts contained in the release. When the initial announcement cannot be specific or complete, the need for additional supplementary announcements when and as more definite or different information is available should be kept in mind. Projections of the future, whether of financial data or of prospective operations, should be soundly based, appropriately qualified, conservative and factual. On the other hand, excessive or misleading conservatism should likewise be

avoided. If subsequent developments should indicate that performance will not match earlier projections, an explanatory announcement will be appropriate. In short, the announcement should be made in proper perspective and should be with appropriate restraint and good judgment with careful adherence to the facts.

7. The following procedure should be followed in making public announcements:

   (a) if the announcement is made shortly before the opening of or during normal trading hours, i.e., between 10 A.M. and 3:30 P.M. New York time, consideration should be given to notifying Stock Exchange officials of the Exchange on which the company's stock is listed, if any, by telephone no later than simultaneously with the release of the announcement to the news media;

   (b) the announcement should be made by the fastest available means; by telephone, telegraph or hand delivery to the national news wire services normally used for company announcements, as well as to the local newspapers normally used by the company; and

   (c) consideration should be given to providing the name and telephone number of a selected company official who will be available to answer appropriate inquiries.

8. The *Texas Gulf Sulphur* decision makes it clear that the insiders of a company are not free to commence trading immediately upon release of a confidential matter to the public. Rather, there must be a reasonable delay in order for the announcement to be distributed to the news media and digested by the investing public. What constitutes a reasonable delay depends upon the circumstances, particularly

the complexity of the announcement. A 24-hour delay, under most circumstances, should be adequate.

9. The NYSE has recommended that public companies whose stocks are listed on its Exchange maintain "an open-door policy" with respect to granting interviews to security analysts, financial underwriters, share owners and others who have a legitimate interest in the company's affairs. In this regard, however, a company should not provide information to one party which it would not make available to the public or to another inquirer. During such interviews a company should avoid giving advance information. If, during an interview, non-public information is made available an immediate public announcement of that information should be released. If the company is about to register or is in the process of registering its securities with the Securities and Exchange Commission, different considerations apply and counsel should be consulted before any such interviews are granted.

THE QUESTION OF INTENT

So much for guidelines. Perhaps the *intention* can be clarified by two examples. The first involves a situation that did not have to do with acquisition, a client company that had come upon a loss in its operation and was advised of that possibility of loss by one of its divisions.

They immediately sent a three-man task force of the executive committee to determine the extent of the loss. Upon returning to New York they decided to make a release disclosing that they would have a loss in the quarter and estimating that the amount of that loss would be equal to 60% of the previous year's total earnings. The reasons for the loss were cryptically stated in two typewritten lines. The announcement would be a shock to the investment community since the company had actively and widely discussed improved results across the board in each of its divisions for the year.

They made a terse release, and the stock dropped about five or six points, which was about 15 or 20 percent of its value. In my opinion, had it been handled differently there was no reason for the stock to have dropped that much.

Technically, for those who follow stock charts, it put the stock in a very dangerous position of falling even further.

More important, what the company had done was to issue its release in very cryptic form, to try to comply with their understanding of the new disclosure directives. In so doing, it literally slipped a note under the door of the analysts and said, "We are losing money," and left the analyst community uninformed of details and very much ill at ease with management and its credibility.

That day we were called in, and after learning the details of the problem and monitoring Wall Street's reaction to the disclosure thus far, we arranged a meeting in New York for about 150 analysts from the New York, Boston and Philadelphia areas. The meeting was pulled together in 26 hours.

The invitation was extended by telephone and telegram. Its purpose was to permit the president to discuss the background of the loss and answer any questions posed by the analysts—just as if the information meeting had been part of the initial disclosure strategy.

Once the meeting was over, the analyst community and, through press coverage, the investing community at large, felt more comfortable with the loss. They understood what had happened. They understood it was of a non-recurring nature. Most important, by openly addressing its financial public, management regained the confidence of the investment community and reopened lines of communication that had been unnecessarily and temporarily closed off. The stock turned around and came back to the point where it was when the initial disclosure was made.

If the management had not reacted so quickly to what it regarded as a threat of disclosure, but rather had thought through how it could release this news in the fullest form possible, with all its implications, it is conceivable the stock would not have had the drop it had.

In the same vein, a lot of people who sold the stock on the basis of insufficient information might not have sold at all.

The second case involved an acquisition company in the initial stages of seeking to acquire another public company. It was necessary to bring in an outside consulting firm to evaluate the selling company's technology.

According to the New York Stock Exchange disclosure requirements, once information goes outside the family—people who don't have a continuing interest with the company—a release should be made.

Fortunately, in this case the consulting organization had been used before on several occasions. As a consequence, they could be considered insiders—a group that had a continuing relationship with the company. We did not make any release.

The technological studies came through. It was positive, and now we are proceeding with more definitive negotiations.

The company which we hope will be acquired has a very lean capitalization. If we had made an announcement at that point, disclosing that our client company was in merger negotiations with this smaller company, I don't think it is difficult to see that the stock of this company would have taken off.

Had the technological evaluation come through negatively, or indeed, had other things come through which could have broken down the merger negotiations, there probably would have been a lot of difficulty in trying to find a bottom for that stock after the first surge.

Each day people are forming attitudes toward companies, and certain of these attitudes are daily resulting in decisions being reached as to whether securities should be bought, sold or held. These decisions, positive and negative, are reflected in the trading volume and price movement of these securities.

The purpose, requirement and opportunity of corporate communications to the financial public should be to facilitate informed investment decisions on the part of present and potential shareholders. Through proper, consistent and programmed communications directly to present shareholders, and through formal and informal analyst meetings and financial press coverage, there is opportunity to help shape the attitudes that lead to investment decision. Disclosure, viewed in this light, should become an opportunity, not a problem.

Question: Can you say anything about disclosing information to company employees?

Mr. John P. Kehoe: There is a sequence to disclosure. We pointed out that officers, directors, consulting groups who have a continuing relationship with the company, are the insiders in the transaction. You would not get down to the employee level—as I understand the question—until such time as you have made a public release. I think at that point you could not hold the information.

If you start giving it to all the people in the plant, or all the people in the office, it has to be made public.

I was involved, fortunately only as an observer, in one situation where an announcement was made and just by a timing mess-up, it was released over the wire about half an hour before a meeting was to be held of the key employees to advise them that the company had been acquired. It created absolute havoc.

I think it is important that the employees be advised of the disposition before reading it in the papers, or before their broker calls them.

Question: How early would you let them know?

Mr. Kehoe: You would communicate to the employees concurrently with the announcement itself going to the *Dow Jones* or *Wall Street Journal* or to the public relations wire services. You would arrange a meeting with your key employees, and tell them what has happened. But you would not do that before you would make a public announcement.

Question: How does the seller keep his office force—bookkeeper, etc.—from knowing this when the buyer sends his accountants in to go over the books? They know there is something going on.

Mr. Kehoe: If you're talking about a very small company, but a public company, and if the bookkeeper is the man who is going to be opening up to the acquiring company, you have a potentially serious problem. If management concludes there is the possibility of a leak at that level, I believe you would have to disclose at least the fact that there are preliminary discussions going on.

If you are talking about a private company, I do not think it is that critical. They probably would not know who the fellow was to whom they were opening the books. But in terms of a public company, if an acquiring company is coming in and you are opening your books to them, I should think more logically that all the journals and whatnot would have been held up the line—given to either the executive vice president or the president to open to the buyer. I shouldn't think it would be handled at the bookkeeper level.

If, of necessity, that is the case and you are concerned that your employee is going to find out, then I think you would go back to the acquiring company to say that you feel you have a disclosure problem, that you would want an announcement made.

Question: Wouldn't a situation like that just be covered with the announcement or the leak that you just had an IRS man coming in to look at your books?

Mr. Kehoe: The idea is to keep it from getting to the point where people who could be considered insiders, the bookkeeper in this instance, having information from the company first-hand, could begin to buy and sell shares in the company which could materially affect the value of the shares of the stock.

I am certain that if someone asked a question: "Gee, what do you need the books for?" "Well, we have an IRS audit," if it could be gotten around that way, that is fine.

I am not for premature disclosure. I agree with Mr. Loomis' remarks that too often companies create an excitement by announcing initial discussions which never seem to come off. I think it is particularly damaging in terms of price structure; I think it is particularly damaging to companies being acquired, when the company makes an announcement, "We are talking."

What has been happening lately is that other firms are coming in and making competitive bids, and your company, being an interested seller with just this one, all of a sudden is known to be "on the block."

So the idea is holding back disclosure during initial discussion until the point when it is obvious that there could be a leak—as reflected either in the price of your securities or just a rumor around the plant. You wait until that time.

Index

(Figures in italics represent pages containing illustrated exhibits)

A

Accountants, use of, 251-261
Accounting rules, 255-256
Acquisitions
 accountants, use of, 251-261
 alternative methods of, 118-120
 business synergy package and, 33-38
 contact, establishing, 56-58
 contracts, preparing, 245-247
 decision-making and, 15-29
 empathy and, 7-14
 financial package and, 33, 43-47
 financial specialists and, 89-104
 graphic approach, value of, 285-286
 lawyers, use of, 235-249
 making, techniques of, 18-19
 marketing approach to, 179-190
 mergers distinguished from, 71-88
 negotiations and (*see* Negotiations)
 pension plan and, 257
 personal contact between decision-makers, 24-26
 positive orientation and, 15-29
 program of, launching a, 7-14
 proposals, oral vs. written, 60-62
 prospective, yardsticks for measuring, 284
 risks and, 17-18, 21-24, 167-178
 seller and (*see* Sellers)
 seller's management package and, 34, 38-41
 strategy development and, 21
 succeeding with, where others have failed, 31-47
 taxable, 214-215
 timing and, 147-165
Advisers, lawyers as, 239
Agreement, merger, 265
Agreement in principle, 226
Analytical Approach to Merger Negotiations (MacDougal and Malek), 281-303
Anatomy of a Successful Closing, The (Scharf), 263-279
Anti-trust problems, 240-241, 273-274
Appraisals. *See* Evaluation(s)
Appreciation, relationship to, of cash and common stock, *293;* of cash and preferred stock, *295*
Art of Making a Seller Happy, The (Salgo), 7-14
Assets, buying and, 81

B

Bankers, investment, use of, 89-104, 176-178

Bargaining
establishing price range for, 105-123, 284-285
mergers and, 77-78
Basis, taxable, 214-215
Book value, 114-115
Brokers, investment, 89-104, 176-178
Business synergy package, 33-38
Butler, Marshall, article by, 191-203
Buyer(s)
advantages, 222-225
approaching a prospective, 217-218
incentives of, 210-211
prospective, other, 219
returns, 215-216
rules for, 171-174
Buying
assets and, 81
definition of acquisition, 257
objectives of, 16-17, 259
reasons for, 51
timing and, 150-151

C

Case study, 286-303
Cash flow, seller's, analyzing, 109-112
Castle, John K., article by, 31-47
Check-lists, 16
contingency payouts, 142-145
Checkpoints, 226-230
Climate, negotiating, establishing the, 74-75, 100, 191-203
Closing
date of, setting the, 158-160
successful, anatomy of a, 263-279
Conditions, 259
Contact, personal
between decision-makers, 24-26
establishing, 56-58
Contingency payouts, 119, 125-145
Contracts, preparing, 245-247
Covenants, 259
Creating a Favorable Climate for Negotiation (Butler), 191-203

D

Day, H. Corbin, article by, 89-104
Decision-making, acquisitions and, 15-29
Details, importance of, 99
Dilution, 210-214, 290-292
replaced by appreciation, 290-293, *292*, *294*, *295*
Disclosure, 242-243
attitudes toward, 307-308
common-sense approach to (Kelly), 305-316
guidelines, 323-328
intent of, 306-307, 328
lawyers and, 309-310
positive approach to (Kehoe), 317-333
rumors, reacting to, 314-315
timing of, 311-314

E

Earnings, seller's, analyzing, 109-112; per share (EPS), 284-285, 294, 296
Effective Handling of Risk in Acquisitions (Fillion), 167-178
Effective Use of Timing in Acquisitions, The (Snyder), 147-165
Empathy, negotiations and, 7-14

EPS, *see* Earnings per share
Evaluation(s)
management, 232-234
mutual, 227
of investments, 284
of offer, 95-97
of risk, 17-18, 170-171

F

Factors, added, 225-226
Fillion, E. P., Jr., 167-178
Financial criteria, basic, 206-207
Financial package, 33
designing the, 43-47
Financial relationships, meaning of, 283-284
Financial specialists, use of, 89-104, 176-178

G

Goals, formulation of, 107
Graphic approach, value of, 285-286
Growth rate(s), impact of, on earnings, 290, *291;* purchase prices and, *292;* various HFE, *291*

H

Haskin, Warren G., article by, 235-249
Hayes, Warren B., article by, 15-29
Historic Family Enterprise (HFE), 286-292, 294, 296-297
How to Establish a Price Range (Keidan), 105-123
How to Make the "Impossible" Merger (Shad), 205-234
How to Succeed Where Others Have Failed (Castle), 31-47

I

Inspection, plant, 232
Insurance coverage, 258
Intelligent Use of Accountants in Acquisitions (Wintrub), 251-261
Intelligent Use of Lawyers in Acquisitions (Haskins), 235-249
Interests, pooling of, 269-270
Investigation, coordination of, 274-275
Investigators, lawyers as, 238-239
Investment bankers, use of, 89-104, 176-178
Investments, evaluation of, 284

K

Kehoe, John P., article by, 317-333
Keidan, Harry W., article by, 105-123
Kelly, Crosby M., article by, 305-316

L

Lawyers
disclosure and, 309-310
use of, 235-249
Liabilities, contingent, 229-230
Liquidation value, 114-115

M

MacDougal, Gary E., article by, 281-303
Making of a Negotiator, The (Putnam), 49-70

Malik, Fred V., article by, 281-303
Management
  appraisal of, 232-234
  positive approach to, 38-41
Market price, 114
Market value, measuring true, 218-219
Marketing Approach to Acquisitions, A (O'Connell), 179-190
Merger(s)
  acquisitions differentiated from, 71-88
  agreement, 265
  agreement in principle, 226
  appraisals, mutual, 227
  bargaining and, 77-78
  closing and, 263-279
  financial specialists and, 89-104, 176-178
  "impossible," how to make, 205-235
  liabilities, contingent, and, 230
  management appraisal, 232-234
  misconceptions concerning, 205-234
  negotiations and (*see* Negotiations)
  objectives, formulation of, 77-79
  operations, analysis of, 227-229
  plant inspection and, 232
  price and, 75-77
  seller's incentives, 208-210
  successful, financial realities of, 205-234
  tactics, 217
  taxable, 213
  tax-free, 208, *209, 212-213*
  trade checks and, 231-232
  transaction, structuring the, 94-95
  warranties and, 257-258, 273

N

Negative factors, handling, 62-63
Negatives, seeking out, 231-232
Negotiations
  accountants, use of, 251-261
  agreement in principle, 226
  approach to, 79-80, 281-303
  business synergy package and, 33-38
  case study, 286-303
  climate for, establishing, 74-75, 100, 191-203
  closing and, 263-279
  details, importance of, 99
  discussions, starting, 97-99, 219-220
  empathy and, 7-14
  financial package and, 33, 43-47
  lawyers, use of, 235-249
  negative factors, handling, 62-63
  price range, establishing a, 105-123, 284-285
  proposals, 281-303
    oral vs. written, 60-62
  seller's management package and, 34, 38-41
  successful, strategy behind, 49-70
  team for, selection of, 52-53
  timing, 63, 147-165
  understanding the proposition, 50-51
Negotiators
  lawyers as, 237-238
  making of, 49-70

O

Objectives
  achieving, 259
  formulating, 107-109
O'Connell, Thomas C., article by, 179-190

Offer, evaluation of, 95-97
Operations, analysis of, 227-229
Ownership, degree of, relationship to, of cash, common stock, preferred stock, purchase prices, *297*

P

Payouts, contingency, 119, 125-145
Pension plans, 17
Plant inspection, 232
Pooling of interests, 269-270
Power of Positive Orientation, The (Hayes), 15-29
Price
- establishing, financial specialists and, 93-94
- market, 114
- maximum, setting a, 115-116
- mergers and, 75-77
- over-all approach to question of, 13-14
- provision in agreement, 255
- range, establishing a, 105-123, 284-285
- value versus, 188

Price/earnings ratios, 113
Pricing concepts, use of, 112-116
Pricing schedule, comparative, 218-219
Projections, financial, 230-231
Proposals, 281-303
- oral vs. written, 60-62
- tailoring, 9-12

Proxy statements, 243
Putnam, Donald H., article by, 49-70

R

Registration, question of, 270-273
Registration statement, 243
Replacement value, 115
Representations, 273
Return on investment, (ROI), 284-290; at various growth rates, *289*
Returns, buyer's, 215-216
Reum, W. Robert, article by, 125-145
Risks
- evaluation of, 17-18, 170-171
- handling of, 167-178

Risk-taking, perspective on, 21-24
ROI, *see* Return on investment
Rules
- accounting, 255-256
- for buyers, 171-174
- for sellers, 174-175

Rumors, reacting to, 314-315

S

Salgo, Nicholas M., article by, 7-14
Scharf, Charles A., article by, 263-279
Securities
- marketability of, 220
- problems concerning, 241-245

Seller(s)
- approach of, 217-218
- attracting the, 208-210
- convincing, to sell, 26-29
- earnings and cash flow of, analyzing the, 109-112
- effect to, 215
- empathy and, 7-14
- incentives of, 208
- intentions of, gauging the, 8-9
- motives behind, 52
- problems of, 220-222
- problems of, seeing, 78-79

Seller(s) (*continued*)
proposal to, tailoring the, 9-12
real, identifying the, 54
rules for, 174-175
timing and, 148-150
understanding the, 7-14, 41-43, 55-56
yields, 215
Seller's management package, 34, 38-41
Shad, John S. R., article by, 205-234
Snyder, Stephen F., article by, 147-165
Specialists, financial, use of, 89-104, 176-178
Steele, Thomas A. III, article by, 125-145
Stock. *See* Securities
Strage, Mark, 335
introduction by, 1-5
Strategy, development of, 19-21
Sullivan, Fred R., article by, 71-88
Synergetics Corporation, case study, 286-297

T____

Tactics: The Distinction Between a Merger and an Acquisition (Sullivan), 71-88
Tax-Free transactions, 208
Team, negotiating, selection of the, 52-53
Technicians, lawyers as, 239-240
Techniques, acquisition, 18-19
Timing
acquisitions and, 147-165
buyer and, 150-153
disclosure and, 311-314
negotiations and, 63, 147-165
seller and, 148-150
Trade checks, 231-232

U____

Use—and Misuse—of Financial Specialists (Day), 89-104

V____

Valuation, estimated, example of, 121; as management budgeting problem, 116-118; notes to, 122-123
Value(s)
book, 114-115
concept of, 182-183
creative approach to, 179-190
liquidation, 114-115
of graphic approach, 285-286
price vs., 188
replacement, 115
true, determining, 58-60

W____

Warranties, 257-258, 273
Wintrub, Warren G., article by, 251-261

Y____

Yields, seller's, 215